Adelaide

INDEPENDENT MONTHLY
LITERARY MAGAZINE

Year IX, No.68, September 2024

BOOKS

ADELAIDE BOOKS

New York / Lisbon

2024

ADELAIDE
Independent Monthly Literary Magazine
Revista Literária Independente Mensal

Year IX, Number 68, September 2024

Ano IX, Número 68, setembro 2024

Published by Adelaide Books, New York / Lisbon

adelaidebooks.org

Editor-in-Chief: Stevan V. Nikolic

For any information, please address Adelaide Books LLC at editor@adelaidebooks.org

ISBN: 978-1-958419-92-2

Printed in the United States of America

Contents

Short Stories

Essays:

Poetry:

SHORT STORIES

A PORTRAIT ON THE BEACH

by Richard Eddie

Hilton Ross had spent many hours on the beach, watching the anemones, the pebbles change colors, and the ink squid migrate into their home, and enjoying their time during the low tides. He thought that would inspire him to paint, and he felt that they were all encouraging him to do so.

Any day was a perfect day to be on the beach, regardless of the season, and Hilton had painted many portraits filled with timeless beauty, but the fall of 1930 had somehow compelled him to spend more time on the beach like never before. During the fall of each year in Kingston, some had found the beach more appealing, and was not so worried about the cold air and cold water affirming that it was indeed fall.

Hilton Ross had purposefully left his art paper, paintbrushes, and all of his supplies at his cottage. He would just sit on the sand in his best clothes even when the wind would make the water choppy and pleasant at the same time; the air and the smell of sea salt had awakened him nauseated him at the same time during the late afternoon. He got up from the sand to walk where towards the ink squids loved to be, and they were gone.

The particular part of the beach that everyone in Kingston loved was the ink squids brought beauty, wonder, hope and magic, and they had suddenly disappeared. Where could they have gone? Hilton walked further along the beach, and he saw a little girl filling a basket. Even though he could see far away, he could not tell what the little girl was filling the basket with.

As Hilton got closer to where the little girl was, he was clear to him that it was not a basket, but more like a pot, a that was used for holding gold or treasures. The girl was humming a nice tune, it sounded like it was perfect for the beach, and matching what she was doing. "Good Afternoon, sir. You are the artist that everyone is always talking about, and you think that the ink squids can help you paint. They have asked me to tell you that they cannot provide any help with your work, but the sea can."

Naturally, Hilton was stunned because he did not know the girl nor recognized her. She looked at his feet and saw that he was wearing shoes and shook her head as if he committed a violation. "Have we met before, or do you live around here?" He looked down at his shoes, expensive black and white shoes had sand dust on the tops of them.

"I have lived around here for an exceptionally long time. You know that smart and talented people like you knows that you should not wear shoes while walking on the beach. The ink squids wanted me to rescue them from your shoes. They are not mad at you, but they hope and ask that you do not do that again." Anyone could or would think that the girl was beyond her years; Hilton liked her.

"Well, I certainly do not want to offend the beach, nor the ocean; the ocean has its own rules, and I respect that." Hilton did not know how to swim, but he still loved the water and the myths of it. "How would the ink squids know that I was not wearing shoes?" He thought that he should humor the child by being imaginary right along with her.

"Mr. Ross, you work with colors every single day, and they are part of your life. It is just possible that the ink squids want to help to add more color." The girl was halfway done with putting the ink squids into the pot, but then she stopped and looked at the sea. "I believe that this would be a good time for you to paint, Mr. Ross, and there is no need for you to run to your cottage to get your work supplies." She had finally finished putting the rest of the ink squids into the pot, with a wishful look that there were more.

"You are right, I do feel like I can paint right now," said Hilton with excitement and gladness. The little girl had turned her attention to the grassy hill further down the beach. She took Hilton by the hand, and he allowed her to guide him without any questions; he trusted her, and he was open to what she was going to show him.

"My father was just like you, he was an artist, and he painted many, maybe even hundreds of paintings." The experience and atmosphere was wonderful, and it was as if Hilton was in a dream. He and the girl were the only people who were on the beach. They walked up a precipice to a cottage, and outside the cottage, there were paintings in large portrait frames surrounding the cottage.

"I do not live here, but my father used to come here to paint and work on the beach. These are all of his paintings." Hilton could not believe his eyes; it was an oasis of paintings with vivid colors, and colors that were rarely seen or heard of. Just when Hilton Ross thought that was no other talented painters in Kington, nor the village, he was astonished and very wrong.

"My father's name was August Kitner, and he knew and admired your work, Mr. Ross; he has even bought some of your paintings." Hilton obviously did not know what to say when it came to the wonderful cottage, the magnificent paintings highlighting themselves, the mysterious child and all that she was revealing to him. The secrets or hidden treasures of Kingston is what made it more fabulous and majestical, prompting some to move there permanently.

"Your father was August Kitner?! Talk about surprises! I, too, own some of your father's work…" Was Hilton too proud to admit that others did inspire him, and admitting that to a young girl, no less? "My father passed away and leaving all of this to me along with plenty of money, not that matters."

The young girl who refused to tell Hilton her first name, led him to the supply shed, had opened a large glass candy jar, but it was not filled with candy. It was filled with antique paint brushes, some used and unused, and underneath was a jewelry box and it contained watercolors. "My father made his very own watercolors; he said that he produced the colors that reflected his moods and fears… you are welcome to all of this, Mr. Ross. I have no need for any of this."

The girl acted and portrayed herself as if she were a grown woman living on her own and her own terms. Hilton was relieved to hear people on the beach, but there was no reason for him to feel apprehensive, especially with a child who seemed to hold her own. He heard laughter and happiness, and he liked it. "This is very nice of you, Ms. Kitner. May I call you Ms. Kitner?"

She put on gardening gloves that were two sizes too big for her hands and tended to her plants. Sometimes it gets very lonely being in here all alone, listening to my father's emotions as well as seeing in his work. My father was a quiet man, and that is fine, because I am quiet, too. Before he passed, he said he believed that the sea could save him if he became too unhappy; he said the same thing about his painting. I could not understand why he left so early when he had me."

Neither did the girl nor Hilton say another word to each other, and the girl had disappeared. Hilton stepped out of the cottage to look for her; there was no sign of her. He walked back to where the girl was sitting, where the pot of ink squids, and there was a black sheet draped over a portrait of the little girl and her father painting on the beach.

***Richard Eddie** started writing back in 2002, and has been writing ever since. His favorite authors are Daphne Du Maurier and Agatha Christie. He lives in California, and reads and writes in his spare time.*

A JANUARY MORNING

by Colette NiReamonn

The frost was spread over the field like splintered, glittery glass, turning the stalks of grass into jell-styled stiffness. There was silence of the kind that hovers over a neglected graveyard where nothing moves. The trees with their stark silvered branches were still as though listening for some descending tremor that could be felt only by their deep-set roots. The lake was a sheet of platinum beauty. A robin flew off a thorn bush its wings the only sound in the hush of early morn; its rich brown and red startlingly alive against the motionless, white tipped things. It called out but there was no answer. The sun became braver and lifted its watery skirts to sweep away the edges of night that clung to one side of the sky as though wanting darkness to linger, to hide some unworthy thing from the truth of daylight. In the vague uncertain distance, a horse whinnied, and a cow mooed. Then the silence returned to dominate the fields and the lake. Soon life would shake itself out of its sleep stupor and reluctantly begin to move into the chill of the day. The day would make no impression on A6-22 for she was lifeless.

The robot body lay on the grass by the lake as stiff as everything else in sight. She had lain there all night. Her light blue coat was covered by a layer of white and her dark glossy hair glistened with thick frost. Her red lips were pursed as though she had said 'ooh' but didn't close her pretty mouth after it had escaped her. One side of her head had been brutally bashed in and her throat was gashed, a line as red as the colour on her lips. Around her head and neck a small pool of petrified, synthetic blood had spread. She had experienced one summer, one autumn and a taste of winter. But would the summer warmth ever again beam on A6-22's face and make her smile into the face of the man with whom she had lived and to whom she had given joy.

Garda Tim Higgins and his chief Michael O'Connell were walking the lane leading to the lake. The Gardai had been alerted to the fact that the 'machine' had been discovered. As Higgins had shut off the engine and both men alighted, O'Connell spat in disgust.

'That thing's been nothing but trouble since it arrived. What in Christ's name am I supposed to do with this 'murder'? It's not a human.'

'But murdered she has been, and we need to cordon off the crime area.' Higgins said quietly bending his knees to get a better look at the corpse. 'She belonged to young Sean Flynn who knew her as his wife; he'll want justice.'

'Justice my arse! Are you out of your bloody Dublin mind, man? It's not a she, it's an it!'

'She is very definitely a 'she'. And she was beautiful.' Higgins murmured.

'Have you one of them things at home these days?' A sneer was spreading across the alcohol-flushed face. The man's rank had often forced Higgins to hold onto his professional opinions and his tongue, but Aisling was personal. He knew the older man's dig was because his wife was nearing the end of her pregnancy. He ignored the remark and continued searching. O'Connell wasn't letting it go.

'It's a bloody nuisance when women are in that condition and can't give a man proper sex.'

He should know, Higgins thought, his senior had impregnated his wife seven times.

'We've a hand in getting them into that 'condition', don't we…sir? And my personal life is not for discussion with anybody.'

'I'm not anybody, Higgins.' O'Connell pushed his face close to his companion's and then to Higgins' annoyance walked in circles around the body. 'I wouldn't want to put my long John into one of them.'

'We're lucky to have real wives…sir. There are lonely people who are greatly helped by these…creations. And whoever did this did it with full force of malice and violence. To have that kind of maniac loose is dangerous. If he or she felt inclined to do that to a machine…for whatever reason, they need psychiatric assessment before they might make the next step a person.' Higgins felt a surge of sympathy for a work of art desecrated.

'At least she can't have felt pain.'

'You fuckin' need psychiatric assessment if you think I'm wasting manpower and energy on investigating the 'death' of a bloody robot.'

'Give me the case; I'll look into it. Can I send to…'

'You'll send nothing nowhere. Do you want us to be the laughing stock of the country, man? You do what you can to keep young

Flynn from breakin' up the town, and wind it up quick. And don't be expecting overtime either.'

Cathal Flynn's mouth was open; speech had temporarily forsaken him. Higgins gave the man time to recover his composure as the farmer sagged into a kitchen chair.

'Jaysus, me son'll go beserk when he hears…'

'Where is Sean?'

'He went to his Aunt Sadie's to pick her up; he doesn't know yet. Sean took Ellen there yesterday evening so Sadie could measure her for a new dress. She has to do that while Dan, her husband, is out.'

'So, the robot…Ellen was with your sister last night?'

'Well, she was in the shed behind the house. Dan wouldn't let her bring Ellen into the house when he's there.'

'How come you didn't pick her up after the fitting, Mr. Flynn, and bring her home?'

'We had an invitation from the institution where Sean goes for therapy sessions, a kind of belated New Year party and we didn't want to disturb Sadie as she sleeps early. Sadie promised Sean she'd cover Ellen with a blanket and make her comfortable. She can be switched off. It took me an hour to make Sean understand that she can't feel the cold like us once her switch is off.'

'Why won't her husband let Sadie bring Ellen in the house, Mr. Flynn?'

'He thinks she's an abomination.'

'Do you think she's an abomination, Mr. Flynn?'

'Would I have bought the feckin' thing if I thought that, man? I paid a mint for it, and it's been worth every cent. Sean has never been so content since he hooked up with her. You're new here, aren't you?' His eyes examined the younger man's face.

'But you know by now, I imagine, that my son is what they call…' Flynn laughed ironically, 'socially challenged'. But he's my lad and I promised my late wife I'd do my best for him.'

'Look, Mr. Flynn, as far as I'm concerned a murder was committed last night and I want to get to the bottom of it.'

The door burst open, and a distressed young man came through it.

'She's dead, Da! My Ellen is dead. Some bastard killed her.'

Sean Flynn banged the door shut behind him and paced the floor fast and furious, slapping his hands against any object he came up against. He ignored the young policeman as he spoke rapidly to himself, each word accompanied by an expletive.

'Sean, Sean, sit down lad, come here. I'll make you a cuppa tay.' Cathal Flynn's distress was almost equal to his son's.

'Don't want tay; I want Ellen…my lovely Ellen. Where is she? I want to see her.'

'Sean, this is Garda Higgins and he's going to find out who did that awful thing to your wife, OK?'

Sean stopped pacing and looked at Higgins. He sat in a chair opposite and stared into Higgins brown eyes. The pale blue stare was unnerving in its intensity. Higgins had heard about Sean and his robot 'wife.' but this was the first time he had met the man.

'That shite O'Connell will do nothing. He hated Ellen, he told me so. Do you know what he called my wife? He called her an abomination. I brought her into the pub one evening and he and some of the other tough nuts made a jeer of me.'

'I'm not O'Connell Sean, and I'm going to do my very best to find the perpetrator.' Higgins had seen a report of the incident in the computer log as he familiarized himself with his new surroundings; the infuriated young man had to be restrained from beating the daylights out of the police chief.

'He probably killed her.'

'We don't know that Sean. Look, give me a little time and I promise I'll keep you in touch with everything I find out, fair enough? I can't let you near the crime scene now because it's cordoned off, I'm going over it and the more people walking round the more difficult it becomes to find any traces, do you get me?'

Sean nodded; his face washed with tears.

'Fair enough.' Cathal Flynn sighed. 'When can we have her back to bury her?'

'We're not going to bury her, Da. Maybe we could fix her.' Hope leapt into Sean's eyes.

'Sean, son, I spent all the savings I had to buy her for you. I don't have enough to send her back to the States to be fixed. I'm sorry.'

The lad sank back into the chair. 'I don't want to put her in a hole. I'll clean her up and put her in the spare room. You have to give her back, haven't you?'

'Of course, Sean.' Higgins attempted to touch Sean's shoulder, but he quickly drew away. 'I'll get your Ellen back to you.'

Aisling ran her fine fingers through her husband's dark hair. He was sprawled on the big couch in front of the fire, his long skinny legs and big feet dangling off the end, his head leaning gently against her belly thrilling to the movement of his child inside her. His contentment was sharply tweaked when a thought crashed through it:

'Aisling, d'you think they'll ever make a robot that can give birth?'

'Given the way technology is galloping through our lives, who knows?'

He adored her. He had from the first moment he'd laid eyes on her at the birthday party of a mutual friend. She had her back to him as she stood with a group of young women. It was obvious from the faces turned towards him that she was telling them a story that had their rapt attention. It was the hair that had first drawn him, long copper-red, delicate glossy waves rippling down her back almost to her waist. Then they were laughing heartily at whatever she had said, and he murmured to himself.

'Turn round, let's see your face.'

It was almost as though she had heard him. She turned to place her wine glass on a nearby table and her eyes held his gaze for a moment before she turned back to her company. He found his friend and asked for an introduction. She mesmerized him. The eyebrows were a natural line of red brown above eyes of vivid speckled green. Her lashes were thick and the same shade as her eyebrows, the nose straight and perfect. Aisling McFadden had a mouth a lipstick advertiser would kill for, and Tim Higgins longed to kiss it. He felt his heart sink. No way was this beauty going to be interested in him. But she was and they were incredibly happy.

He took her hand and kissed it.

'This really has you spiked up; hasn't it love?'

'It's a tough case, Aishie; I've no precedent to go by. Abomination is often used around here to describe her, passed around like drink at a wake. There's not much acceptance locally for her or sympathy for Sean. I called the lads in town on the sly, but they were as stumped as I am. All I can do is treat this the way any other crime would be treated because to Sean Flynn she was as real a wife as you are to me.'

'His father amazes me, to be that advanced as to buy his …'

'Socially challenged son' is what they call him.' Tim smiled ruefully.

'A robot wife.'

'From what I gather from our canteen lady, it was out of sheer exhaustion with Sean's moods.'

'No mother to help out,' Aisling sighed, 'a young man like that with all the urges of his age and unable to socialize with the opposite sex…terrible frustrations leading to terrible outbursts. It's sad. And the debate goes on as to whether it's a good or a bad thing for a human to copulate'…Aisling said the last word slowly with a smile, 'with a machine.'

'She looks so incredibly real, though. The father sent all the way to America for her. I went over the whole scene with two of the locals but there was nothing to find, nothing that leapt out at me. That heavy frost covered any tracks. Anyway, it's not as though I'm an expert or there's any kind of specialized equipment I can bring to investigate properly. O'Connell is just glad to have me out of his way for a few hours; he doesn't give a damn who did it.'

'Was she raped?'

Higgins sat up and stared at her. 'Jesus! I didn't check. Jesus! I totally forgot one of the most important parts of procedure in a case of that kind because…'

'Because she wasn't human?' Aisling ended for him.

'How could I tell if a robot was raped…I mean would her synthetic body show signs of forced entry, sorry love, I don't know what else to say…'

Forced entry?' Aisling raised an eyebrow at him.' You're on the wrong page of the police instructions manual, Higs.'

'I couldn't think of the right phrase…'

'Anyway, I looked it up on the internet while you were busy. The company that makes them has a pretty explicit site that tells all the advantages of that particular model and one of the advantages of A6-22 is that she has a sac that is easily removed from her passage chamber…their term not mine…to enable upkeep of hygienic conditions.'

'You mean you can remove the sperm and clean the area?'

'Yes. Apparently, the way this one works is that when sex is finished, and the man withdraws his penis a…gap closes.'

'Ouch! Not sure I like the sound of that.'

'It's perfectly safe according to them as the inner parts are as soft as human tissue; the closing is merely two edges over locking so sperm can't escape. It wouldn't circumcise you…in case you're thinking of replacing me with one.' Aisling kissed him lightly, laughed and continued.

'The sperm is thus maintained…their term…'

'Not yours, go on.'

'It can be ejected by pressing a tiny button at the base of the spine. So…if you want a DNA sample, it's there for you.'

'Provided the killer isn't robot savvy and has already taken it away if he did rape her.' He paused.

'I need help on this. I can't go poking around inside her…robot or not.'

'Call Irene.'

'Your cousin, the G.P.?'

'She's delivered God knows how many babies in this town. If any person has been up close and personal with the female undercarriage, it's her.'

'Now whose work glossary is showing, Missus Flight attendant?' He grinned, pulled his coat from the hall stand and started for the door taking out his phone as he did so.

'Where are you going?'

'To the mortuary where I sent Ellen, to check if there's any semen still there. Hallo, Irene, I have a job for you.'

Dr. Irene Collins was a tall blonde, well-toned Amazon approaching fifty with smoky blue eyes. Her hair, short at the back, fell in expertly cut meshed wisps over her high forehead. Irene was one of the reasons Aisling had been keen to give birth in her small hometown near her family. Tim had put in for a temporary six-month transfer and got it when Aisling heard through the grapevine that a vacancy had opened up, her large family had a certain amount of clout in the area. O'Connell had not been pleased as he had been hoping one of his cronies would step in and he lost no opportunity to remind Higgins that he was an unwanted temp. Irene's deft fingers pulled on rubber gloves.

'You owe me, Higgins, calling me out at this time. Jack was hopping mad, and the brood was yelling for Pizza.'

Irene had four youngsters all full of energy and demands. They knew their mother was a hard worker being one of only two doctors on call locally, but that evening she had promised them a pizza and the biggest prize of all – her undivided attention. She escaped the house only because she promised to add to the pizza cinnamon apple pie and the biggest tub of caramel ice cream on sale. Her husband, long used to her being called out at all times day and night, had sighed resignedly, and told the kids to shut up.

'I can tell you one thing for sure,' Irene examined the cut on the neck, 'this was made with the kind of knife used to kill pigs.'

'How do you know that by just looking at it?'

'I'm a country girl, Tim, raised on a farm. I've seen pigs slaughtered. God, this is weird. I've never examined a robot bottom before. It's so…realistic. Go over there and sit down. I won't have you looking up the poor woman's privates.'

'I had no intention of looking up her privates; that's why I called you.' Higgins obeyed.

'She's flexible, which is a gift, because a human at this stage wouldn't be so easy to examine.' Irene began her examination.

'Was she raped?'

'Hard to tell considering, there's no external damage from what I can see.' Irene removed the chamber.

'Oh, oh…as clean as my Aunt Bridie's fridge. No sperm to help you here Tim.'

Tim sighed, thought a moment than said.

'Can you give me a few swabs and some sterile containers?'

'Have you any suspects?'

'Not yet. I have to see who would be so offended by a robot…'

'Or be curious enough to find out what exactly she felt like sexually before getting rid of her?'

'That too…but I don't know the people here well enough to have any suspicions. I need to ask the boys at the station if there's a ruffian capable of that measure of aggression in the community. I'm just hoping…stupid maybe, that if whoever it was sees it's not going to be passed over, I might startle or trap them into an admission - if I'm lucky when I wave the swabs about. Semen needn't be mentioned. They've all seen enough police procedurals on the telly to know it might be saliva, hair or a number of things.'

Irene covered Ellen up and took off her gloves. As she threw them in a bin, she told him.

'The closer to the bone the sweeter is the meat.'

'You mean it might be the father?' Tim was shocked; Cathal Flynn didn't seem the type.

'No, I don't think so. Flynn is a good man, and he loves his son, promised his dying wife he'd take good care of Sean…I know, I was with them she died. No, I was thinking it had to be someone who knew the moves…knew she would be in the shed that night.'

'That narrows it a bit. Are you thinking of Sadie's husband…what's his name?'

'Dan Maher…a ruffian if ever. It's no secret he's beaten that poor woman up on many occasions. O'Connell always turned a blind eye when I asked him to have a word in person after I'd patched her up; they're drinking pals. But he's another bloody male chauvinist. Sadie's also to blame, though, wouldn't charge him. Just as well there's no kids there.' She added the paper surgical gown to the gloves in the bin.

'Where does he work?'

'Out of his home, he fixes things; everything from clocks to gas or paraffin heaters. That's why Sean didn't bring Ellen there during the day, he's scared of his uncle, knew he hated the robot.' She grinned as she rattled her car keys on her way out.

'And he gives a hand on days when farmers need to slaughter stock, very efficient he is too from what I hear.'

Tim Higgins was beginning to think the women around him had more detective potential than he had. God bless them.

Maher was in the driveway his head stuck inside his car bonnet when Higgins drove up. He lifted his untidy head and glared at the Garda, then went under the bonnet again. Tim stood beside him and waited till Maher realised he wasn't going anywhere until they spoke.

'What'd you want? Does the O'Connell know yer here?' The eyes were slits in a fleshy face that had gathered itself up into thick folds of skin above his eyes and around his broken nose. The mouth was thin and unattractive; Higgins wondered what Sadie had ever seen in him.

'O'Connell gave me the case to investigate and that's what I'm doing.'

'Case! Investigate! Jaysus, you must be hard up for somethin' t'do trying to find who bumped off a fuckin' machine.' An empty laugh cracked the mean face.

Higgins took a swab and a sterile container out of his pocket.

'I need to take a sample of your saliva, it's mere procedure for all those who had contact with Ellen recently.'

'You will not! I wouldn't touch that thing with a pitchfork.'

'Well, we can do it here or at the station.' Shit! Higgins heard himself roll out lines from a movie script.

'And if I don't want to give ye me spit?'

'There's no choice here, as I said, this is a friendly request, we can make it legal if you want but one way or another it will be done.'

'What do you hope to gain from that?' Maher was looking edgy.

'It's procedure, as I said. Criminals often leave traces on or around the victim.'

'The victim! It was a fuckin' bloody machine, not a person. It's not murder to get rid of a thing like that; it's not human.'

'That's not for you to decide, Mr. Maher. Can we go in the house now and…'?

Maher shoved his way past Higgins.

'Do you possess a butcher's knife for killing pigs, Mr. Maher?'

'An' what if I do?'

'That kind of knife was used to slit Ellen Flynn's throat. But, being a non-human, that didn't 'kill' her. The blow on the head did that. The throat was simply a brutal gesture.'

'She wasn't a Flynn; he only called her his 'wife' No church would sanction that bond. She was an abomination. Who would want to poke that and then have to clean her out after it except a retarded twit like Sean?'

'How do you know he had to clean her out?'

'Sadie told me. The Sean fella tells her everything.'

'There's a good possibility that the camera inside her head might be retrieved.'

Maher froze. 'What camera?'

'The one that helped her recognise her partner.' Higgins gave another silent thanks to Aisling. 'His photo and his body proportions were programmed into her memory, and she wouldn't...copulate with any other person without his programmed permission. Now can we go into the house and take that swab?'

The house was a bleak affair, the dull furnishings merely functional, the atmosphere abysmal. Love didn't ring any bells in this home. Maher took Higgins into the kitchen and sat at the table.

'Is Mrs. Maher home?

'No, why? D'ye want to swab her as well...you think me wife is a butch?' His laugh was harsh and shallow. The door leading to the living room opened and Sadie stood there glaring at her husband, her face a mass of bruises and her left eye so swollen it had closed.

'He did it; he killed Ellen.' She glared at Maher. 'I should have taken me brother up on his offer to move in with them ages ago, but I stuck with you for better or for worse, and worse it was most of the time. I've put up with you hurtin' me over years, but I won't have you hurtin' Sean and gettin' away with it. He's been cryin' non-stop since you killed her.'

Maher stood up and rushed towards his wife his fist balled. Higgins tripped him with a Judo flip, and he went down.

'I'll sue ye, yeh bastard. Yeh've put me back out.'

Higgins took out his mobile and called one of the young guards he knew he could reply on telling him to come to the Maher house at once.

'What possessed Sadie to tell you?' Aisling asked her husband.

'I think something in her snapped out one beating too many, and out of sympathy for Sean.'

'What's the story behind the killing?'

'He came in that evening drunk, picked up Ellen's dress that Sadie was ironing and started swearing at her. He went out into the shed and brought Ellen back in, asking Sadie if this was her new baby she had to dress up. He shoved his hand down Ellen's breasts and up her skirt and Sadie said she could see his expression change.

'Jaysus! She fuckin' feels real enough.'

'Did the robot react?'

'No, she'd been switched off to conserve her battery. Then he demanded to know how to switch her on and when he did, he tried, for a laugh, he said, to have sex with her in front of his wife, but Ellen wouldn't oblige; her thighs clamped together.'

Maher had lost his temper, Sadie told Higgins, and he hit Ellen on the head with the iron. Then he drove off with her and that was the last Sadie had seen.

'Apparently, he keeps his pig knife in the car and cut her throat out of sheer fury, she was already flatlined. Then he threw her over the hedge into the field.'

'Now what?' Aisling asked.

'There's a pack of journalists outside the station, he's being held for assault and battery on property, which is not 'murder' until someone can figure out a proper charge. One of my 'pals' in town leaked it to a journalist friend. O'Connell is beside himself. My life will be miserable for as long as this lasts but blast him anyway, all I care about is you two.' He slowly massaged her tummy.

'Irene called me,' Aisling sighed, 'she stitched Ellen's throat, and the undertaker did his best to fix the outer damage and got her back to Sean, poor lad. It's sad, both the father and the son without wives, lonely people.'

'Yeah, but with Sadie moving in there'll be at least a woman's comforting presence in the house. Do you mind if I walk over for a bit, just to see how they are?'

Higgins, off duty, had a large glass of whiskey in front of him as he chatted with Sadie and Cathal. The doorbell rang and Cathal went to answer it. Outside stood a short man with perfectly groomed hair, smelling of expensive aftershave. He carried an expensive leather briefcase in his right hand and his shoes looked as though they had been handcrafted from the softest leather.

'Mr. Flynn?' The voice was deep and cultured.

'…Yes?'

'May I come in?'

'May I ask who you are first?'

'Of course, here's my card.'

'Come in.' The man sat opposite Higgins and Flynn introduced him. 'This is a Mr. Bailey.' He handed Higgins the card.

'I passed by your home Garda Higgins and your wife said you were here, so it's a case of killing two birds with one stone, so to speak.' A smile showed a set of well cared for teeth.

'And what can I do for you Mr. Bailey?' Tim wondered if Maher had in fact sued him.

'I have heard a great deal about 'Ellen', and I believe you investigated the crime scene and discovered who destroyed her.' The voice was cultured and soft.

'I would love to represent the young man whose eh, wife, was allegedly 'murdered' by a Mr. Maher. I think it is one of the most intriguing cases that could ever come my way. It will be Pro Bono of course.'

By the following snow-cold January, Aoife Rosemary Higgins had come into a welcoming world and found it very good. The robin went about his business and the farm animals continued to call as they always did. The field where Ellen had lain all night was once again covered in white.

Sean lay in bed, his alarm having woken him ten minutes earlier, talking to his darling who was lying next to him, stroking her face carefully, treating her with the delicate touch of love a parent bestows on a baby. He did that a lot now, talked to her, and Ellen had started talking back. Her speech was not always clear and most of her functions were damaged but that didn't matter; he could hold her gently and kiss her, she was warm again. He had combed the wig Sadie had bought for Ellen over one eye to hide the dreadful wound. He had recharged her battery every night even though he had been told she was technologically dead. And yesterday she had opened her good eye, smiled at him and told him haltingly she loved him too. Sean was over the moon but from now on, only his father and Sadie would know she had come back. No one was ever going to hurt his darling again.

Colette NiReamonn: *Retired. Worked with Cyprus Broadcasting Corporation live/recorded, on TV and radio in various capacities: news reading/interviewing, including script writing, creating music programmes, acting as location finder and fixer for foreign crews. Had four short stories on Cyprus used by BBC World two of which were forwarded to the Commonwealth Magazine. Worked in various media forms here, magazines (commissioned articles for national air carrier), short stories in an art and culture quarterly In Focus, features, interviews, opinion pieces for newspapers. I now have a column in the oldest English language paper here. I write songs as a hobby.*

SCALE FORWARD

by KoRaan Williams

The doctor clears the stones off the glass scale that is tipped in the direction of the empty seat. The scale is once again balanced. "Next patient!"

The patient walks into the doctor's office. He looks around with uncertainty at the overflow of books on the mahogany shelves and takes a seat in the empty black velvet armchair next to the scale.

The doctor notices the diamond ring on his finger as he nervously grabs hold of the chair's armrest. "First time you've had a therapy session?" she asks.

"And my last," he replies, as he turns his focus to the picture of a kid reaching his hand in a cookie jar with the word Integrity at the bottom in a bold font.

"Never understood those kinds of pictures."

The doctor grabs her note book from her desk and sits right across from the man, underneath a portrait of a woman holding a child.

"So what brings you here today?" she asks.

"I think people are useless. I don't understand why they won't listen to me." he replies.

"That may be a little vague, but I'm sure you have your reasons for why you believe that." she says, while grabbing a black box beside her seat. Handing it to the patient.

Inspecting the box before opening it, he shakes.

"Is this a gift or something? You're too kind," he says.

The doctor chuckles at his remark.

"I would like to think so. Actually I have a lesson for my first-time patients that require what's in the box and that glass scale next to you. I noticed you weren't totally on board with the idea of therapy since you entered my office. Your participation will be needed in this exercise."

The patient sighs and sits up straight in the chair. He opens the box and pulls out a handful of stones.

"Now, in this exercise I'm going to be getting to know you a bit better and try to understand why you're truly here. How does that sound to you?"

The patient rolls the stones in his hand. " OK!" he says.

"I'm going to make some statements and I want you to place a stone on the scale if the statements apply to you," she says.

The patient nods.

"It's hard for you to compromise with others. You prize your idea of perfection above all," she says.

"That's two statements doc," he replies.

The doctor stares at him with a blank face. He turns to the scales and places two stones on the scale.

"You want love from those same people."

He adds another stone.

"From what I understand, you seek validation and separation from everyone. I don't believe those can coexist as easily as you want them to," she says.

"I'm not following," he says.

"You want them to love you but not know you. Doesn't that feel unfair?" she asks.

"I want what I want. If I can't live the perfect life I see for myself. I at least want the closest thing to it," he replies.

"I think you are obsessed with something close to unattainable," she says, while taking notes. "It doesn't mean it's impossible, but sometimes we try so hard to craft the life we want without being able to actually enjoy it."

The patient drops his head in his lap, showing signs of frustration. The doctor hears him mumbling something under his breath.

"Maybe you're right, maybe what I want is unattainable," he says.

"I believe what you're looking for has been right in front of you the whole time. Raise your head and take one final look at the scale," she says.

He takes a deep breath and looks up.

"The closest thing to perfection," she says.

He stares at the glass scale seeing the three stones resting. The scale is barely off balance. He faces the doctor with a smile on his face.

Ko Williams*: "I am from a small town Sumter, South Carolina. I am currently attending Full Sail University for my creative writing degree. I have been writing music and screenplays for some years now, I understand the magic a good story can bring to people. I truly enjoy what I do and hope to take my talents far. My dream is to inspire and create for the world!"*

THE MAN OF YOUR DREAMS

by Kate Niestrom

The doctor suggested that Lena get a hobby.

She laughed. "I'm admitted into the hospital for exhaustion and you want me to do more?"

He shrugged. "You need to do something for yourself, Lena. Something apart from Jesse and the kids."

Lena laughed at the prospect of having time for that, but the doctor insisted that surely she could spare thirty measly minutes for self-care. Lena eyed him warily. Collapsing in Hy-Vee had been the first moment of quiet she'd experienced in years. Did this appointment count as thirty minutes to herself?

She sighed. "What do you suggest, Doctor?"

"I don't know," Dr. Kelp said. "Some people paint or crochet."

Lena stared at him.

"I like to unwind with long-distance running, myself."

Lena's eyes narrowed.

"Or," the doctor said, eyeing the broken-spined paperback peeking out of Lena's bag. "You could try writing. Maybe exercising some creativity could be good for you?"

Lena sagged back into her chair. She couldn't even come up with a way out of this conversation, let alone write a competent story.

"It doesn't have to be good," Dr. Kelp said. "You just need to use your brain in a different way. Give it a break, you know? Doctor's orders," he laughed.

"Fine," Lena said. "I suppose it beats marathons."

#

"I wish I'd picked running," she said the next night, sitting at the kitchen table as her husband poured her a glass of Sauv Blanc.

"You don't mean that," Jesse laughed. "You majored in literature, this should be right up your alley."

That had been a long time ago. Lena barely remembered that person, the girl who would spend entire afternoons sipping coffee and losing herself in a thousand-page classic. It felt like a fantasy now, when there was always a thing on her to-list that never got to-done, a million people she needed to be in order to make sure her kids made it from bed in the morning back to bed again at night.

"Are you sure you've got bath time? Cooper just gets so fussy..."

"Relax," he said. "He's basically a potato, he barely knows the difference between you and me. And Ella's four now, I can just stick her in the shower, right?"

Lena started to get up.

"I'm kidding!" Jesse said, holding her shoulders. "Hon, you don't have to write if you don't want to. Just take a break. Stream a show. Paint your nails or...something."

"I just…" Lena stared at the blinking cursor on her empty Word document. "I don't know what to write."

Jesse shrugged. "Write what you know."

Lena took a deep breath.

Lisa was running late. The frigid November cold blew her hair back from her face, freezing tears in the corner of her eyes and making the tip of her nose sting. She burst into the warm embrace of the cafe and breathed a sigh of relief. Her professor wasn't here yet, and there were two open seats.

She took one and set her bag on the other, grateful for a moment to prepare before presenting her thesis to Professor Lumley.

What she was not prepared for, however, was to look up into the warm eyes of a handsome stranger.

"Hi there," he said, and suddenly she wasn't in such a hurry for the professor to arrive. Suddenly, she had a few moments to linger in this kind man's gaze.

Lena sighed and pressed the delete key. She didn't need to rehash the night she first met Jesse only to arrive years later back on the linoleum tile of Hy-Vee.

But this is fiction! A voice in her head whispered. This doesn't have to be you and Jesse, it could be Lisa and… Jamie.

Lena set her fingers back down on the keys.

What Lisa was not prepared for, however, was to look up into the mahogany eyes of one of the most beautiful men she'd ever seen.

"Hi there," he said with a flashing grin, and suddenly she forgot all about the professor and her thesis and why she had come to the cafe in the first place.

It seemed so obvious to her now. She had come here for him. For Jamie.

#

Lena woke up the next morning filled with ideas for Lisa and Jamie. As she started getting breakfast ready for Ella and Cooper, she imagined the lush brunch spread the couple would be eating filled with savory eggs and delicate flutes of mimosas. As she kissed Jesse goodbye on his way out the door, she found herself picturing Jamie, who, with his coffee-colored skin and crooked smile, resembled her husband, but with a slightly more chiseled chin and the hint of a sparkle in his eye.

"Goodbye, my love," she said as he buttoned his coat.

Jesse raised an eyebrow. "Oh, uh, okay. Have a good one, hun."

But Jamie would not have been able to leave for work. He would have pulled Lisa in and kissed her neck, breathing in the scent of her shampoo and entwining himself with her until his coat was off along with the rest of his clothes, the two of them a tangle on the floor.

"MoOOM"!" Ella screeched, banging her fork on the kitchen table, breaking the spell. "Where are the hearts? I want the hearts!"

Lena set a plate of limp, heart-shaped waffles down before her daughter.

She spent the rest of the morning daydreaming about her characters and the various ways they'd lace themselves together and tear themselves apart. Ways in which their exciting attraction could exist between the spaces of Lena's own navigation of feedings and playtime.

When Cooper spit up all over the couch, she pictured Lisa home from a night on the town, trying to get over her undeniable feelings for Jamie. Where her daughter sat, playing with her purple Furby, Lisa's best friend and confidant would have been perched, rubbing Lisa's back and telling her that instead of drinking Jamie away, she just needed to tell him how she really felt.

That night when her husband got home, Lena couldn't skip off fast enough to her laptop, abandoning her previous worries about Jesse not being able to properly care for their children on his own. She spent the entire delicious evening falling deeper and deeper for Jamie.

"I don't know, Jamie. Our spark is undeniable but how am I ever supposed to trust you again? Why didn't you show up?"

"Lisa," Jamie said, cupping her face with his hands. "There's nowhere else I'd rather be than by your side. I was on my way to the airport to meet you when my taxi crashed. I tried to hobble on a broken leg, if you can believe it."

Lisa gazed up into the stars of his eyes, feeling oceans arise in her own. "You…did?"

Jamie laughed. "There's nothing I wouldn't do to be with you, crazy girl."

He looked at her and she saw the same face that caught her by surprise in the café that first night, the face she would love for the rest of her life.

#

Lena reread her last sentence again. She'd spent the last six days pouring everything she had into Lisa and Jamie's love story and knew it was time for their happily ever after. But something about them spending the rest of their lives together made her feel nauseous.

She looked up at Jesse, pressing the bottom flap of a diaper closed around their son's waist. Is this what her beloved characters had to look forward to? Is this all she truly had to offer them? She slapped her laptop shut and got up, pushing her husband to the side to fix Cooper's diaper.

"Done writing for the night?" he asked.

She nodded. "I think I'm done for a while. I need to give my story some space."

"Does this mean I can finally read it?"

Lena went white, realizing she never wanted Jesse and Jamie to meet. Her character belonged to her, and he felt too intimate to share with her husband.

"I mean, okay," Jesse grinned, "I read over your shoulder a little bit the other night and I saw that it's about the night we met at Racy's..."

"You...what?" Lena felt the tips of her ears start to burn. "It's not about us, Jess! And it's private."

She pressed Cooper to her chest and stormed out, thinking about how Jamie would never make Lisa feel this way. Jamie would have respected Lisa's privacy. Jamie would never be so…so oblivious.

Jesse is not Jamie, Lena thought to herself. And then she let herself think the thing that had been crawling out from the back of her mind since the night she'd written Jamie and Lisa into existence, the thing that had grown harder and harder to chase back. But, god, do I wish he was.

#

Later that night, after bath time and bedtime were done, the kids were down and Jesse was blissfully snoring on his side of the bed, Lena unfolded her laptop and deleted the happy ending she had given her characters. "They deserve more than this," she muttered to herself, giving her couple one last passionate kiss to remember each other by before shredding them apart forever.

"It's better this way," she whispered to them. "Go be free."

She felt a tension lift from her shoulders and a wave of exhaustion come over her. She pushed her laptop away, content in the knowledge that everyone had ended up where they were supposed to. Jamie and Lisa could go on to experience any adventure of their choosing and recall their fervid affair fondly.

Her husband let out a loud fart next to her.

Lena exhaled. She had saved them.

#

She woke up a few hours later to find Jesse's face illuminated by a fluorescent glow, eyes unblinking as he focused on the screen of her laptop with a grim-set mouth. Lena's blood rushed to her cheeks and she scrambled upright.

"What are you doing?"

He looked up, that kind gaze she'd first seen over the counter at Racy's coffee shop gone, now filled with ire and betrayal.

"Me?" he asked. He shook his head at the screen. "You took our story and bastardized it."

"I…I…" she sputtered. "I told you it's not about us!"

Jesse scoffed. "Come on, Lena. Lisa and Jamie meet at a coffee shop while she's waiting on her professor to get advice on her thesis?"

"Okay," she mumbled. "It may have started out about us but it became something entirely different."

"I can see that," her husband said, pushing the computer off his lap. "I mean, what even is all this, Lena? Is this your subconscious way of telling me you need more sex or something?" Lena scoffed. "And why…" he rubbed his eyes, the anger and indignation deflating from his voice. "Why don't they end up together?" He looked up at her. "What are you trying to say, here?"

Lena swallowed, feeling tears well up in her eyes. When was the last time she'd cried? She never felt like she had the time to get emotional anymore, always needing to show the kids a brave face.

But there were no kids now, just her and the man she had once looked at and thought was so handsome she forgot the stress of presenting a college thesis. Just her and the man who concocted specialty coffees based on her mood every day of her final semester to get her through to graduation. The man who had followed her to a teaching position halfway across the country. Who had cried tears of joy when he found out she was pregnant. Who had understood completely when she said she wanted to quit work and take care of their daughter full time. Who had kept the family afloat when a second baby came and Lena retreated further into herself. The man who she'd spent years thinking was no longer enough.

What had she been trying to say with Lisa and Jamie?

She wiped her eyes. "Maybe it was some misguided, subconscious need for drama. Some curiosity about if things had been different."

"Do you wish things had been different?"

Did she actually want Jamie, with his strong jaw and tendency to disappear right when Lisa needed him most? Did she want to look back and remember the love she shared with her husband fondly rather than face the hard times?

"No," she said. "I don't." A tear escaped down her face. "But Jess, I'm just so tired and I feel so lost. I can feel myself slipping away, and I miss who I was before. I love our kids, but I miss me."

"Then tell me that," he said, wrapping his arm around her shoulders. "You don't have to do this by yourself." He tipped her chin to face him. "You can write all the stories you like about love and drama and theatrics." She laughed. "But when it comes to something you need from me, you have to say it out loud so we can figure it out together."

She nodded, burying her face in his shoulder. "I love you," she said into his worn college sweatshirt.

"I love you too, Lena."

She looked up at him and saw the same face that caught her by surprise in the cafe that first night, the face she would love for the rest of her life. If not always happily, then honestly. Compassionately. Dearly. Forever after.

***Kate Niestrom** (she/her) is a writer of speculative and contemporary fiction with a degree in Creative Writing and Communications from the University of Wisconsin-Eau Claire. Her non-fiction essays have been published on Thought Catalog. Her short stories and microfiction have made it to the final rounds of NYC Midnight fiction competitions. She lives in Minneapolis, Minnesota.*

THE RUNNER

by Enrique Melendez

I took a breath as my degenerating eyes focused on time slowing down. The echoes around me faded, I knew this was my moment, I got this.

It wasn't my only thought but when I moved my hand towards the line, just close enough to be ready for the fiery shot to ring my dysfunctional ears. BANG! I ran as the echoes behind me faded.

I can make it, I thought, as my legs shook with each step I took.

"You aren't going to make it!" a man said.

I ran into the forest spaced out enough for me to slip through, hoping for a clear path with few obstacles, but I wasn't sure.

"Dang," I said, "my arm—"

I put pressure on it as I hid behind a tree. Grabbing some wild herbs with green stems and white moss around the middle, I noticed the scent of mushrooms off-putting enough to make me nauseous. I sat down to let the herb work for a few minutes. My heart was racing, but I was worried they were going to catch up to me.

I've been through this many times, running away from the people behind me. As a child I thought, one day I was going to make it.

"He's over there," a woman said.

"Don't let him get any further," a man said.

Have to go, I thought.

The sun disorienting my eyes, my legs punching back with every step, I couldn't stop now. I went left then right, weaving the zigzag line of trees in front of me. Running through the dark-mossy, white trees for over a mile, my mind started to wander.

"How far is the end?" I said.

"He's almost out," a man said.

Diverting my attention I plunged down a hill shielding my head as my arms and legs smashed into rocks, slamming into a boulder.

"No!" I said.

I tried to hold back my voice biting my finger hard enough for it to bleed. My eyes poured hopeless tears and the taste of dirt filled my mouth with bitter sorrow, I leaned back on the boulder to rest from the pain for a while taking slow breaths, but after a few moments, I heard someone run past me.

I sat there for some time, I knew I had to pass them to make it out first, but I didn't know how. I looked at my body to see how bad I was and then I saw it.

"No, come on," I said.

My left arm limp like rubber, I knew if I lifted it the pain would shock my whole left side enough that I would throw up. I had been through this before and I couldn't try to fix such a small distraction, being so close to the end. I knew this was a sacrifice I had to take advantage of no matter how bad it was, I needed to get through this forest.

"Where did he go?" a man said.

I peeked my head out after a while to see that the one that passed me was going the wrong way, Dumb ass. I tried to climb, but my shoes filled with dirt and mud made me struggle more. With one arm, it was taking me too long to --

"There he is!" two men yelled.

I saw them closer than before, but I didn't want them to know that I fell. I glanced at my arm, but I had to keep going. I started to stand up and felt shocks of lightning shoot into my heart. I looked forward and saw the opening, the way out, the end, and I knew I could make it. I ran hard, one step after another the wind flowing around me, tripping over big brown roots and branches like a game of rock, paper, scissors.

I stopped a few times to see where he was, the one who passed me. Every time I stopped the cuts and bruises filled me with the rage of a wild man. I intently leaned toward the left so that if I slammed into a tree it wasn't going to slow me down.

"He's almost out," a man said.

I didn't know how close I was, but when I looked to my left, I saw the man who had passed me and realized how close he was. He turned to face me, his eyes became wide and psychotic as he rushed in my direction.

"Dumb ass," I yelled.

"Go, go, go!" the crowd said.

The echoes I heard before faded back as I got closer to the end, not knowing if they were for me or not, I knew I couldn't slow down to look. I was a one-armed man running through the forest, I'm sure I looked ridiculous, but I didn't care. I went left, right, left, and right again. I jumped over a bolder so big I could have been jumping over a mountain.

The forest disappeared when I landed and then I saw it --The End, two words so enlightening not even God could stop me from getting there. I slowed down for just a second and realized that the man behind me was still rushing toward my direction, eyes burning to steal my soul if I went any further. I stared back, a smile so disturbing I could have looked insane. I took one more deep breath and burst down the last quarter mile.

"Yay!" the crowd roared.

I made it to the end with one less arm and blood dripping down from parts I didn't know the names of, but I knew as a Cross Country Runner, that I was the best even though this was my final run.

Enrique Melendez *is a writer from Full Sail University who favors thriller, suspense, and mystery genres. He became aware of his storytelling capabilities from a young age when he began to write poetry. He continues to grow his stories to try to affect others on his path to screenwriting.*

ALL THAT REMAINS

by Joe Ducato

A fly walked the edge of the hardwood floor left mostly deserted by bargain seekers and treasure hunters. All that was left, in the middle of the room, were a grand piano, a wooden bench on which an old woman was sitting, and an oil painting of 3 white birch trees in a snow squall. Even all the chairs had been taken. Outside curtainless windows, heavy clouds mimicked uncles at Thanksgiving; too fat and too full to move. In the driveway, the boss lady sat in her running car crunching numbers and sipping from an Arby's cup.

A car pulled up and a tall man with an umbrella got out and walked up the drive. The boss lady watched him through the rear-view.

'This guy's no buyer,' she thought, 'Money stays with him like an in-law at Christmas.'

She went back to her numbers. The tall man walked past the car then entered the home, ignoring the sign with the hours of the sale. He came upon the room and stopped as soon as he saw the piano and the old woman.

"Guess I'm late to the party again," he joked, setting the umbrella down.

He stared at the painting.

"Simplest things are beautiful through the right eyes."

The woman on the bench nodded.

‘ “Did you come to make an offer?” she asked, then:

“The lady in the car. That’s who you’ll need to talk to.”

“Thanks, I’ll keep that in mind.”

“She’s making deals today,” the woman added.

“I’m sure.”

He turned his gaze to the piano.

“Does it play, the Steinway?”

The woman put a hand to her cheek.

“Oh no, it’s not a Steinway. It’s a Hamlin and Mason. My father couldn’t afford a Steinway.”

“Does it play?”

“It did,” the woman replied, “I mean it probably still does. You’ll need to talk to…”

“…the lady in the car,” the man finished.

“That’s right.”

The woman lowered her head.

“That’s ok,” the tall man said, “…but it is stunning, the piano.”

“Stunning,” the old woman repeated, “Funny word to describe a dusty, old piano.”

The man paused.

“Well to me it is. I don’t know why anyone would part with such a thing.”

He unbuttoned the top button of his coat and looked out the window.

“Feels like snow. The first of the season though the hill tops may have had a dusting.”

“Because it’s unmovable,” the old woman blurted, “…and it certainly won’t fit where I’m going. Why most of it would stick out a window.”

“A ready-made balcony,” the man grinned. The woman laughed into her hand.

”The piano? Is it yours? Do you play?”

“I did,” the old woman replied.

“We never forget,” the man noted.

“A long time ago,” the women went on, “I took lessons when I was a girl and then as a young woman, before the work.”

“Yes,” the man nodded, “The work. So, is this the one you learned on?”

“Yes.”

The woman thought.

“Not one offer.”

“Just as well,” the man replied, “I wouldn’t want to see it go to just anyone. Why somebody might buy it just to bust it up for firewood. That would bring tears to my eyes.”

"Tears to your eyes?!" the woman cackled showing a couple of broken teeth.

The man smiled.

"A weakness of mine. I could cry over a perfect bowl of spaghetti."

The woman shook her head.

"Nobody will buy it. It's not what people want. People don't want an albatross."

"You know, I think you might be right," the man said, "In my neighborhood I hardly ever see anyone walking their albatrosses anymore."

He laughed.

"Say, tell me if I'm out of line, but would you mind if I tried it, struck a few notes?"

The woman stood and shoved the bench back.

"I didn't know you…'

The man laughed.

"Oh, I can't play a lick but I know how they work. I had an uncle who fixed these. He taught me because I, well - because I was the only one who cared - really."

"The boy who cries over spaghetti."

"Yes ma'am."

"Do you miss him? Your uncle?"

"I do."

The tall man stepped forward, stood at the keyboard, put his hands in position then pressed a key, producing a note.

"Needs tuning, but rich. So rich."

"That's a good word."

The woman thought for a second, then:

"I always thought it was a little off. I wanted to have it looked at a hundred times, but my husband insisted it was my ears that were off. Damn fool. Besides, he always said, 'Nobody plays it anymore anyway."

She lowered her head;

"He was right. Nobody played it anymore – not since the boy."

Her voice trailed off.

"… not since then," she said mostly to herself.

"I'm sorry," the tall man said.

He didn't know what to say, then:

"They're very fixable. That's the beauty of it. Everything revolves around a series of pullies, hinges, and adjustable screws. It's complicated yet simple. The first time my uncle showed me what happens when you strike a key, why it was like being handed the keys to the universe. Most likely it's just a tweak or a slight warp, a small crack in a hammer or maybe it's just replacing a fifty-cent drop-screw. I could look at it. Wouldn't cost you a dime."

The woman sat again and put her hands on her lap.

"No need to," she said.

"Well can I look anyway? Just to see what it might be? Another fault of mine. I just have to know."

"Help yourself," the woman grinned.

The man lifted the piano lid and peered inside.

"I swear to God, it's a disease I have," he said sticking his head almost entirely inside the piano.

The woman picked at the tips of her fingers, then looked at the window.

"There's a fly on the glass. It survived. Even in all this cold, it survived.

"Amazing isn't it?" the man said, but the woman wasn't listening.

"Wasn't my husband's fault," she said, "Wasn't nobody's fault. I said it until I was blue in the face but he couldn't hear. He was already gone and he couldn't come back. Just couldn't - poor man. Now it's just me and the other one, the beauty himself. God!"

She laughed.

"Now it's off she goes - into the closet with all the other dirty laundry!"

She looked around.

The door opened revealing the boss lady.

"I have to meet another client, Margaret. Is your son coming?"

"Yes," the woman said, "6:00, that means 7:00."

The tall man pulled his head out of the piano and straightened. The boss lady moved closer.

"Fifty percent off," she said, "Sixty if you take it all. I'm basically giving you the painting for free."

"Oh," the tall man tipped his head, "Thank you but I think I'll just be on my way."

'I knew it,' the boss lady thought.

The tall man turned to the old woman.

"Mostly fixable. Most times we just don't realize it."

The old woman eyes turned gentle, "I hope there's a Mrs. Cry Baby somewhere. Would be a shame if…"

The tall man turned just as the boss lady shoved a calling card into his hand.

After the boss lady left, the tall man turned back to the old woman who was staring at her hand.

"I can't even hold a tea cup."

The tall man smiled.

"We always surprise ourselves."

"They say there's lots of nice people there," the woman said, "Lots of activities day and night. Never stops they say."

"I'll bet."

The man looked around then stood near the door.

The woman got up, slowly pulled the piano bench close to the piano, then sat on the bench and laid her hands gently on the keys. She took a deep breath then started to play, slow at first, then her playing become faster and smoother. The tall man said:

"La Campanella."

"That's right," the old woman smiled.

The tall man opened the door and stepped into the cold. Darkness had come. He found himself in the glare of the boss lady's headlights. He could still hear the woman playing. He buttoned his coat. It started to snow.

Joe Ducato *lives in Utica, NY. Publications include The Santa Barbara LIterary Review, Modern Literature, and Home Planet News among others.*

THE DAY OF THE DAMNED

by Russell Frietze

I lost my parents shortly before The Day of the Damned while they were in their home. I was out on a run gathering the ingredients I needed in order to do a spell I devised as a surprise when I heard high pitched whines before crashes were heard followed by screams. I ran as fast as I can down the trail leading to their home while I managed to dodge fireballs that continued to land around me. When I returned home only to find that their home was in ruins, I desperately moved the ruins only to find their hands grasping each other in their final embrace. Dammit! As I stood there overcome with dread another fireball landed near me that sent me through some trees causing the wind to be knocked out.

I had to get out of there or I was next to die. I grabbed my pouch to for what I needed to open a portal out of the area. When I looked up to see another one heading for me, I stepped through the portal behind me just as it crashed in front of me. The place I ended up was foreign and strange, but something felt strangely familiar about it. The air had a distinct freshness in it and the trees seemed different from my land, also there was a struggle for magic to be free in the air.

The support of the people came with quite a challenge, most people ran when I told them that I could give them peace by raising their loved ones. The first few times I did raise their loved ones they ran from me with names like "monster" getting thrown around. I retreated to the mountains so I could study my spells to find out what I missed with raising the dead, only to find out that it would be impossible to do so without the Gloom Flower. It was very rare but with the help of William the herbalist in town I was able to acquire and use it to separate the body from the soul. Since I was able to retrieve my spell book before leaving home there was a spell that allowed me to speed the process of growing more of the Flower.

With a decent supply of the Flower I was able to give aid to those in town to get closure. I was eventually given the title "Peace giver." Granted I wasn't too keen on the title at first but it grew on me. They even started leaving tokens of appreciation for my help and at first I tried to refuse it but started to show my appreciation by casting spells that resembled fireworks. The Day of the Damned celebration preparations started shortly after this. I was informed that the veil between the living and the dead would be weakest and wanted my help bringing closure to everyone at once.

I took the time to get rested and fed. I was bone tired and was feeling my parents loss all over again. I had to fight off the drowning feeling of it so I took a little time and ingredients to cast a smaller ritual to see my parents. A few moments had passed and I started to think I did it wrong when finally they appeared before me. We spent some time talking about how we felt. As we spoke they came in and out of focus since I only had used a little bit. A few moments later they began to fade away with teary eyes. Afterwards I decided to lay down close to where I casted the spell.

Scene break

I lined up what herbs and concoctions I have available. A scream was cut off abruptly by a loud crash. I spread my wings to launch myself up to get a rough idea of where the source of the crash was only to find smoke and fire in the distance. Once I landed, I spotted something embedded in the ground. A strange black orb that was smooth but hot to the touch. While I inspected the area I eventually saw the hand of a small child undeath the sphere. This ended up putting a hamper in the plan to cast the ritual because I felt horrible bout this unfortunate loss of life.

The orb I thought was heavy ended up be pretty easy to lift when I touched it. Once I was able to get it off the child and set it down I returned to the child to carefully lift the body. Once again I spread my wings to launch myself up to return to town. It took me a few moments to reach the town square. As I was coming down I spot a pure white three tailed fox that I was told is a spiritual animal that would appear when I needed it. I casted another spell to make my voice louder to announce I found a young child in the mountains and inquired who the parents are. I continued to stand in the square for the rest of that day and the only person to come up to me was a little girl in grungy clothes.

I took the time to give the child proper burial before I returned home to take a further look at the orb. Once home I spotted the orb floating in the of middle the floor and this took me off guard. As I moved around my home it seemed to follow me around which was pretty creepy but I had decided to deal with it another time I was pretty whooped. I nod and I speak the words necessary for the spell.

When the final words have finished a green wall circles the town square along with the ghosts of loved ones. The little girl yelps in shock at seeing her friend appear. Standing there admiring my work at pulling this off my parents appear before me. I looked upon the square to see all the people reconnecting with their loved ones happy with the success of the outcome. Tears well up as I look upon my parents once again. With a sadness in their eyes they tell me "We're so proud of you. We love you."

The celebration took all day and into the night when the spell began to wear off and the spirits returned to where they came from. From what I was able to ascertain everyone had a great time. Everyone as they passed by to go to their homes gave me their thanks. While I was receiving their thanks I kept thinking of the mysterious orb in my home just floating there. I spread my wings for another time and take to the skies for a flight to think about the orb and what it's possible purpose may be. As I flew around to get my thoughts in order about the orb and decided to get home to do some research.

After a night of close studying and prodding the orb. It responded to my every touch and command. Gaining ground on the orb was difficult but eventually something happened. I don't really recall what I did but at some point the orb disappeared and in it's place was a box with my name engraved in the top. What the hell is this? Maybe it is something from my parents. I carefully lifted the lid off to find a note letting me know that this box will hold everything I put in it and if I was to reach into it all I would have to do is think of what I'm reaching for and it'll rise to the top.

I decided to test it out for the first time by taking all my things and putting them in the box and waited a few moments before reaching in to recall my spell book. I watched as it rose to the top amazed by the sheer magical feeling that I may not have to limit my collections anymore. I pulled everything out of the box and catalogued everything that I have left after the ritual. Once I completed this I wrote down that the box's magic is akin to a bag of holding but my parents modified it for a box instead to give it more durability. As I sat there trying to decide what I am going to do with the box so that no one will take it I heard claws padding there way up to me. I looked up to see the fox again padding its way up to me. I spent time trying to wrack my brain on why now did it show itself but glad it did.

SNOWBOUND LOVERS

by Victoria Windapo

The windscreen wipers smacked against the snow. Ethan squinted, the streetlights flickering like the ones in a horror movie scene. He was late, with a familiar aching in his stomach. But then, a flash on the pavement caught his hazy gaze. Hera. His ex, in a red coat, extended his thumb into the blizzard. There's no car in sight.

A confusing urge, a tangled jumble of sorrow and lingering affection, caused him to slam on the brakes. The automobile skidded in a controlled spiral, ending up facing Hera. She beheld him with surprise in her big, snow-dusted eyes.

"Ethan?" Her voice was hardly audible over the wind.

He rolled down the window, the sting of cold air a pleasant surprise. "Stuck, are you?"

"Every taxi app says no thanks to this weather," she said, a hint of defiance in her voice. He knew her too well.

Offering a ride was an act of self-sabotage, ignoring the voice in his head urging him to continue driving. "Same way. Get in, or you'll be an ice sculpture in the morning."

Hera paused, her attention shifting to the dashboard, where a half-empty bottle of whisky always sat during their carpool days. His stomach turned. Although he had denied it, she had a nagging sense.

"Look," he groaned, trying to sound lighthearted, "either freeze or get a not-so-princely ride."

The decision was apparent. Mumbling to herself, she climbed in, slamming the door with finality that reflected the closing of a chapter in their lives.

The silence inside the car was heavy, interrupted only by the repetitive thud of the wipers. The air was dense with unspoken words and the faint aroma of her vanilla perfume, which had once captivated him but now served as a bittersweet recollection.

Suddenly, the automobile jerked abruptly, its tires whirling against a wall of white. Ethan cursed as he white-knuckled the steering wheel. "Damn it, I didn't see that drift."

Hera turned around, her eyes sparkling. "Ethan, you were speeding! "In this weather?"

The rage in her voice ripped the frail thread of his equanimity. "Maybe if you hadn't spent the entire relationship nagging me, I wouldn't have needed to drink myself numb all the time!"

The words lingered in the air, weighty and accusatory. The automobile was silent again, with the only sound being the hiss of the malfunctioning heater. Shame boiled bitterly in Ethan's throat.

"That's not fair," Hera finally murmured, her tone softening. "You were unhappy, Ethan, but you never mentioned it. You simply shut down, buried yourself in work, and..." her voice drifted off.

He let out a fake laugh. "And the whisky, correct?

"Like a bad cliché.-"

"It wasn't just about the whisky," she explained, her voice steely. "I wanted us to work, but I was scared." I'm afraid you'll abandon me like everyone else."

The tenderness in her voice pierced the wall he'd created around himself. "I wouldn't have," he answered gently, his voice tinged with sorrow and prior promises. "I just..." I didn't know how to be joyful, so I blamed you for it."

This time, the silence was softer and tinged with a hesitant understanding. They discussed the raw, messy portions of their relationship, rather than the wonderful times. Her desire for control, his destructive inclinations, and their incapacity to communicate.

As they talked, the snow piled up, burying the car. The towing company, phoned in exasperation, would not arrive for at least an hour.

"So," Ethan eventually replied, the strain in his shoulders relaxing. "What now?"

Hera gazed at him, a slight smile on her lips. "Well, are we stuck here? We might as well make the most of it.

The air between them was lighter, with the sting of the past replaced by a new understanding. They dug out the glass with a credit card, giggling as snowflakes fell on their faces. She told him about her new photographic project, and the spark in her eyes brought back a forgotten warmth in him. He told her about his plans to finally pursue his love of writing, and the fear was replaced with a renewed determination.

By the time the tow truck arrived, the snow had ceased, and stars twinkled dimly in a cloudless sky. As they stepped out of the car, the environment around them appeared a little brighter and less harsh.

Hera responded, "Thanks for the ride, Ethan," with a sincere smile.

"Anytime,"

TRAPPED

by Gloria Frazier

"Damn it," Karin muttered as she yanked on the icy handle of the walk-in freezer door. "Yeah, keep yanking on the door that's clearly frozen shut. Just face it, we're trapped until someone realizes we're missing and comes to save us," I said leaning against the wall with a sigh of frustration. She shot me a quick narrowed glance, rolling her eyes before turning back to the door.

"Thanks for the brilliant insight, Professor Lexi," she replied, her tone heavy with sarcasm.

We've been trapped in the walk-in freezer at our job, Margot's Ice Dream for about a while now, our manager left out early, leaving Karin and I to close the store. We used to be great friends but, she's hated me ever since her boyfriend got wasted and hit on me last summer. I pushed him off me and ran to tell Karin, she got mad and started a fight with me in the bar.

The icy freezer air was starting to pierce my skin. What if no one notices until it's too late? I thought to myself.

"Shit! Hey Lexi, why don't you get off your ass and come help me!", Karin hissed. I whipped my head around ready to rip Karin a new one when I noticed her hands.

"Uhm, Karin can you feel your fingers?" I asked.

"What the hell are you talking ab-..." her voice drifted off. She stared down in her hands with a petrified look on her face. Her hands are completely numb, and it seems like they're becoming too stiff for her to move. She started to have a panic attack. "We're never going to get out of here!" Karin cried.

Puffs of frosty white air escape our mouths as we exhale. With every breath I feel my body getting colder and colder, the air of the walk-in cutting through my skin like daggers and chilling me to the core. Karin and I are now cuddled up right next to the door, the area in the room that was furthest from the vent that was constantly pumping cold air into the room. Our bodies are shivering so hard that you could hear our teeth chattering between the hums coming from the vent. I can feel my toes starting to go numb.

The familiar sound of the alarm signaling that someone has entered the store. Karin and I both made eye contact. "Did you hear that?" she asked. I nodded, we both jolt from where we were seated, hands nearly frozen, we began banging and screaming on the freezer door making as much noise as we could.

Then we heard it, the beautiful sound of the locking mechanism clicking and the door opening. There stood Margot, completely frozen with shock and disbelief. "Wha- what on earth?!" she exclaimed stammering over her words. Margot grabbed her phone from her bag and began dialing 911.

Karin collapsed into Margot's arms; her icy skin sends shocks throughout Margot's body. "Oh, my goodness! How long have you girls been in here?" she asked while wrapping us in her big winter coat. I couldn't give her an answer, I was blacking out…

When I came to, I was lying on my back my eyes were immediately flooded with a bright light. Once my eyes focused, I realized they were hospital lights, I looked over and saw my mom, boyfriend, and surprisingly Karin waiting for me. They explained everything; the door to the freezer has an electronic locking mechanism that just so happened to malfunction while we were both inside subsequently trapping us.

Karin also apologized to me, she explained how she was just drunk that night and overreacted. She felt terrible about the whole thing after she talked to one of our mutual friends about it and they confirmed my story. But by then I wanted nothing to do with her, so she decided to hold onto the grudge. I don't know if this experience brought an old friend and I back together, however I'm glad we made it out alive.

Gloria Frazier *is a student at Full Sail University.*

THE FLAK HOUSE

by Harvey Huddleston

August 15, 1945

Betty shows me her scar. Dark purple it runs six inches down her belly. She says it's ugly and I say it'll fade in time.

Drove through town on my way back. Jap surrender is all over the news so people hold up two fingers for victory. It's when I get away from the crowd. I hit the gas and can't let off. Car speeds up but still can't let off so I hook my arm under my leg and sit up hard pulling my foot up with me.

Stopped on the side. Scary as hell. Take some breaths and try my leg. It works so I pull away. Slow this time and make it back here.

Martins are outside. He won't stop talking. I tell them her tests are normal and she'll be home with the baby in a week. That little dog stares like it wants an answer but I don't have any. All I have is the question. Why did my foot stick like that again?

That time with Betty in the car. She snaps at me to slow down. My leg unsticks but she's still mad so I say we have to burn off the factory oil. She gives me a look and then we go on like everything's normal. And it was. Until today.

I sat in here earlier. Curtain stops high in its arc. Falls back and starts all over again. That crowd before my leg froze. Dancing. Hugging. Almost got out but didn't. Their faces. Such happiness.

I should be the happiest guy in the world. War's over. I have a son and wife. That job back home waiting. We can do it all now just like we planned so what's wrong?

Haven't looked at this notebook since Kimbolton. At the bottom of my grip but I put it aside. Need to be there with donuts by eight. That powdered kind she likes.

In bed early but then comes a dream. One I never had before. Someone I don't know. Saying something I can't hear. I try hard to listen but this roar in my ears blocks it out and then there I am again. Awake. Soaked in sweat.

It feels different in my hand now. All soft and beat up.

Maybe if I read through I can put that year in the past. Back where it belongs. Or find an answer. The answer I need.

And maybe that's why my foot stuck today. It's telling me to get out now while I still have the chance. If I can't fix this before they come home that's what it has to come to anyway.

May 10, 1944

At intake Doc Spencer wants to know if I ever froze up before. Says if I come up with anything to write it down so here goes.

We're on a weekend pass in Piccadilly. Kal says one of the Red Cross girls is giving him the eye so we all laugh. He says watch this and goes for a refill but it's about then I decide to head out on my own anyway.

You might think Piccadilly Circus is full of clowns and elephants but it's just a big city intersection. An old guy tells me Park on the right so I go that way keeping right.

London has a smell. Dirt and rubble but you can't really say what that is. Burnt brick. Not fresh burnt old burnt.

Buds on the trees. Without all the big guns you might think there's no war at all.

Further in is a bandstand in a clearing. No one there so I sit on a bench. A couple comes through. They keep going so I stay. It's quiet.

Then I wake up and don't know where I am. I try to get up but can't. I try again but still can't so I just sit there and it comes to me. There's no war on that bench but when I get up it starts all over again.

A woman and kid come at me. She has a newspaper. Makes like she's folding it and pushes it to the sky. I figure she wants me to make an airplane for that kid so I take it and start folding.

It looks pretty good but when the kid tosses it it crashes. I'm all set to try again with less pages but that woman looks at me now like I'm one sorry ass plane builder. Maybe the worst she's ever seen.

She drags the kid away. I think what the hell was that all about and take off to find the guys.

May 11, 1944

An RC girl says no GI issue in the dining room so look in my closet. I do and find a shirt and some pants there I have to roll the cuffs up on to keep from tripping.

I set my tray on a table when that same RC girl brings me a coffee and sits down with her own cup. She looks at the wraps on my hands so I say frostbite. I guess that's her cue because then she starts up about perspex waist ports on the new B-17s. It's kind of funny but she knows her stuff so I listen.

I was going to give Spencer what I wrote but then left it here. I tell him instead about not being able to get up from that bench. He says maybe I don't want to. Big difference but I let it go. Spencer's like that mad scientist in the Frankenstein movie so now I'm looking for Igor to walk in.

He asks if I like it here. I almost say best damn flak house ever but don't. Then he asks if I have any questions so I ask when I can get back with my crew but he don't answer that. Next time he wants one time up there when I didn't think I'd make it back.

He tells me to lose the wraps. So much for frostbite. Frostbite of the brain and they all know it.

I know now why I didn't take what I wrote. It was my file there on his desk. Just one more thing to use against me.

So here's the deal. I'll tell Spencer what he wants. Maybe even write it down but what I put in this notebook is my business. Then I'll decide if he needs to hear it.

May 13, 1944

They say ignorance is bliss. Which means the less you know the happier you are. It follows then that learning something new costs some happiness. But people learn new things all the time so that means your whole life you become less happy.

The inverse then has to mean forgetting things brings back some happiness. So why remember anything? Maybe I don't want to. Maybe I don't have to.

Most people don't go up in airplanes to drop bombs on people.

Spencer wants one time when I thought I wouldn't make it back but that would be every time. Add to that it's all mashed up in my head now anyway. What sticks out I guess is the first one. When I first found out what I'd gotten myself into.

We thought it might be a milk run like they sometimes give a new crew but then they pull back the curtain. Schweinfurt is deep inside Germany. Our mission is to destroy their ball bearing factory. Stopping production there can end the war. That's what they say.

Last time there in the fall our group lost a quarter of its planes. But you can't know anything until you do it yourself and this was my first mission so I was ignorant. Not happy. Just ignorant.

We take off at dawn and don't cross the Channel until 1140. The bomber stream goes as far as you can see in front and behind.

About a half hour over France some Mustangs show up in my waist port. I point them out on the headset and we're all glad they're there. Then they're not. We learn later some fighters lured them off leaving us to face their main force alone.

Some chatter on the headset. Then Whitman on top turret yells they're coming in a voice so high I don't recognize it. He opens up with his Double Fifty and the rest of us do too.

They come head on rolling over while firing. Then they hit the group to our right and I see three forts go down. One with its tail blown off and two trailing smoke.

Some chutes open below. I watch as far as I can follow.

Closing on Schweinfurt their ground Eighty-Eights open up. Flak pings off our hull over the engine and wind noise. Black puffs appear out my waist port and inside the close ones I see that red glow. What they call the red monster and now I know why.

Our bombs are gone but it's still three hours back to England. They had time to land and re-arm so the only question is when. Just before the Channel they come from all sides.

I stay on one all the way in. He's gone when I realize my body is up in the air behind me. I land on the casings and see Kal yelling at me through a cordite haze.

Coastal batteries throw up one last barrage. A fort in the distance takes a direct hit. There it is one second and gone the next. Then the Channel appears beneath us.

Kal says when I locked on that FW I kicked him in the head. He thinks he's hit but then sees my legs up in the air so I tell him I'll keep my feet on the deck next time.

Back on my bunk not sure how long. That's when it comes to me if that's number one how will I ever make it through twenty nine more.

May 14, 1944

Tough session with Spencer today. Only thing I say about Schweinfurt is watching those chutes go down. He wants to know about that so I say it was like them passing into another world.

That perks him up and I want to bash his head in with that paperweight on his desk. He says I'm here to help. I say you're here to get me back into a B-17 so just sign my paperwork and I'll be on my way.

He asks about that other world. I say it's a world of hate. How the farmers down there are waiting to pitchfork us while the guys under those chutes watch us go on without them. All they got anymore is that world of hate below.

Next time he wants to hear about my freeze-up. Says I should make use of the facilities here. That I should enjoy myself. So how do I do that with my crew back there carrying all the load. I say I will.

May 16, 1944

I take a shortcut to the driving range and get lost. That's when it comes to me to just go tell Spencer that's it. I'm done flying. So I'm all set to do just that when I ask myself who I'll be then. A quitter for one thing and that ain't so easy to fix once it's done.

I don't tell him I got lost. Who gets lost in a clump of trees? Then something pops into my head. I tell him about this buddy when I'm a kid and how at the start of the school year he's not there. Then I find out he's held back and wonder if he's stupid.

Spencer asks what it means and I ask him why it has to mean something. He says my buddy got left behind. Same as those guys under the chutes.

I see where he's going so I say there's a difference with me. I plan to catch up. I'll just volunteer for extra missions when I get back. When you give me the okay. I say that last part like a question but then he switches to my freeze-up.

I say it's our eighth mission. Montdidier. No fighters all the way there and back so I'm looking out at some clouds thinking this one's in the bag. We'll be back in an hour with more than a quarter of our missions done. That's when they hit us.

He asks what I think then. I say it ain't fair and keep going..

I'm on one but then here comes another. Cannons flash round in my sight so I give him a burst. He keeps coming so I give him another and then another. And then. My fingers won't let off. I stay on it until it gets so hot it jams. Back on the ground my fingers are still stuck so the medics come on to pry me off. I say it's frostbite. They take me to the infirmary. And that's it.

He makes a note and checks my file. Then he asks about what they call me back home.

I have to think back on that one and tell him it's like those clouds before the fighters jumped us. One time instead of my chores I get caught laid back on this hill looking up at the clouds. All those shapes. So my little sister Tippy gets a big kick out of it and starts calling me Leisure. Then they all start up.

He asks if it bothers me and I say no. I do my job. Like my football team back in school. We were good because we all did our jobs. Same with my crew. Ask any of them. That freeze-up just snuck up on me but it won't happen again.

He asks if I've written home. I say not until I know what happens. He says I should. I say maybe and we leave it at that.

May 17, 1944

Been here a week now. He wants to know about Betty.

I tell how she lives in St. Louis and don't want to live in Memphis. How she won't listen when I explain about my job. I tell him about our last day in Forest Park and how I wish it went better.

What I don't tell him is I decide right then to write to her as soon as I leave his office. So I do and tell her we'll find a way to make it work.

Funny. Right after I mail that letter I want one back and then the next morning one shows up forwarded from Kimbolton. Before even reading mine she answers me almost word for word everything in it.

Spencer says I should mix in more here so I say I'm going to toast marshmallows Friday night. Colored signs everywhere. Punch and cupcakes for all.

May 18, 1944

He wants me to go back through my missions. Wish I wrote them here all along.

We skip a day after Schweinfurt. Then go three straight. Kassel. No Oranienburg is first. Aircraft factory. We peel away from the main group as a diversion. No losses.

Then Kassel. It was destroyed in February but they rebuilt it underground. We lose one fort while our sister group loses three.

Third day is to a V-1 rocket site at Sottevast. Some Focke Wulfs and light flak. Whole mission lasts only four hours.

Next day I sleep in but then keep popping up like I'm missing something. That's the day I meet Fred. He's already got fourteen missions and I can't even imagine that many.

He asks what I think about killing innocent civilians down there. I say it's our job and he nods. Then he wonders what it's like getting hit with a five hundred pounder and I tell him there's nothing to wonder about because there's nothing left. At that he just stares with that far off look.

Number five is to Landesberg outside Munich. A new type Messerschmidt is built there. Some groups from Italy are supposed to link up but all I see is what looks like the whole German Air Force.

Rail yards at Hamm-Bonn is six. I'm looking at a runway crack thinking that concrete was poured way too fast. It's about then we all are wondering what happened to the land invasion. Even the brass knows we can't win this war by ourselves.

Seven is to Berlin. Seven hundred forts and nothing goes right. High winds and clouds the whole way. Over the target we lose five forts and count very few chutes.

Fifty men. Same chow line. Throwing around the same football. Gone. Just like that. That's when they give us the two-day pass to London.

I try to make an airplane for that kid.

On the train back people out the window do the normal things people do. And we feel normal too after our thousands of miles traveling together. Difference is we ain't in a goddamn airplane.

We get back. First the quiet. Then the gear missing from the middle bunks. End crew ignores us until one pipes up. Went down yesterday. No chutes reported.

Fred's crew. I hope he's a POW somewhere but there's a better chance he's not. I think at least he won't have to worry anymore about killing civilians.

That look on his face. It's like he knew but then how could he not? You can't keep rolling the dice and expect it to not come up snake eyes. The law of averages. It has to catch up.

Berlin's the first time my hands freeze. I'm plugged in so I figure it's a bad connection. I take my gloves over to the equipment chief and he hands them back saying they're fine. I think he's telling the truth.

May 19, 1944

I try to tell about Fred but then don't have much to say. That's when Spencer brings up me taking the Pentothal. Nothing to it he says. It relaxes you so you can talk.

And spout off any dumb thing in your head. What he's really saying is I have to take it if I want back with my crew while at the same time saying it's my choice. Funny how that works. He tells me to sleep on it.

Then I go to the marshmallow toast. GIs and RC girls. A crowd at the fireplace cooking marshmallows.

It feels tight in there and then something jumps the rails. This RC girl acts like I should say something. I try to smile but that's wrong so I go for the punch. Then I think I might throw up so I head for the door and make it outside.

I lean against a bicycle rack when this other RC girl comes out and offers me a cigarette. I see now she's that one from my first day.

I tell her I don't smoke so she lights up and lets out a long contrail.

She checks her watch a few times and asks if I want to go for a ride. Then she hops on a bike and tells me to grab one. Next thing I'm following her down the driveway and I don't think anything's ever felt so good as riding that bicycle through the night.

Almost bright out except for the tree shadows. We go a long way and then turn down a lane that ends at a fence. She hops over and heads off into a field. She stops to check her watch again so I strike a match and ask if she needs to be somewhere. All she says back is give it a minute.

You feel the hum before hearing it. Then comes that rumble that gets louder until the ground shakes. A Lancaster comes over the tree line followed by dozens more. It's RAF since they only fly at night but she knows that.

I say Limey and she says blimey.

She's from New York so I call her a Yankee. She says that's what her husband calls her but he shortens it to Yank. I ask where he is now and she points up to that bomber stream. So that's it. We're here to see him off.

Her eyes stay on that stream so I shut up and watch too. I also watch her face and it reminds me of something. Something I lost track of.

Back at the house all she says is I got heart and goes in.

There's still that answer I owe Spencer. I can turn down the Pentothal. Get a ground job maybe. Or I can take it and try to get back in the war. After being out in that field earlier turns out there's not much choice after all.

May 20, 1944

Bug Juice. Truth serum. I say I don't need that stuff to tell the truth and that sets him off but good.

He says it's not to find out if I'm lying but to reveal what we don't know. Think of it as peeling back the flesh on an infection to flush it out. He's wound up pretty good so I tell him I already said okay. Let's just do it.

I report in the morning to a small clinic behind the main house.

May 27, 1944

What's fair? Kids say that's not fair to each other. Some people say we lost the game but we played fair. And then for others it don't matter at all.

Been a whole week since writing here. Sent another letter to Betty. Told her I want to take a trip together when I get back. And it don't matter where.

I knew we were killing people by the thousands. Guess I had to see for myself.

I want to go hunting again. Not to kill anything. Just to be there. I want to see Betty again and see how we do together. I want to live a little more like anyone else in the world and there's nothing wrong with that.

But there's no guarantee. That's the important part. Some die and the rest go on. There's nothing fair about it. The other side is you have to live with yourself and if you can't do that you don't have anything anyway.

My plan to catch up is over. Those guys must be halfway through by now. They've gone on and I hope they keep going on just like I plan on doing when the time comes.

May 28, 1944

If your mask fills with puke you choke. But you can't pull it off. No oxygen so you fight it back down. You fight the FWs too. But then something wants to take you away. You want to go but you have to stay on that Fifty. So you do it and then do it again. And keep doing it. Until you don't.

Spencer reads from his notes. He says some remember everything under the Pentothal while others like me almost nothing.

Yelling over the headset. 17s falling out of the sky. The cold. Spencer says it's okay to cry and I tell him why it's not.

Then he brings up Jimmy Stewart. He flew the lead fort to Berlin that day. They say with a movie star leading us we shouldn't mind following. I remember all this.

After the mission we find out they turned him back over France but then we see a newsreel of him getting the Croix de Guerre for leading us to Berlin. It's a crap lie and Stewart gets cussed out pretty good that day as just another newsreel hero.

But that's not fair and I say why. Stewart's flown more combat missions than all those other newsreel heroes put together. Maybe he did have engine trouble but that's not the point anyway. And then there it is staring me right in the face. It's not fair. I yell it out and wait for an answer but nothing.

Fair is for another time. Another place. And who am I to judge what's fair anyway? Maybe those newsreel heroes know something I don't. Maybe they know to not get themselves in a situation where they freeze-up. Maybe they're doing the best they can with this rotten mess and that's all you can expect of anyone.

Only other thing I remember is getting up from that table soaked in sweat.

May 29, 1944

Got my okay today. A new directive says B-17 crews will now be nine men instead of ten. Half the waist-gunners will train on the radio and split time between it and the Fifty. Spencer thinks I can be one of these radio-waist gunners.

He says my problem is all the waiting. Too much time to think so doubling up on the radio suits me better. I'll be on the Fifty when the fighters come but the rest of the time will be all dots and dashes.

It's up to the brass at Kimbolton but with my experience you can bet they'll find a place for me.

Only thing I can't figure out is how much to tell Betty. In my letter today I only say I had some down time. I don't like lying to her but if I try to explain the censors will leave in some and block out the rest. It'll only confuse her more.

So that's where I leave it.With her and me it's all about the future anyway

Harvey Huddleston*'s short fiction has appeared in The RavensPerch and Mystery Tribune among many others.*

AN AGREEMENT

by Daniel Senser

Justin and Theresa were walking back to their apartment after going to see a movie on Saturday night. It was mid-July, and the air was balmy. There were many people out and about, coming from restaurants and going to bars and cafés. They stopped off at an ice cream parlor and got cones, which they enjoyed as they walked along slowly down the thoroughfare. They both agreed that the movie they had seen had been very sad, and Theresa especially seemed very pensive.

They had been together for five years after meeting in medical school. They worked in the same hospital—he as an oncologist, she in internal medicine. They liked their jobs, lived in a very nice apartment, and both had good friends who they could depend on. As their relationship had developed, they had come to an understanding—and even an agreement—that they would not get married, deciding that marriage was a needless institution, and that they would not have children, mostly because they were both career-driven people.

Lately, however, they had noticed more of a distance developing between themselves, which neither of them could explain. They seemed to have less to talk about, less things in common, and they fought, though their fights were passive, and rarely if ever did either raise their voice to the other.

As they walked along, Justin tried to engage Theresa by recalling various scenes from the movie, but she showed little interest. Then, suddenly, Theresa stopped in her tracks in front of a woman's clothing store, and looked in through the window at a dress on display. It was a little girl's dress—green with a pleated skirt and a yellow sash. "That's a pretty dress," she said.

"It is pretty," said Justin. "But it's a little small, don't you think?"

"Of course it is," said Theresa, playfully. "It's a girl's dress. But I like it. You don't see dresses like that anymore. At least on grown women."

"That's why it's a girls' dress," said Justin, who knew this subtle jab would go over.

"You know what I mean," said Theresa. She looked at the dress for a long time, then sighed, turned and started walking.

She was very pensive. "What are you thinking about?" Justin asked her.

"Oh, nothing special."

"The movie?"

"No! Though, it was a sad movie. But I'm over it. It was just a movie. Movies can be sad, but I think life can be a lot sadder, don't you?"

"I suppose," said Justin, not sure what she was driving at. "Are you sad?"

"Me? No. Not sad, really. Just..."

"Anxious?"

"Anxious…No, I wouldn't say I'm anxious, either. Dubious! That's what I am. Dubious."

"What are you dubious about?"

"Well, it just makes me wonder…If you can't know for certain that you actually want something until you have it…or rather, no. What am I saying?"

"I don't know. What are you saying?"

"Well, let's say I were to go and buy that dress."

There was a long pause. Justin was waiting for her to finish her thought, but she didn't.

"Yes?" he said.

"What I'm saying is, I am not certain of anything anymore."

"Not certain? You mean, about you and me?"

"No! I am certain that I love you. But…Oh, let's drop it!"

"Are you sure?" Justin asked.

"Yes, I'm sure."

When they got home, they each took up their reading material and drank a glass of wine, then went to bed. As Justin slept, Theresa lay in bed. She couldn't get the image of the little girl's dress out of her mind. Finally, she put her hand on Justin's shoulder and shook him awake. "I want children," she said.

Justin looked at her for a long time through the darkness. "Are you sure?" he finally asked.

Theresa nodded. Justin sat up.

"When did things change?" he asked her.

"They've been changing slowly, incrementally. And then tonight, that really depressing movie, and then seeing that dress…"

Justin was silent.

"Well, what do you think?"

"I don't know," said Justin. "Both of our careers have just started. Are you sure you want to bring children into our lives?"

"I don't see what our careers have to do with it. I want children. More than I want anything else. Are you afraid?"

"Yes, I am afraid," said Justin. "Aren't you?"

"Maybe. Only, my desire outweighs my fear. I guess, somehow, I am getting over my fear. Can't you?"

Justin thought. The idea of having a child made him realize that he had been afraid the majority of his life, and this was unsettling to him. There had been minor fears which he had overcome, but they all seemed so paltry to him now. This new fear—which had really always been there—seemed to rise from the very depths of his being. It seemed to be overcoming him. But then, right at that moment, Theresa kissed him, and then the fear disappeared. They fell onto the bed together, both knowing that their love was now much greater than it had ever been before. Every kiss seemed imbued with more passion, every touch with more vitality. Their embrace seemed to make of them a single, preternaturally powerful being, one which had the potential to create something even more powerful, and knowing this, they were both afraid and exhilarated, and yet calm and empowered at the same time. As Justin let out his final, unmitigated moan of pleasure, it was as if his love for her had found its true purpose, and he fell, exhausted and satiated, into her arms, feeling her warm embrace like the embrace of a great goddess, a mother who would hold him till the morning came.

Daniel Senser *is thirty-eight years old and has been writing for nearly twenty years. He works as a receptionist at a gym in Cincinnati, Ohio.*

MY FIRST "BATTLE"

by Irwin Benitez

The transport ship descends through the atmosphere of Proxima, and my breath catches in my throat. The planet is beautiful, a tapestry of lush forests, sparkling rivers, and rolling hills that stretch as far as the eye can see. The sky is a deep, serene blue, dotted with fluffy white clouds. Birds with iridescent feathers soar gracefully, and strange, colorful flowers blanket the ground below.

The ramp lowers, and we march into formation. General Khan stands before us, a giant man nearly seven feet tall, his right eye glows red from his scouting transplant, and he has a scar across his right eyebrow. "Listen closely soldiers, today we face an enemy unlike any other. These people are ruthless, and you must have your guard up," says General Khan.

I tightened my grip on my weapon.

"Due to the nature of our enemy, we will be infiltrating their camp by unit. Alpha battery will go first, followed by bravo, and then charlie."

A roar comes from the formation, I join along pumping my fist in the air, the veins in my neck bulge out, and my head gets hot. I love this feeling I think to myself.

"Settle down, there is much to be done," said General Khan. The entire formation was quiet almost instantly. General Khan paces back and forth looking into the eyes of the soldiers, as he reaches the middle of the formation he stops. "We will march out at sundown do you understand?"

"Yes sir," yelled the soldiers.

General Khan salutes. "Dismissed."

All the soldiers scattered. One of the men from my unit walks up to me and extends his hand out. "Welcome to charlie, kid," he says.

I shake his hand. "Thanks, it's an honor," I say with a smile.

"You're damn right it is," he says. "Now c'mon, we got a planet to save."

***

Flames engulf the huts around me, painting the night sky with a grim glow. The air is thick with smoke and the cries of women and children yanked brutally from their huts. Men are herded together and forced onto their knees.

"Help…help." The voices ring in my ear from my translator implant. I tap it, turning it off.

A soldier approaches, his heavy boots crunching on the ground. "Why are you just standing there?" he asks.

"I thought this was supposed to be a battle," I say, barely above a whisper.

The soldier scoffs. "First timer." He shakes his head and runs off.

I remain still, my eyes fixed on the horrors ahead. More men are dragged into line while the women and children are shoved next to them. Unable to bear the sight any longer, I turn away and walk back toward the transport ship. I spot a woman and her child hiding near it and tap my ear, activating the translator.

As I approach, the woman cowers away. "Don't hurt us," she pleads. She is beautiful, with red hair, tan skin, and bright purple eyes.

"I'm not here to hurt you, but they will if they find you," I say, pointing at the soldiers. "You have to follow me." I extend my hand.

"No," her daughter replies.

"Is that all of them?" General Khan asks.

We all turn toward the general.

"Yes, sir," says a soldier from a nearby hut.

"Very well, now kill them." The general walks away. Soldiers raise their weapons and fire.

I flinch and look away, into the purple eyes of the red-haired woman. "Please, just follow me."

The red-haired woman wipes a tear from her cheek. "Okay." She grabs her daughter, and we head to the ship.

"Everyone, get in formation!" yells the general. The soldiers assemble in unison, ten to a row.

"Hide in there," I point to an open room. The girls run in. My heart races and sweat pours from my forehead and palms. I poke my head around the corner of the entrance.

"Attention!" yells the general. The soldiers stop shuffling their feet, straighten their backs, and lock eyes with General Khan.

"Proxima is ours," General Khan declares. A loud applause rises from the formation. Soldiers shake hands, wide smiles on their faces as the huts burn behind them.

My stomach churns as the smell of burning wood and flesh fills the air. I look up into the sky. General Khan's voice booms, "There is nothing to celebrate. This is only the beginning." The stars fade, swallowed by thick black smoke.

The cries of the woman and child fill the ship. I glance back at their tear-streaked faces and then outside at the celebrating men. My fist clenches and trembles. I close the hatch and run to the girls.

The soldiers rush toward the ship; their shouts pierce through the metal. They bang on the hull, some even open fire.

"Follow me," I tell the girls, leading them to the cockpit. "Sit here and put this on." I grab the seatbelt and wrap it around the red-haired woman's waist. She repeats the motion with her daughter.

"This is General Khan." His voice echoes through the speakers. "What is the meaning of this?"

I run back to the cockpit and press the communications button. "You told us these people were the enemy. But I see now... the real

"This is treas...—"

I yank the communication cable from the console, then turn on the map function. A hologram of a planet springs to life, glowing softly in the cockpit.

"Shall we proceed to Planet Keplar?" asks the AI assistant.

"Yes," I reply, breathless.

With a thunderous roar, we surge into space. Through the viewport, I see a distant spot of light piercing the vast blackness. I look back at the red-haired woman and her daughter; the light twinkles in their eyes.

NO SUGAR IN MY COFFEE

by Christian Gonzalez

I love morning cups of coffee. Waking up having a burning hot kiss of Colombian dark roast on my lips. Energizing and warmed up as if I got a good morning text from... well, maybe not her. Either way being in this tranquil environment with the smell of brewing coffee warms me up. Different gossip being exchanged between people as we wait for our lovely orders. The old speakers struggled to play; Baby Come Back by The Players throughout the shop.

The customers coming bring the chilly winter breeze. It is the type of frost that will make you want to take a double shot of espresso. I am always curious to see the new souls that this old coffee shop brings in. I couldn't believe it was her. The only person in the whole world who orders one thing from every coffee shop.

"Hi, Welcome to Pete's Coffee shop. What can I get you started with?" asked the cashier in an Indian accent.

She ordered, "I am going to have a black coffee with two cups of cream and a lot of sugar."

"That will be three dollars," said the cashier as he opens the cash register.

She pays the sweaty cashier and makes her way to the napkin dispenser.

Her face glowed with a blue glare texting on her phone, probably to her new boyfriend. I noticed that she had cut her hair and dyed it blonde like she had always wanted to. Well, I gotta say it looks great on her. Still wearing that grey hoodie that she stole from me, that night when we were dancing with the stars in the park.

Instead of the dim light of her phone lighting up her smooth tanned skin, it was the moonlight that had accented her glow. She shined like the miracle star you see on Christmas nights. How can I forget those big brown eyes? It was like looking into a black hole, pulling you into a void where you were lost to both space and time. Scary to think about but it always pulled me in to stay.

I thought about not only her eyes but those moments when we got lost in space and time. How we used to dance to Earth, Wind, and Fire in her kitchen. Watching Strangers Things on that old green couch she had in her living room. Even remembering each other's coffee order. I miss her. I miss those memories we shared. Just like wishing on a star. I wish she would tell me why she left me. Did I not make her happy? Did I not give her the stars, the moon, and sun?

I thought I had finally moved on. A part of me still wants her back or while the other half is telling me let her go; move on. I wanted her to notice how much I have changed too. How I finally decided to cut my hair short like she had always asked me. Hopefully, she will hear how I changed my coffee order too. I reached over to the side of her going in to grab some napkins.

"Excuse me," I said to her.

"Ooops, I am sorry," she replied.

"It's ok, I really like your hair."

"Thank you so much... Oh my God Antonio!! Is that really you?"

She reached out and gave me a hug. It was the type of awkward hug you give to family members you meet for the first time.

"Yeah. It's me," I said smiling hiding my emotions.

"You look good. I didn't even recognize you. You finally cut your hair."

"Yeah. It was getting too much to handle. But me, look at your beautiful as always, Briana." I said, grazing the little buzz I had on my head.

"I see you're still rocking that hoodie of mine.

She awkwardly laughed as she crossed arms and looked down at the floor. We caught up on each other's lives. Asking how work is going or if we added any new songs to that old school playlist we used to listen to together. My heart pounding as I gazed back into those brown eyes. Just like old times I was lost in space and time. It was just me and her.

"Colombian dark roast with extra cream, no sugar, for Antonio," yelled the youthful employee.

"That's me!" I said, raising my hand as I grabbed my coffee.

Briana asked "No sugar? You couldn't have coffee without sugar when we went out together."

"Yeah, I outgrew it I always loved creamer anyways."

"Antonino... I want to apologize. I am sorry for leaving you. Although we were never official, I have always tried to find you in every guy that I met. I never found that special bond I had with you. I wanted to call so many times, but I was scared that you had blocked me or were going to lash out on me. I guess, I want to know if you wanted to make up?"

I took a moment to take it all in. I could see the truth in her eyes. I guess all those times talking to the moon paid off. I sipped my coffee and looked down at the steam leaking from the sipping hole. I thought how much I used to love having sugar with my coffee. I looked back into her eyes and pulled her hair behind her ear. We leaned in to lean for our "Disney" kiss. Kissing her on big forehead that stretched pass the milky way. Pulling back, I smiled looking into her big brown eyes. I then turned to the front door carrying that smile as I left back into the cold world with no sugar in my coffee.

THE CROWN'S HONOR

by Mike Robles Vazquez

The day's presence was heavy, with dark gray clouds surrounding the kingdom of Patmos. Such a beautiful island now engulfed with the worst reality imaginable for its inhabitants. The absence of their beloved king. A kingdom living its glory days to suddenly losing what sustained the glory. However, the queen remained but had made no presence to her people, causing an uproar of distrust and anger across the kingdom.

In the meeting room where the king would hold private audiences with his most trusted advisors, was the queen. Stationed there to not forget the presence of her husband. Her eyes glanced at everything that reminded her of him. From the pictures that sat on the brown table with other great leaders from the kingdom and neighboring kingdoms to the frames on the wall with all his accomplishments of war, to the famous chair. The chair was framed in gold that was so bright it could be a source of light, with a white cushion to sit on and lean your back on, in its sides were dark gold statues of roaring lions defining who the king was. It was the throne of the king.

Suddenly, the door opened and the queen's attention to the throne was disrupted, and she glanced to see who had interrupted her period of grief. When she saw who came through, she said, "Oh, it's just you, General Iroh."

General Iroh entered the room and bowed his head as courtesy for the queen. He was about six feet tall, with gray long hair reaching his shoulders, a gray beard that covered his face but taken care of. He wore the uniform of the military which was blood red with details of bright gold. In the left side of his uniform were all the medals that proved why he was the general of the kingdom of Patmos. "Your majesty," he responded.

"What brings you here, General?"

General Iroh paced towards the queen all the while looking at the former king's throne. "Well, Your Majesty, it's about the late king."

The queen glanced in the direction General Iroh had his eyes focused on. "What would you like to discuss about my husband."

"As you know, the king was an integral part to the kingdom of Patmos. He lifted the kingdom from its dark age and brought forth a renaissance era, returning Patmos to its former glory."

"I am aware."

"Because of that reason, the people are requesting a mourning period to honor the late king."

"Of course, the people are allowed to mourn him in their homes. As is customary."

"Actually, Your Majesty, the consensus is to perform a public funeral for the king."

The queen paused and gave General Iroh a stern look. "I will not allow it. It has always been tradition for the people to mourn the passing of a monarch in private. The funeral services are held in private with family and close friends. Opening it to the public breaks tradition, destroys the precedent set in stone, and devalues the prestige of the crown."

"Does tradition really matter in times like these, Ma'am? The people are desiring to honor their beloved late king, and we would refuse to give them the opportunity to publicly honor His Majesty?"

"General. A monarch should never be seen in a state of weakness. That is why we have the traditions we have. I won't let the people see my husband in the state of death. That is not how he should be remembered."

The room stood still as the queen let out all her pain in just that statement. General Iroh responded, "With all due respect, Your Majesty, while the late king was your husband, per tradition, once a monarch receives the crown, he or she must place the kingdom above everything else. Even when death takes them away."

The queen stood in silence, holding her hands together as if she was squishing a stress ball. "I stand by what I said, General."

"It seems that when death enters the room, our emotions confuse our roles and duties in life. The crown takes precedence. The king would have wanted for his people to honor him."

"My emotions are not confusing me, General. I refuse the request and that is final."

Both stared at each other in a standstill. Realizing the conversation was going nowhere. "Unfortunately, the conversation seems to be going nowhere productive, Ma'am. I shall take this issue to the new king then."

"You would dismiss me because it is not what you wanted?"

"Your Majesty, the council voted to take this matter to the new king immediately, but I convinced them to bring this to you first. Out of respect, of course. But as I stated, the crown takes precedence, and while, Your Majesty, is to be honored and respected, She, is not above the wishes of the crown."

"But I am his wife."

"Was, Your Majesty. Understand that in the end we serve the crown and that includes you. That is what your late husband always reminded us. I am very sorry, but I must inform the king. Please excuse me." General Iroh bowed to the queen and exited the room.

The queen fell to her knees in distraught. She felt as her world was breaking into a million pieces with no chance of it being rebuilt. Tears poured out of her eyes as she cried out, "Arthur, why did have you to leave me."

MY SISTER-IN-LAW HATES ME

by Christina Langford

It smells as if I am in an all-boys gym class. No windows and it is freezing. Everyone has gone home for the evening. That is everyone but her. She is standing in the small, tight elevator on the other end. I can feel her piercing gaze through my back. I turn to look at her.

She looks at me like a hawk ready to attack her prey. Her eyes are the color of the scarlet scarf she is wearing. Her lips are fixed as if she has eaten a whole bag of lemons. She is scowling at me.

"HOW COULD YOU LET THIS HAPPEN?" she screamed in my direction. I jumped at the tone of her voice. I'm thinking to myself, trying to figure out why this woman hates me so much. After all, I am married to her sister. I ignore her yelling and make her even angrier. I pull out my phone to see if I can get a signal to text my wife so she can send help; what do you know, no signal.

I look over at my sister-in-law. She is shaking as if she is cold, and her lips are turning blue. The building we are in is as cold as the arctic. The small elevator makes it twenty times colder as the walls are made of metal. I can't help but think of the fowl smelling person that left their body odor in the small, enclosed space that we are stuck in.

"Sylvia, are you cold or hungry?" I asked politely. I did not eat the lunch my wife made me, and I was willing to share because it looked as if we would be in here all night. I also wanted to offer her my throw blanket that I bring from home every day. We might not get along, but she is my wife's sister, and I will always have her back.

"I don't want anything from you. I would rather starve and freeze to death before I take anything from a demon like you," she responded in a tone so evil, it felt as if she had stabbed me in the heart and twisted the blade inside me.

I do not know what I did that was so bad to make Sylvia hate me as much as she does. I'm determined to figure it out and fix it before we get out of this smelly elevator.

"Sylvia, what did I ever do to you to make you hate me so much?" I asked.

"You stole my best friend from me. Ever since you married Angela, I don't get to see her or talk to her. I know you said something to her and now she does not even call me anymore," she replied. I looked at her like a deer in headlights. Suddenly, my mouth became as dry as the desert. I opened my mouth to speak but no words came out. I could not believe she was blaming me for Angela not calling her.

I have been married to Angela for over a year now. I have always encouraged her to reach out to Sylvia and continue to have that strong sisterhood they have always had. It was Angela's decision to not call Sylvia. She decided that she needed to focus on getting her degree and preparing for the baby that will be here any day now.

"Sylvia, I would never come between the bond you and Angela have. This decision was all Angela's doing. In fact, I always told her to call you. She is just focusing on her last year in school."

Sylvia looked at me. I could tell she was trying to read my facial expressions to see if I was lying. A few minutes later, she started to chuckle. I was confused and a little scared. She ran up and hugged me.

"Bryan, I am so sorry for the way I have treated you. I just assumed you were the reason Angela stopped talking to me. If the offer is still on the table, I would appreciate part of your lunch and the blanket," she said with a smile on her face.

We sat and ate the meal I had, and I gave her the blanket. About an hour later, the elevator started up again and we were able to leave. Once we got outside of the building, Angela was waiting to meet us with open arms.

"How did you know we were here? Sylvia asked her. She had a look of shock on her face that quickly turned into a huge grin.

"I called mom, and she said you had a meeting at work and never returned. I thought about it and realized Bryan also had a meeting and never returned, so I called the office manager, and we got the elevator fixed. I am so glad you both are ok," she said.

I went to put my things in my car to give Angela and Sylvia some privacy. A few minutes later, we were on our way home. I could not wait to shower and get in my bed. I am glad that Sylvia and I were able to mend our relationship for the sake of Angela and our baby.

Christina Langford *was born in Charlotte, NC. She is currently enrolled in Full Sail University where she is studying to get her Associates Degree and will continue on to get her Bachelors Degree in Creative Writing. She loves to cook and entertain her family and friends. Her ultimate goal is to write inspirational stories based off of her life experiences.*

DEAR SNIPER

by Ali Ramtahn Hussein

Translated from the Arabic by Essam M. Al-Jassim

Dear Sniper,

I'm the boy you killed a few days ago.

Regretfully, resolute and unwavering sniper, I cannot introduce myself to you because, having lived for little more than a dozen years, I had no significant achievements to boast of—nor did I have an illustrious heritage. A small, inconsequential being in this vast world. Only a marginal soul in this life. My identity was just taking shape when you delivered my end.

Simply put, I was merely a young boy with a pulsating love for his country. I knew nothing about the murky, unsavory realm of politics. And yet—and yet I'm dead.

Despite what you might think, I seize this opportunity to applaud you! I salute your impeccable aim and precise shot. I'm, in a strange way, proud of you—yes, proud of you! —for being an Iraqi who can snipe with such accuracy. Your skill is a testament to rigorous training and unflinching dedication to your profession.

Yes, proud of you!

Your bullet struck the dead center of my forehead, as if you aimed to perforate my very being. The projectile was mercifully fast. When it pierced my skull, I felt nothing. I commend you for the speed with which I fell. Surely, your commander is impressed by your valor, and an appreciation letter awaits you for your courage. What command unleashed such a force, full of your unidentified rage?

As I have been so suddenly wrenched from mine, I wonder if you have a family. Do you miss them? The separation must weigh heavily on you. They must miss you, too, and worry about your safety. I hope you assure them that you're completely safe, properly protected by your gear. I'm sure you will visit them when you are on leave. You will have the opportunity to see them, hug them, talk to them, and enjoy their company.

My dear sniper, will you tell your family about the bullet you put through my head? Will this act of death-dealing add to your achievements in their eyes? I'm asking to know if your taking my life was at all worthwhile for you.

Recount for them the story of the unarmed boy you killed. Please, give them the full account. Try to weave a plausible tale or create a heroic narrative. Try to turn something ugly into a beautiful anecdote.

I don't think you will be able to.

Perhaps you can tell them I was as young as your brother's son, Ahmed, or as old as your sister's son, Alaa. You can explain how I was standing with my friends, cheering and chanting of my love for my homeland. Tell them the boy you killed had dreams of mending the terrible ruptures that have torn apart this land and our society. Tell them he was a passionate boy who was simply trying to stand up for what he believed in. He was not harming anybody, any property, any soul. Tell them he was not a threat to you or your puppeteers.

Tell your wife, as she cuddles your daughter in her loving arms, that the boy you killed was rallying to support the creation of a decent healthcare system for the next generation. Assure her of this – it will give your story a poignant, unforgettable flavor.

My dear sniper, tell me about your daughter. Do you love her? I picture her on your lap, her smile brightening as you gently stroke her soft hair. It must feel soothing, to her and to you. I want you to caress her brow and try to press one finger on the center.

Push her forehead a little. Then apply more pressure.

Can you? I don't think you can.

Why?

Because the pressure would hurt her, and you care for her deeply.

The discomfort she might feel is but a fraction of the anguish my parents endure. I felt nothing, but they suffer the searing pain of your bullet. They'll carry it forever. They'll mourn helplessly, their hearts shattered, clinging to each other in piercing grief.

Ah, the tender bond of a mother, the compassionate embrace of a father. They'll live through each other's agony.

Don't forget to tell your loved ones the little boy you killed was a false enemy. I was not trying to attract the soldiers' attention. I wanted nothing to do with the imminent war. I posed no threat, standing in front of you with a face mask and a bony bare chest. I was innocent, kind, good-natured, and poor. Yet, inexplicably, you confronted me with a sniper's deadly precision.

One last question, sniper: WHY did you kill me?

*This story was written during the protests that erupted in Baghdad in 2019 over high unemployment, poor basic services, and state corruption. Many protesters were killed at the hands of the police force and snipers.

***Ali Ramthan Hussein** is an Iraqi writer. He is an associate research professor at the seismology, University of Sumer, Dhi Qar, Iraq. Beside his scientific studies, Mr. Hussein has this knack for poetry and fiction. His short story 'Dear Sniper' has attracted divergent critical acclaim and praise for its emotional depth.*

***Essam M. Al-Jassim** is a Saudi writer and translator based in Jubail, Saudi Arabia. Mr. Al-Jassim received his bachelor's degree in foreign languages and education from King Faisal University, Hofuf. His writings and translations have appeared in a variety of print and online literary Arabic and English-language journals. Essam compiled and translated the recently published anthology of flash fiction Furtive Glimpses: Flash Fiction from The Arab World (White Falcon*

THE BOLTS ARE LOOSE

by Heather N. Sloan

"Please don't make me ride this," I say.

"It's just the Ferris wheel, Abigail, come on I'll hold you," replies Linden.

"You don't understand, I'm traumatized due to the Ferris wheel, and I have a fear of heights. When that ride stops at the top to let people on or off, I can't handle the anxiety that takes over inside me. All I hear inside my head is the bolts are loose. Then the damn seat rocks back and forth, making those rickety sounds that confirm the possibility of a loose bolt, and scares the shit out of me. No thank you."

Linden stands behind me with his arms completely wrapped around my torso in a warm embrace. "Sweetheart, life itself is about taking risks. Don't let it control you. I'm here and I'll protect you."

Linden has been my best friend since High School. Everyone thinks we're an item, but we're young and just having fun. Not to say he isn't perfect for me, because he is, no one knows me like he does.

It's our turn to load onto the ride. I'm trying to remember to take deep breaths, because right now I'm a nervous wreck. I begin shivering as the wind blows on my neck while the metal of the cart is cold to the touch.

We sit down and I brace myself. The ride rocks back and forth momentarily. My heart beats rapidly and I'm ready to get right back off this thing and onto the safety of the ground below me.

"Can I stay on the ground and wait while you ride it?"

"You can do this, I got you."

The ride operator locks us in and then the ride moves slowly into its next position.

As Linden is wrapping his arms back around me, we hear a loud snap. The ride operator yells something about a belt and disappears. The cart starts to rock back and forth from the abrupt stop and a tear falls from my eyes.

Stuck? As in, I'm stuck on this nightmare of a ride until it's fixed. That's outstanding. Lucky me.

"Aww! Don't cry, we're going to be okay." Linden pulls me into him.

"I won't be. This is traumatizing being stuck here. Maybe you didn't grow up being told the bolts were loose as the Ferris wheel went round and round. And you as a child waiting for what would happen, scared the ride would fall apart with you trapped on it" But, Linden holding me tight feels very comforting. I take in the scent of hot sausage sandwiches at a nearby concession stand.

The operator returns and eventually the ride starts again and stops to unload some more people. My heart racing, I hold on tight to the lap bar. I look up. There's a cart above us. Oh lord if those bolts are loose that cart will fall and kill me.

The cart moves upwards again.

Okay I can do this. I look down. Holy shit I shouldn't have done that! We're not even close to the ground anymore. HELP ME!

I begin to feel sick, vomit coming up my throat. "I can't do this. Get me off this thing." My stomach is in knots and my hands are sweating profusely. STOP THIS RIDE!

Linden pulls me in closer to him. A sense of calmness and relaxation replaces the vibrating intensity of my anxiety. Linden nudges my head towards his shoulder, so I rest my head and close my eyes. I breathe. My body sinks into his. Safety. I can do this. I'm doing it. I let out a breath and sigh. I open my eyes, look out across the fairgrounds and take in the scenery.

The ride begins and I look up at Linden who is smiling. I smile, too. His hand squeezes my shoulder and I know I'm going to be okay.

When the ride ends, we get back into line and ride again.

THE FUNERAL

by Robert Gamer

I must allow that those who are planning my funeral happen to have done a banner job. The carved top mahogany casket is fit for a regent. The flower arrangements ordered-the assortment of carnations, lilies, orchids, chrysanthemums, casket sprays, and roses- absolutely dazzle the eye. Even the Right Reverend Alastair Cuthbert Sniggins, Jr., has agreed to perform the last rites. And my resting place, the plot on a hillock overlocking the Peabody Institute Library, happens to be in my beloved spot. All in all, an estimable job in these funeral arrangements by any respect.

The only drawback, of course, has to be to be that I am not even close to breathing my last. The fact remains that, at the moment, I could probably pass a physical with flying colors. My state of health hasn't perturbed those fortunate enough to be on the list of invitees to the funeral ceremony a bit, though. In fact, I have heard hissing fits breaking out among the poor souls not getting invitations. Word has gotten back that a cousin all the way in Sausalito, for example, tore my framed photo off her library wall and smashed it on the floor when she discovered that she had not made the cut.

Now to provide a perspective, having what was diagnosed as stage 4 pancreatic cancer, I had been placed in a hospice in Danvers to live out my final days. After going through dozens of chemotherapy sessions, with a shaved head, losing my appetite and not eating for weeks, skeletal, I did look the part of someone about to meet his maker. Imagine my shock and surprise when a team of doctors came to my bedside bright and early in the morning and announced that a terrible mistake had been made: my chart had been confused with another person with the same name. Well, almost the same name. Instead of my middle name, Elliot, this person spelled his middle name Elliott, double t. So very sorry! came their cry. These MDs appeared, in fact, so crestfallen, so totally broken, that I actually felt for them.

My close ones would have been elated by this miraculous turnaround, that is, had any member of my immediate family actually bothered to stop by to pay their final respects to me at the hospice. But ,as matters turned out, I had been left to pass on my own. No wife of 43 years, son or daughter, five grandchildren, former business associates, friends, club members, golfing partners. For all intents and purposes, I had been abandoned. Forsaken would have been the better way to put it, already given up for dead. Granted I had been on a morphine drip which made me dopey, but please, make an effort to show a modicum of consideration for me all things considered. But no, I had apparently been dropped from the cast.

Anyway, when I was sure there weren't any witnesses in the corridor, after dressing and packing a little suitcase, I ducked down to the bottom floor where they keep the caskets of those about to kick the bucket. Closing mine, I slipped out the side exit. With the high turnover in the hospice, I was banking on my disappearance being lost in the shuffle. When the nurses didn't find a body with a pulse in my bed, in the bureaucratic confusion, they would likely assume that my remains had gone through the cogs and be downstairs awaiting pick up to the funeral home.

Naturally, when the hospice manager finally realized I had skipped out, the alarm bell went off. As for the doctors in charge, with the catastrophic error that had been made in my identity, their teeth must have been chattering, their bones shaking, about the mega malpractice suit for $ hundreds of millions in damages that likely awaited them. Their medical practices, would be ruined, their reputations in tatters. Still in the dark as far as anyone detecting what had happened, a deal was hurriedly made between the hospice and doctors, with a false death certificate signed and forwarded electronically through the channels to give the appearance the proceedings were legit, above board.

Still having access to the checking account as far as I knew, I grabbed an Uber to my local bank. Withdrawing a thousand dollars, I had enough for a hotel and expenses. Skipping the wake at the funeral home, I patronized the bar at the hotel-a local Marriott- and got so stinking drunk on double extra dry martinis I could barely stagger back to my room. Before drifting off to sleep, I set the timer on my cell phone for 8 sharp in the morning. Rest assured, nothing was going to keep me from getting the most out of witnessing my own funeral. Anyone who tried to prevent me would have to commit murder on my person.

In order to truly appreciate the solemnities of the event, I made sure to arrive at St. Paul's Church on time. The doors opened promptly at 11:00. Before making my way past the stewards, I noticed a woman sobbing into a handkerchief on the entrance steps. Stopping by her, I recognized the woman as my sister-in-law, Amelia-or Amy, as I called her. "Now, now," I tried to comfort her. "He wouldn't want you to cry, would he?"

Turning her face to me, her cheeks turned crimson, her eyes scorching. “What the fuck are you talking about? If your reservation at Cote d Azur fell through because you had to attend this side show, you’d be bawling just as loud, you infernal asshole!”

“I’m sorry, so sorry!” I tried to comfort her before continuing up the steps to the entrance.

Once inside the sanctuary, I had to marvel at how, in all the years I had attended church, for the first time I felt at ease, relaxed, liberated, instead of feeling crimped, caged in, a prisoner. The pews no longer gave me the impression as cell blocks. Even the crucifix beyond the altar affixed with a writhing Jesus, somehow did not strike me as an instrument of torture and utter agony. As odd as it may sound, I found that, at my own funeral, I was overcome with lightness and levity.

When the steward asked me which side of the family I came from. I murmured, “Just a dear friend.” He directed me to the Baxter, my wife’s side. I took a seat in the next to last row to give me a full view of the viewing audience. Wearing thick dark sunglasses, my clothes way too big having lost so much weight, I assumed no one would recognize me. What unnerved me a bit was that it wasn’t until 11:20 that a trinkle of attendees passed in. My cousin, Aubree, proceeded down the aisle. As she was going by, I said, “Glad to see you.”

Stopping, she peered at me. “Do I know you, sir?”

So nearsighted she wouldn’t catch sight of a bull charging in her direction until about to get gored, she believed wearing glasses or contacts would be unbecoming to a society lady of her social standing. “Yes, we’ve met before.”

"You don't look familiar," she nodded her head before being helped on.

My son, Barrett, unaccompanied by his wife entered the church. The eldest, he was dressed in a tailor made pinstripe black suit. The Patek Philippe Skeleton watch glittered on his wrist. He didn't even glance at me as he jaunted by, heedless.

Next came my wife, Everly. Wearing sunglasses, no doubt to conceal her rummy bloodshot eyes, she looked dashing in a coal black double breasted cap sleeve ruffle dress. The sparkling, three stone 11 carat sparkling diamonds on her wedding band did not leave any doubt as to where she was on the social ladder. Wearing her draggy, dyed golden blonde hair in a bouffant, every line of make-up had been assiduously applied.

Behind her came Paisley and Lillian Baxter. Paisley, who was in the middle of a torrid affair with my wife, looked totally a mess. In a rumpled suit, a blue dress shirt that did not match, and hair uncombed, the terribly troubled expression on his face made it appear that he had just barely survived a car wreck. He was the only one who did a double take coming upon me before proceeding on. The Baxters went on to sit directly behind Everly.

When the last mourner had filed in, the ceremony began. What struck me had to be the low attendance. With just a few rows occupied, the church appeared almost empty. With the wide number in my social circle, club members, chums, the prep and college crews, associates in the business community, only a thimbleful had, in fact, showed up. Even my younger daughter, Tabitha, had not arrived. Nor had Meredith, the lady who I had been seeing off and on.

Plumping herself by my side as the Right Reverend Alastair Cuthbert Sniggins, Jr. started out was my younger sister, Georgina. In a shrunken form that appeared you could blow her over with a puff of a straw, her gas tank had read empty when she had reached my pew. "She won't get the insurance," she snarled over the cracking voice of the reverend. "Did you know the measly bitch just upped the life insurance policy, or should I say, policies. Not satisfied with being the beneficiary of the estate, the homes, the trusts, the whole kit and kaboodle. No, not our Miss Fancy Pants!"

I don't think Georgina realized who she was addressing. In all fairness, for all intents and purposes, we were, for all intents and purposes, complete strangers. Sent to boarding schools as wee ones, and then on to college, our paths almost never crossed. "And carrying on all these dalliances," she was muttering under her breath. "I tell you that her hi-drive libido would make a slut blush!"

As the pallbearers and acolytes were carrying the empty coffin to its place by the altar, we stood. I could not help but admire the stately sight of my casket going past. Fit for a sovereign! "The poor bastard!" I heard her groan. "The poor duped ninny is all I can say!" With what passed for my family already seated, the usual entry rite of the liturgy, with family members following the casket, apparently had been suspended.

I'll skip the liturgical part of the service, quite heartening I have to say, and go to the choir numbers. The cantor led the choir in two of my true favorites, Out of the Depths I Call and A Mighty Fortress Is Our God. Quite stirring pieces to be sure!

Finally, the time I had been waiting for had arrived, the time for remembrances. When the Right Reverend Alastair Cuthbert

Sniggins, Jr. announced that, due to the wishes of the loved ones, none would be offered, I was horrified, stunned, shattered. Something welled up in me. I could not let this pass. Standing up, I brushed by Georgina, , who grunted, to the aisle.

Hobbling my way up to the altar, all eyes were upon me, that is, those that had not closed for a little snooze.

Taking my place, I adjusted the microphone to be heard. Looking over the attendees, as no one seemed to recognize me, clearing my voice, I began: "Seeing as there are no other speakers, I would just like to say a few words on behalf of the deceased. Hunter Lester Thornton was known to all of you, who cared for him deeply. There isn't anyone present who doubts his selfless generosity, beneficence of spirit, good will, dedication to the church, a bulwark to the community, and, all told, a bounty of love. Hunter Lester Thornton-we-we will truly miss you!"

Tears had begun to wet my eyes as I stepped down from the pulpit, giving the casket a nice, firm pat as I passed. I was still sobbing when I reached my seat. When I had sat down, Georgina stuck her lean elbow in my side forcefully. "Who the fuck was that jerk? What a load of donkey shit, huh?"

Returning to the altar, the Right Reverend Alastair Cuthbert Sniggins, Jr., clutched the lectern to steady himself. "Anyone else?" he asked sarcastically. With a worn, tired look that suggested that he had seen and heard it all, he surveyed the sparse number of those in the pews. "Okay then," his voice crackled, "according to the wishes of the family, there will be no Eucharist. Also, as the family changed from a burial to a cremation there will be no graveside service." A look at the altar boy sent the adolescent over to spray the casket with incense.

When the altar boy returned to place, the Right Reverend Alastair Cuthbert Sniggins, Jr. breathed a sigh of relief, having reached the close of the ceremony. "Into your hands, O merciful Savior," he crossed himself, "we commend your servant, Hunter Lester Thornton. Acknowledge, we humbly beseech you, a sheep of your own field, a lamb of your own flock, a sinner of your own redeeming. Receive Hunter Lester Thornton into the arms of your mercy, into the blessed rest of everlasting peace, and into the glorious company of the saints in light. Amen."

Although I believe that I was the only churchgoer I heard utter an amen in response, I couldn't think of more fitting words to close. After the choir did a rendition of the hymn, Jesus Christ Is Risen Today, the Right Reverend Alastair Cuthbert Sniggins, Jr. raised his voice to startle those in the audience who might have drifted off: "Let us go forth in the name of Christ. All those who are able to stand, let the family members exit first."

Everyone instead rose in unison to make their way out. I had to nudge the old prune at my side to bustle her. "What the fuck!" she uttered, her eyes snapping open.

"Time to go."

Needing no more encouragement, she didn't waste a moment gathering her bones up and into the aisle.

In minutes, when the sanctuary had cleared, I was left to myself. Just me and the empty casket. I must also add a horsefly I noticed creeping at my feet. He must have been an old-timer judging by his weary walk. Within striking distance of me, he couldn't seem to gather the strength to fly away. Seemingly resigned to his fate, each forward movement of a tentacle appeared to be his last.

After observing him for some moments, I took out a tissue and plucked the drained stoical old bug up. Placing the critter in the center, I neatly folded the tissue up. It had come time for me to depart. Taking a last look at the splendid casket, I had to admire that my remains were being sent off in such becoming style. There was no question in my mind, not any reservation whatsoever, that the bereaved who had planned my funeral were going to get my highest recommendation.

Once outside, I reached into my pocket for the tissue. Going over to a shrub beside the entrance, I deposited the forlorn insect on a top stem. The fresh air must have suddenly resuscitated him because he took to immediately to wing and buzzed away in a flash. As I watched the bug disappear from sight, I felt a curious sense of elation. No longer condemned, a captive of circumstances, this common horsefly had been given the freedom to enjoy life anew. Blessed that I had had the opportunity to be an onlooker at my own funeral ceremony, my mortal remains on their way to be cremated, was there any reason anymore that I couldn't do the same thing, take to wing? Perhaps become a barker at a peep show. Or get a job as a longshoreman. The sky now seemed to be the limit.

THE UNIVERSE...

by Lucas Perelo

Chapter One, like a Monday morning

I feel like my first day at school, writing the foundation was extremely enlightening, I needed to find my forgiveness, all my friends died, and Ed I miss you more than the others, and I salute you brother. I stayed, I'm here, living in the present, this is not a party where people know your name, if you stay with me one more night. If this were a TV series, if I stayed with you one more night. but this is not a party where they know your name. Go, or don't go, why don't you stay one more night, go or stay with me one more day. "This isn't a party where people know your name"

So many lost dreams, all those faces, where are they now, we wait for their return, but I still hear them, when there's no one else around, this is my life, I can't turn my back now, I'll be here, for a while I've been waiting for you all my life, but I'll walk away, "if you love me, let me go"

The universe got in touch, he arrived without knocking on the door, it was a kick in the head, wow, I was losing my sight, losing my reason, I just wanted someone to say that all the little things were going to be okay.

But nothing was right, nothing was right, I cried, I cut my life into pieces, I lost my sight, I lost and cried. Imagine me and you, I think about you all the time, so happy together, imagine that the world could go very well without both of us,

Because the skies would be blue all the time, so happy together. And I, who dreamed of writing songs, am simply leaving an instruction manual for my future SELFs, so happy together.

I thank the universe, that my words are all directly from him, that I am a simple radio connecting your frequency, that I can vibrate your light, that I can be a father to you, that I can make you fly, the wings are in you, look inside, I want to share everything with you, so that you reach me, and together we can feel the night, the memories passing quickly, the night coming out of nowhere in rays of light, I want to share everything with you, and soon it will make you feel alive. "feel alive, feel the night"

And I think I'm this adult, the universe just told me that it's my inner child screaming...

A pause, talking about the universe is talking about love, in the next few days I will try in words to describe the universe, the stars and their planets, I will humbly allow myself to listen, in silence writing, just breathing and exhaling, an analogue digital antenna that is supporting my pyramid, may my light make a hole in the sky, and may you feel the divine hand in your heart.

The true love way. I rescued my heart from all the prisons I put myself in, I met princesses, elfs and demons, it's a difficult path, but it's the way of love, because we will be so free, happy alone, there are babies who stay if asking and walking around.

Ah, the universe, how magnificent and unimaginable, its mysteries, its entrances and exits, black holes open to knowing, the biological mathematics that is being, and its present space and time.

It's in the water, it's where we came from, they cry to see your face, it's in your daughter, and all the glory she will bring, beside her they stood, vibrating only an energy to the future, an energy of peace and love, and all his glory will form them.

I need to find my home every day, like a breathing Rolling Stone, that I never lack love on my journey, that I don't let myself be blinded again by the Sun, that I understand and respect our distance, on my knees I surrender to you, In my hands I carry love, in my words I will carry peace, and so I will get lost in the four corners of the world, everything is planned, your flying saucer will be waiting for you at the end of the map.

Follow your path, build your roads, write down your story, tell a sincere story, made with heart and dedication. That night you pray, don't take anything, just thank you, walk in peace, confess to yourself, and embrace your Hail Marys.

It all started with a photo, now we need accurate information, so swallow it and after downloading, this new sensation gives you pleasure, my friend, make your own kind of music, make your own type of sound.

Chapter two, enjoy the silence

Rebirth, a new story, a good beginning, a new love, there will always be a new dawn, so enjoy the silence, the world is a reflection, as Rumi said, bring your anger and your pride at your feet, and make it a ladder, and climb the highest one. The universe tells me so many things, gives me that touch of gray, but I'm going to get by, try to keep a little grace.

For it is in the silence of the night, that I have the dimension of your greatness, Einstein said, the true sign of intelligence, is not knowledge but imagination, once we accept our limits we go beyond them.

For this journey of self-knowledge my friend, I will need you to free your imagination. You will have to walk this path alone, so be patient. I will teach you how to walk again, I believe you have waited long enough, where do we start?

Close your eyes, find yourself in your darkness, feel yourself growing strong, touch yourself, learn to talk to yourself, forget the walls, free yourself from all ties, see yourself as a floating energy, everything is within your reach, learn to say goodbye, let go of everything and everyone,

This journey has no tenants, it will be you against yourself, tears come, smiles too, but none of that matters, because the moments you will be speechless will be the most exciting, and I give you, I say the name of the game, we call it riding the gravy train. The universe is wonderful, may you enjoy this journey, may I show you all the secrets that nothing holds for you, may I give you a vision, a taste of what it is, may you have the desire to grow in your imagination.

May you be able to free yourself, free your mind and your body, may we built this city in rock and roll, welcome to my mind, through these lines I will show you frequencies, it just depends on you, which ones you are looking for, but remember that, I can't create anything in your head, only you will have this power, what I can do is simply show you the paths, the doors and the trapdoors.

Acceptance and patience my dear padawan you will have to have, the universe will show you the signs, but you have to believe, and when you are ready it will show you, you will have doubts, this is normal, but believe in a force and in yourself

Even though it will be vital, all its energy comes from your imagination, from your power to feel the now, and channel your mind and body, your boat will have to sail, leave the slopes, there will be days of storms, days of pain, without direction , do not be afraid, it will be your baptism of fire, you will walk on the coals, but you will not fear, because your greater power will be at your side, the faith that is within you will be totally lost, and only then will it be restored,

It will be something new, it will be from the inside out, it will be the eternal fire of your soul. But remember, your eyes can deceive you, don't trust them, your focus will determine your reality, you have to unlearn everything you've learned, do it or don't do it, there is no such thing as trying.

I read gestures and intentions... words don't fool me anymore... when they're just sounds. To listen to the universe, you need to have unconditional love in your chest, a trail of lit and healed chakras, on the back of your head is the connector of your connection with your superior, on your forehead is your blank screen, your notebook, take your notes and create your book,

when the eyes betray, believe in your faith, walk on invisible bridges, let the universe guide you, kneel to it, and find gratitude in your steps, stop forgiving yourself and stand up,

There is no more need for forgiveness, from now on simply have gratitude, and never forget to say your prayers. Circular model, the law of vibration, as it makes sense, a curve was necessary to be able to see ahead, all these ups and downs, it was scary for a while, I got lost in my arrogance, I didn't know how to thank you the first time you appeared, this time It will be a Fourth of July,

You are original, you cannot be replaced, everything leads you to your perfect door, you just have to turn on the lights, and own your night. Be fireworks, boom boom boom, it's always been inside you, and now it's time for you to let it go.

On this journey we will have darkness and light, a circular line of love must form in the shape of a figure eight lying down, the darkness passing through the light and vice versa, find this within your being, you will need a love that makes you happy, it seems a little crazy That's all, but baby you don't want to make me happy.

Life is a road, put the top down on your mind, and enjoy the view, there's a world out there around you, where the blues won't hurt you no more, this is the road and these are the hands, we are survivors ,

I've already driven all night, this distance between us, when we look into each other's eyes, I tell you again, life is a road, if you come with me, we'll walk all night, my love, country roads, always I will be this metamorphosis, to enter the universe, I needed to close my eyes, be born and die, learn to fly, forget gravity, surrender to everything that love brought to my life, the universe will enchant you,

it will tell you a story, nothing is by chance, everything has its direction, an intention, it's playing detective with yourself, your innermost secrets, the way you want, the way you need, my life was told by rock bands from the 80s, I opened my heart to the universe,

I gave in my darkest desires, it was a conversation that lasted years, a game of chess, I was patient, I waited my turn.

The law of action, faith is not enough without the necessary action, the way of love, a little blue note, the universe is a million songs. I was lost in the room one ten zero nine, waiting for a connection, I was already high on you, may the good lord shine a light on you,

Ah, angels, wings and halos, what a magnificent vision, believe in angels, believe in yours angels, may they lead you to the door you are looking for, don't be afraid of what you will find, stand up and be grateful.

Life is perfect, never complain again, breathing and walking is necessary, salvation, salvation, salvation is free, don't feel alone brother, you were never alone, not for a second, we are all in you, we are one, for That's it, today, feel loved, embrace yourself, love, because salvation is free." Zelda... do You hear me... find me in your dreams... see me in the close of your eyes... my daughter, there I will be... by your side... in a place of our own, among the light and dark. .. "

You will need your inner child to see the universe, you will have to walk hand in hand with it, because to see the universe, you will need your imagination, and only in your inner child will you find self-love, just company, your mind goes through this line of magic and science that exists in your being, whatever happens will be ok.

Come anytime, welcome to the universe, knock and enter. Be grateful as you float, as you lose gravity, let yourself go, just distill and relax, look around at nothing, the stars and black holes, imagine yourself in an expanding octagon, forget the passwords to enter, your DNA is engraved in their existence, the use of names will not be necessary, know their importance for the universe.

The law of correspondences, they are manifestations of the spiritual world, contaminate the environments with happiness. If all I do is try, that means I don't believe, fear is the path to the dark side, fear leads to anger, anger leads to hate, hate leads to suffering, confronting fear is the destiny of a Jedi, and to say that if a Jedi dies, the light dies, that would be pure vanity.

It takes strength to resist the dark side, wars don't make you unique, when you understand the force, you will see how small you are, and how little you know, focus on the moment, feel, don't think, believe in your feelings. Instincts, if you define yourself by the power to take a life, the desire to dominate, to possess, then you have nothing.

The law of Karma, it will not be easy, there will be losses and sacrifice, but we cannot give up just because of fear, at this time we need to get up, because nothing happens by chance. Everything in life has a price.

I'm going to give you an example of how the universe works: you want to play the music track, and it simply doesn't happen, so stop, listen, soon tomorrow will come, chance pushes those who cling to denial, the support is that Soon tomorrow comes, bite the bullet to start over.

Open your eyes now and allow yourself to listen, what is left will be scars. Meeting of souls, words of love, I feel your perfume, your voice is soft and smooth, congratulations, be rock, be you.

A happiness, I never saved money for the sunset, it was always an adventure, I always took candy from strangers, it was a journey of love and nights and days, thank you sir, I had a love that keeps me happy, from flesh to bone, I needed a love that would make me happy, my Rolling Stone heart, if my guitar could speak, I don't know what that song would be yet, but practice and be practical, let it be just love. off LINE, with all the music inside me, just a click away, life is a road.

Your love is a lie that my vanity wants, and my poetry of a blind man, cannot see that in my world something has died, our love we invent, we wait, I am an exaggerated eternal, it is in my veins be like this, a thousand roses and all stolen, and a while ago, for you I would give up everything, money, career and straw.

This cruel passion, all my mistakes, I wouldn't be able to breathe if you didn't notice me, even on the most banal backs, for me it's all or never again, I adore and admire an invented love.

Crazy life, since I can't take you, I want you to take me, and in a short life, let it be light, because no one will forgive us, I'm tired of so much nonsense, so much carelessness, of this eternal lack of anything to say.

Ah immense life, I want you to take me, our crime doesn't pay, my machine gun full of sorrows, but know that the dice still roll, and so I survive without a scratch, I see the future repeating the past, time doesn't stop, It's all a museum of great news.

All the love there is in this life for you. the luck of a peaceful love, with the flavor of bitten fruits, and some change to provide security, for poetry that we don't experience, to transform boredom into a whole body like a hurricane, and some medicine that gives me joy.

Wow, wow, listen to the músic, ALL the time.

The twelve laws of the universe, about thinking I will, let's start at the beginning, the law of energy, the universe is made of energy, nothing is lost, in string theories energy fields are formed, energy fields are around us and in all spaces, it is possible to feel the lines vibrating, not with the eyes but with the heart, this leads me to the law of rhythm, everything has its flow, the river will always flow to the sea, in its own time, I already spoke about law of action, what leads us to the law of unity, everything is in interconnection with the spark within you, the strength is from the inside out, but remember that a love so strong, can send you in different paths, the power of the inner child may surprise you, the chemicals are taking their toll on this bed.

The balance of the law of gender, you know how to balance your masculine and feminine sides, as well as dark and light, everything is a circle, which passes through a triangle, inside a square, this is how I can see the universe, through calculations geometric, and with my eyes closed, I need to take a moment, breathe, enjoy the moment, because everything in life has a polarity, the law of opposites, these are mental vibrations, take this moment, and see everything that is given to us, this whole world of information, feel it when you get lost, put a price on this whole life.

Law of relativity, perspective and perception, relativism is in everything, it is a high territory, we are evolving and floating, law of transmutation, everything around is growing, evolving, they die and are born, this is normal, it is the process, life in a fast lane. Cause and effect, law of compensation, we reap what we sow.

The best known, the law of attraction, forget about all the others, we are what we attract, what takes us the law of correspondences, everything done with great affection and love for you, see like a blind person, talk to a mute, listen by turning a deaf ear, the universe dwells in silence, signs continue, transmissions of love, use your imagination, don't get caught up in a look, raise the fire in your heart, see the sky tonight, all in mother wings crossing the skies

We will leave flowers on your grave, because the sky is so far away, You have to get up to go down, I live in Senna's S, you have to get up, get up, get up to fall, think and dance, I'm the only one who chooses and makes my own enemies, I do everything for my desires. I served in the army of love, and I realized that you can't save everyone.

Simple notes of anticipation notes, you will win wars, you will build empires, a king without a crown, without a throne, I was once someone, but now I am someone else. I will write thirteen chapters, about the universe slowly I will, passing messages and returning signs, may I be strong, so that in my silence I can speak... Thank you to the universe, may it be my light in the darkness. goodnight.

“we need Ted Logan, that the Jack Traven's of life appear, the Johnny Utah, we are millions of Neo's and Thomas Anderson's, that your mr. Wick brings you comfort and security, good people, welcome.x”

Chapter three, You spin my head, right round, when it goes down...

The universe, set of all existing matter, energy, space and time, planets, comets, stars, galaxies, nebulae, satellites, among others. The universe is, therefore, more than an immense place, it is everything, and encompasses everything that exists. The most accepted scientific and cosmological theory and model about the origin of the universe is called the Big Bang.

The Big Bang theory says that all matter and energy were concentrated in a super dense and hot point, known as a singularity. From this point on, the universe expanded in a process known as inflation, which lasted an infinitesimal fraction of time.

A series of transformations continued to happen for billions of years, until the structure with which we know it today. The universe expanded more and more, so that it cooled, giving rise to the different stars.

More recent studies indicate that the approximate age is between 13.8 and 14 billion years. Planets are solid, rounded bodies that do not have their own light and heat. However, each planet has its own gravity, which revolves around a star. Natural satellites, celestial bodies that orbit the planets.

Galaxies are a collection of planets, stars and gases. The universe has approximately 100 billion galaxies. We live in the galaxy called the Milky Way, where the solar system is located. Comets are celestial bodies that have little mass and irregular orbits. The best known is Halley's Comet.

Stars, spherical celestial bodies formed from plasma and that have their own light and heat, for example, the Sun. Satellites are classified into natural satellites and artificial satellites, satellites are solid celestial bodies that orbit the planets. The best-known natural satellite is the Moon and the artificial satellite is Sputnik.

Black holes are among the most massive celestial objects that exert the greatest gravity.

All of this has been frightening, but enlightening, it has given me fear, and demonstrated confidence, I don't know how it took me so long to realize, the whole and the nothing that exists within me, microcosm to macrocosm, from stars to subatomic particles, everything can be learned in cosmology. Pythagoras said, listen and you will be wise, the beginning of wisdom is silence, if what you have to say is not more beautiful than silence, shut up.

The universe as a whole, within nothingness, is how we should feel when we close our eyes, a train running away, a circus tent, water straight from the source, which you can drink in silence, and manifest in space and time.

You know that poster on your wall, that advertisement on television, the universe is in everything, it talks to you, when I realized that they were signs, that the third eye really opened, and my vision changed, it all came coming like a boiling dream, a priest in his pulpit, and I saw how he transformed me, it was the greatest show.

When it comes in all the colorful colors, we light up, and we won't come down, it's all I ever wanted, all that I needed.

The impossible becoming true, taking over me, this is the greatest show, not even the walls stopped what was happening, everything became small and big at the same time, the universe enters you, like a spirit giving messages, a light from the stars , it was all I needed, a shooting star, a form of energy and heat, I was too tight, my love needed to expand, I had to serve it right.

Redemption, how long it took, the first time I saw you, I should have kneeled at your feet, how everything was new when the universe appeared to me, how my pride and arrogance blinded me, it's not easy to grow up as the chosen one, until we understand that we are all chosen, and that it only depends on you, knowing whether it is you or not, it is all in the power of believing in yourself, remember what the oracle says, it is in you, but not in this life. To deny our own impulses is to deny the very thing that makes us human.

Choice is an illusion created between those with power and those without. Then you'll see that it is not the spoon that bends, it is only yourself.

The universe will grow within you, if you believe in the force, everything will fall into place, the powers in your being are infinite, close your eyes when you catch them, the energy that comes from you will light up roads, keep you company on rainy days, we need silence to hear the universe, its movements are light and coordinated.

Let your heart guide you, when listening to your higher self, believe in it, there is no reason to give in halfway, this will only work if you are 110 percent involved. In a sky with so many people, only a few want to fly, that's not crazy

It's a sweet feeling, it's such a good vibration, only a child knows, it's a hot temptation, my God thank you, I filled my emptiness with love, the universe belongs to me, and I belong to it, through the darkness, but I I feel home, I don't care if I call myself crazy.

We can live in a world we design, I think about what the world could be, a million dreams for the world we will make. With far away stuff, if it all seems like we've lost our minds, just run to a world you draw. it can be big or small, but go to a world that you see, that you close your eyes to see,

What can I say about the universe, red, white and blue, it freed me, I'm rocking in a free world.

What should I say to the universe, well, first thank you, I'm grateful, imagine walking in a tunnel, spiral, and inclined upwards to the northeast, go through this dark tunnel, until you find a point of light, focus your energy on that point of light, until an explosion inside your mind happens, release all the accumulated energy, see the light inside your darkness, and be grateful, simply be grateful, evolve your way of seeing streaming, remember, radio waves, microwaves, everything in the universe It's on.

Outside my window I can hear the train blow, I'll push the clouds out, I'll let the music have its way, 'cause it's almost Saturday night and I'll steal my heart away.

When you hear locomotion, be ready, good times, times of calm, when we look at the universe, and see ourselves inside it, part of it, everything becomes magical, you can create, use your imagination, that's why I talked about waking up your inner child, this lost and found inside you, a little tenderness, oh tenderness please come down.

Your imagination is limitless, allow yourself to connect stars in the universe, see the patterns and shapes that the universe gives you, they are graphs and statistics, have your brush in hand, draw your world, fill it with stars, make better days come, You have to stay, get off the ground, and speak loudly.

Oh lord, what is this world about, in the darkness of the city, I don't have a place to go home, I'm just a stranger in this city, living with the thought away bothers people, if they know the world I have inside of me, how I make myself happy every day, how my soundtrack feeds me, a heart always finds its way, I thank you I thank you, I remain a stranger to this city, my soul is my home, I walk alone through my Darkness, I'm not dying, but can you hear that sound, the midnight rain is coming, I don't wish for any danger, I'm just a stranger, a stranger in your town.

A stranger in the universe, raise your hands and pray, fall in love again, the darkness looks beautiful under the shine of a star, the black in the universe is beautiful, it protects the universe, it works like a protective mirror, what goes around comes around.

The magic of darkness, don't get lost into it, find your source of heat, let it shine. Have your peaceful place in the universe, a place where only you can go, your privacy, your little corner, there you can learn, be at peace, get lost in all the nothingness that exists within yourself, I was always on the outside looking in, but it's at Edge that the sparks explode,

I swear someone is leaving messages for me, on the sidewalk of my street. In time you will leave the past behind, and learn that everything changes, we divide and disappear, see the me and you in all aspects, the universe gives you this vision, the power is in you, from the inside out, disappears to two opposite sides, I just hope the world you find is better than the one you left behind.

It's all in your head, and inside they fight, at three in the morning they wake me up. Oh, getting lost in the universe, what a feeling, letting go, without gravity, without breathing, without time and place, time stops for three whole seconds.

What a magical touch, take time to waste the moment, never ask for forgiveness. Look into your eyes, see yourself, put a price on everything that's alive, Your songs go with you, so my friend, when you're floating, jump, because you're standing, it lifted you up, I can see what you mean, the power of the word, writing dreams, my back is to a recording machine, and I'm not the worst you've ever seen, so jump, just jump.

It's like someone turned on the overdrive, even when the music is off, the universe and its country girls, whatever you have in mind, I must be doing something right, by the look in your eye.

Give me something for the pain, give me something for the blues, a shelter from the rain, something that I can wear and get through the night.

Your imagination is what will guide you through the universe, it's a way that you can use, it comes and goes, and if you lie you lose it, feelings show themselves, so don't let go.

No one is alone until someone leaves, the universe is expanding, and to understand it you need to be expanding too.

A mind must always be open, don't let your eyes deceive you, the mind is your third eye, see beyond reach, wake up the lion within you, be it a cat, a feline, with heightened senses, nine lives, that's it. There are nine deaths.

Sail the sea that exists in the universe, let go. I never felt like I was nowhere, every time I saw you, you were so alive, and all I wanted was for you to shine, shine in this life that was Burnout.

A reaction was all I wanted, but on my own feet, I took a conscious step, so I want to feel, your shine upon me

In the universe I see myself, I feel safe, he doesn't exercise any authority over me, all the songs are in my favorite tone, he warms me like the sun, he lets me breathe, he never says goodbye but always says hello, a magician of pinball, here in the fields, I fight for my meals, so don't cry, take my hand, and we will go soft through the earth

We will be together before we grow old, teenage confessions, eternal lovers, in search of a sun, and a moon, a single light, a greater love, may the peace of the universe be in you, say I love you to him every second, and may you have the humility to hear him say it back, you can be anyone, a fool lost by the Sun, be the one who goes tonight, you are under control, and freedom is a lonely word.

A piece of me will be dancing in the streets all night, a spark, be great to each other, I see the future, it's beautiful, but I can't touch what I don't have yet, we'll be so free, happy alone , sharing a smile, so far from home.

I'm working hard for this, making music, making lies, who doesn't have money, tells stories, basic mathematics, the path of love, towards Santiago I'll go to the south of France I'll start a new journey, making songs, happy alone.

The universe is not for beginners, no one ever taught you how to play, and if you can't handle it, go back to where you came from, take your money and run. global heat has increased, if you can't take it, walk away from the game, go back the way you came.

The universe is cold, you will lose all your friends there, loved ones and loves are the past, all your friends have died, the universe only exists if it is for two, how to find a known soul on the way, let love open the door, let my love open the door, to your home.

When everything seems to be everywhere, the limitless space you allow me, lift me from misery, and it will set me free, love heals your problems, let my love open the door to your heart.

Go where the sound takes you…

A moment of truth in my life, when everything seems like a movie, everything is made to break, a guitar solo, with a beginning, middle and an end, I don't think they understand, I just want you to know who I am, even if They don't understand that everything was made to break.

The love that completes me, makes me smile, makes me cry, but I close my eyes and I see more than a feeling, I think it's a dream, I see myself walking away, so many people coming to me,

I need to walk alone and reaching my heaven, this is more than a feeling, through songs, I rescued my being, I have my traditions and customs, I am free, I am my own planet, we only stop being disciples when we begin to feel, we are masters of our destiny,

The path of love, more than a feeling, is a dream, follow the golden bricks, be happy on rainy days, may the universe show you that everything is possible, the impossible is a matter of opinion, distance doesn't make sense but, For me, space and time do not exist, we are light, energy that vibrates in frequencies, this is the feeling I have when I am by your side,

I was never a person alone, I was always by your side, bad love, no more bad love, because for me everything has always been blue, and I have no more memory to remember, I need something to be proud of, no more bad love.

A free guitar playing the universe, that I know the moments of silence, that the stars illuminate me, and my guardian angels protect me, that with the horse and the sword of Saint George, I make my home on the moon, and feed All dragons, may misery love your company, frustrated and incorporated.

Because I know what you need, I know what you would pay to get. We make the cure, we create the disease, frustrated and incorporated, I have the thing you seek, but I need to take you out of your misery, there is a path of love waiting for you, have you satisfied your greed, submit all your desires, everything incorporated and frustrated within you, like an operating system, like software, the path of love is a path of truth, only you and the universe will follow, may this friendship grow in you, may you see in my eyes that there was something missing ,

That you listen, don't play dead, your love saved me, and we are still together, when I said I love you, I meant that I will love you forever, I just want to keep loving you.

The road, every day opens up more for me, there are no trails for my heart, with my falcon I enter the forest, I make my trails, all of this, because I continue to love you. In my life, so many lost dreams, where are all my friends, the millions of faces, where are they now, I still hear them now, when there is no one around,

I just walk away, this is my life, I can't give up With my back to her, I've been waiting here for a lifetime, and when there's no one around, I can go back and walk down the empty street, where they were, I still hear them now, when no one's around,

I'll walk away, the road continues, don't get lost, admire everything around you, this new friendship with the universe, stop fighting this feeling, and lose your fear and let it show, have the strength to show it, there is no reason for your fear, because at the same time universe side, you are safe, everything is clear, and you will get as close as you can, the universe will show you the dock where you can leave your boat, you no longer remember why you were fighting, you can never fight this feeling , come crawling through the door, the universe will welcome you with open arms, and closed eyes, everything nothing becomes everything.

That you can see the magic of the universe, with your eyes open, that you hold your breath, it's a dark path, and it can kill you, it can kill everything inside you, it's a hard path, but it's the path to love. and I'll go crazy to see your face, 'cause we'll be so free, so far from home, and we'll laugh until we cry,

The universe is going around, spiraling, feel it, as if for the first and last time, spin like a dog , you will be free, happy alone, and you will laugh until you cry, making songs, happy alone

Chapter four, free your mind...

You have your place in the universe, this battle has already been won, your voice is the only vote, your word is king, don't cut off heads, heal and set them free.

Let your imagination flow, you will only see the tip of the iceberg. The rest is submerged in dark matter. go wherever the sound takes you, have a good time.

The universe is polite, it comforts you and feeds you, like a mother, a mother who has been a father all her life.

The universe works like a fedora on my head. I needed to find this man inside me, the universe allowed me to sculpt, and embrace this soul. I don't need anything, except a good time, how can I resist, I just look for good times, it's just that I look.

Take it easy, the universe will not charge you anything, it is a friend of yours, don't let its deafening sound drive you crazy, the silence babe, the sweet lord who will save you. Don't let the sound of your own wheels drive you crazy.

You seek perfection, I heard that only those who wanted it were sad, things that I will now understand, why you are so angry.

Toys and flavors, because you don't show what you're looking for, Seeing tomorrow, living in the present, from a past that no longer exists, a new road, without gates and doormen, just messengers passing by, astronauts without homes, each one on your ship, coming from distant planets, each speaks a language, each sings a song.

Don't mind, we were so young, I still listen to the songs, it reminds me of a friend, my father saying don't worry my son, heaven has a plan for you, see, heaven has a plan. I'm telling you about my contact with the universe, but I can only imagine what it will be like, what my eyes will say, when I'm floating in its glory.

I will dance, sing Hallelujah, and fall to my knees, when I find myself standing looking at the sun, I can only imagine.

Learning to silence others outside of oneself is important, blue in the dark, blind, now I see, the truth, lies in half, wrong cannot be undone, or words from the tip of the tongue.

Tenderness a little tenderness, it will be necessary, what starts with a friendship becomes stronger, don't be afraid, I will give you direction, I will make everything clearer, a candle in the window, getting closer and closer, making you forget, and throw all your pain away forever, and come falling through the door, but stop fighting this feeling, the universe loves you, it will hold hands with you, it will be a friend, a partner and a brother.

A call, because your heart is on fire, it is turned on and lit, in words with flames, speaking the language of love, as if you know what it means, you are simply the best, the best I have ever met, In your heart There is the star, that warms you and illuminates you every day, as long as you are in his arms, everything will be fine,

I hear every word you say to me, and it's time for me to go, that path between my heart and my soul It's full of adventures, it's the best, better than everything else, better than anyone I've ever met, leading me to break in two, and so we will be love.

But time on my hands could be spent with you, and that's why they call it the blues, live every second, without excitement, when just a girl cries in her high heels, time on my hands love, laughing like children, between the blankets, dreams, a simple I love you, time that will be spent with you.

The universe, in a way that you can use, boy don't you know, don't let go. No one is right until someone is wrong, no one is alone, until someone is gone, everything has a way of using, practice will lead to perfection, of being human and completely imperfect, because if you lie, you will get lost, and feelings Will show, I've seen dark skies, but never like these.

The wind blows and time stands still, see the magic around, see the things that are taking you home, keep in view, everything that is good for you, in the darkness there is so much love, your heart goes boom boom boom.

When the illusion is no longer necessary, and you think you are free, just a silhouette, spinning in space, keep the dreams that took you home, keep them all close to your heart, good thoughts, words of peace, a road shines its headlights, no traffic lights, an eternal curve, your speed is measured by your heartbeat, life in a fast lane, law of action, he knew all the right people, he had lines on his face, and lines in the mirror, life in fast lane, all at the same time.

The universe will scare you and heal you, with your eyes closed you will be welcomed into a new world.

Save time and money, you won't use them on the way. I turned the world upside down for you, a very aggressive game. I lost someone a long time ago. For every trip, I had to say goodbye, always starting over somewhere new. I got good at it, I learned how to build my nests , because I need my night's sleep.

Lions and lambs, a vision of ourselves being invented, be a limitless being, there is no end, just a curve forward.

Can't stop this feeling, when you start to believe, hysteria when you're there, intuition, you can hide, I ,,,,believe, I need to know tonight, can you stop this feeling, magic, mysteries and miracles when you're near.

We put soldiers at risk, and I have already taken my share of the blame. They are lions led by lambs. We must change things, hysteria when that happens, when you have that feeling, can you feel it, and start to believe it.

We are not indestructible, some things are worth fighting for, there is no easy way out, there is no short way home, I see these ugly faces, thinking it could be you and me, if giving could be wrong. love, my baby we can share all this, there are feelings that never died, I just want to know why. I have no easy way out, no short way home.

Might as well jump, it took me time to understand, a leap of faith, must be taken towards the universe, we are the people, one by one, we are the ones who are crying, full of anger and full of doubts, and we will break all the rules, we will never choose to be fools.

We are tired of being used, in the heat, and in defeat, we will be the ones who are screaming, full of anger and doubt, I will never be blinded by the fool's eye, Peter my friend, get up and walk, sing your songs with your own voice, your talk box. It seduces you, scares you and makes you feel in between.

Feed the hunger for knowledge, for light to all ignorance, be a master of silence, point to the sun, and build your dreams, go to the origin of your being, in the workshop of the mind, use all the tools you find, don't get attached to visions, remember all your senses, everything around you is at your disposal, it will not be necessary to waste your imagination.

The universe and its plans, with open eyes I will trust them. Every time I look at my future, I see something bigger, Something' big, a dream within several, giving peace a chance, and being able to sing, donate, surrender to the universe.

Thinking that we are alone would be like taking a spoon in the ocean and saying that there are no fish, we only see 1 percent, and we use 10 percent of the brain, the liberation of the mind, the power that is behind the third eye, free yourself sister, free yourself brothers, the universe has in store for you an enchanting journey through love, forgiveness and gratitude, fasten your seatbelts, uno, duno, three fourteen, turning up the sound is necessary,

Focus on the now, faith in your sparks of love, be Sparks of fire, I've been hitting the bottoms of bottles, but look what I found, another piece of my heart there on the floor, and my prayers are working tonight. a piece of my heart, there is on the floor.

The seven seals will be opened, seven sins, chapters of your story, so take me to the wishing well, and throw water in my eyes so that I can see, a mother's love, will open and break the seven seals. the universe just wants to say that it loves you, whatever your type of sound.

Chapter Five, Stop and Stare...

In the beginning, there was nothing, Miles and miles are open to me, I walk through the valley of shadows, I say hello as always, the truth will set you free,, don't worry darling, we can run away from it all, no matter what they say, all the dark in the universe It has a gray feel.

Living in the now, vibrating for tomorrow, the universe has my bed in its home, I am welcome, I feel at home, I see the light. but rest assured, because the men in black will come, be strong, leaders and groups, you see what I see, stop and stare, a universe of a million songs.

I got back on my feet, and looked at what I found, another piece of my heart lying there on the floor, someone carrying me, all the pieces mixed together there on the floor.

Your soul feeds on energy, feeds if it is not necessary, doesn't get attached to anything, learns to love everything, and be grateful.

Use all the tools you find, don't get attached to visions, remember all the senses, everything around you is available, not wasting your imagination will be necessary.

The respect of genders, the evolution of masculine and feminine, in a single curve, a loop, evolving from cocoons to butterfly, being reborn and flying in flames, through nothingness ahead, imagine all races rising, in frequencies, towards a only strength, your soul is freed, neither man nor woman, just an angel, a semi-god, the evolution of a being.

Stop for a moment, breathe, clear the path to your chakras, light up, see the root, create a circle and go up, with your eyes closed, focus on your breathing, and feel the path that the air takes inside you, oxygenate your brain, cleanse all the negative thoughts that are in you, breathe in, breathe out, don't be afraid, there are lives and lives in this process, it's like walking on a machine, the path is to breathe in, breathe out, the blood is in motion, you will be conscious the entire time, as you are a machine head, keep rising, elevating yourself, getting to know yourself, you will not have an instruction manual for your body, you will have to test all the buttons, believe in all the solutions of security, in the blink of an eye everything can change, please allow me to introduce myself, I am a man of good taste, I was there when Jesus had his moment of doubt and pain, nice to meet you, I hope you know my name, for pleasure, is the nature of my game.

It's in your face, but you can't take it, because you want it all, but you can't have it, the law of attraction, have you ever thought about manifesting all our desires, serious life is a mess, a feeling, what it's like to feel, besides to know yourself, for you to understand the law of attraction, you have to be in love with yourself, but be careful, because fear manifests itself too, and we cannot forget that we vibrate in dark matter.

This reminds me of when I was 16, listening to Pearl Jam and thinking that I was right, if I knew that everything was leading me in this direction when I arrived, I would be grateful every day for being alive, I lost all my hopes, but in the end I found love, I am very grateful.

That I never freeze, I can always reinvent, hey ho lets go, what they want I don't know, don't shoot her in the back, everything is in the backseat, get comfortable, and say hello to a very high quality sound, high frequencies just a click away, labyrinths from your mind to your soul, in the jungle, welcome to the jungle, I want to hear you scream, you learn to live like an animal, you start to believe, I will see you please, When you're high, you don't want to be so down.

I believe in something called love, I want to kiss you, touch you all the time, it comes straight from my heart, invades my mind and projects itself into space. make me a man, I don't need my toys anymore, time to give them away, because I believe in the sun going down, the universe makes me better, nothing in the past, the future is his and the now is mine, we are at peace, you have that if you feel like a woman, she will free you, but if you look to me, to free you, I can't, but she will, it only depends on you, my brother and my friend, the thief of the night, the Robin wood of love, You have to be a woman to feel love, it will set you free.

We don't know, so we chase them, answers and questions, what you don't know you can feel, what you don't have you don't need now, be grateful, even if it flows, on my path, I'm alive, I embrace every second, I love myself, even if it flows, blowing in my hands, I'm on my way, I thank you and I walk, smiling more than crying.

If everything was going to stay like this forever, if everything was going to be this good forever, all I ask of you, is not to stop the joker flying overhead, looking at everything, all the people he sees in the light, he flies overhead, everyone the days, and if he takes you, what happens.

I no longer feel alone, my love is in me, with him I am at peace, only I know the good he does for me, I can no longer give up on myself, survive the darkness and walk brother, auto parts record player, show me where look, I lay down on the floor, last year I died, this year I don't die, wake up and sleep, a long step to dreams, love will be there, teach me how to talk, teach me where to find it, let yours shine now, Even mistakes are rights, gain power, give me a sign, tell me what I will think, you are those guys who hate everything.

I grew up in the middle of summer, and I hate everything about you, until love comes and invades you like an old country song, I smoke in the morning and drink my beer late in the afternoon.

If you don't like the way I live, just leave me alone. Don't worry about my soul, I don't ask anyone for anything, because I can get it on my own.

I stopped and stared, now I need to continue, with my guitar I will walk, learn to sing, release my voice, howl at the universe, I was born a Rolling Stone, an astronaut and his elements, the story of a hurricane, which all the authorities want to blame, I only robbed the registers, as I could see, in Patterson that's how it goes, if you don't want to draw heat, you can find a man guilty.

No announcements or interruptions, I'm no stranger to the dark, there's a place for us, when sharp words cut you, to the beat I drum, my skin doesn't matter, we are warriors, this is what we have become, we are glorious, this It's me, and pay attention that I'm coming, I have no excuses, marching towards the sun I will go, and when sharp words cut me, I will follow the fluid forward, this is me, I will drown in love. and the night the cold wind blows.

I don't wanna be buried in a pet cemetery, I don't want to live my life again.

I'm alone in my house, I'm out of the city, I became who I shouldn't have, the city got tired of us, it's time to move, I counted the years, steady hands take the steering wheel, stop and face.

I think I'm moving but I'm not going anywhere, and I stop thinking, will it be just everything I need, firm feet, don't fail me now, I'll run until I can walk, I've become what I couldn't, why here and not there, it's not necessary, it doesn't fit, it doesn't belong to you, to move, it's alive, everyone is afraid, do you see what I see.

A beetle passing by, everything else was greed, if we could come together as a team, One and one and one is three, hear you but don't see, may it be good, may it do you good, the fate of the righteous, young students of universe, may your mind be your pencil, and silence your books, be wonderful to each other, life depends on it, if you want to evolve, learn with your streaming, Premium level, sew up what was torn, at seven o'clock in the morning I receive your message, this is the current situation, it is up to us to join hands, and talk about what we heard about freedom, all its gamma rays, its best days are yet to come, enlightened people at its feet, an energy that will save everyone, a lot to do, until then, a lot to do.

High ground, mr. Wonder what you say, the world keeps turning, I was lucky to try again, the first time was a lot of sins, the world keeps turning, enjoy the music without interruptions. I've been working hard for you, we'll be so free, happy alone, that's what I want now, but I can't touch what I don't have yet, share a smile, far from home, make songs, and make the lies, the universe and its plan, each time I realize myself in a universe, all the lines and their parallels, everything in a giant circle, we will be so free, that we will laugh until we cry, happy alone. welcome to your life.

There's no way back, even when you sleep we'll be there, it's my own drawing, it's my own remorse, there's a room where the light won't find you, and I'll be happy that you're there, what a shame they couldn't, everyone They want to rule the world, it's only sad who does, indecision and lack of vision, say you never needed it, everyone wants to rule the world.

The universe speaks calmly to me now, it taught me to be patient, I was very afraid at the beginning, believing in myself seemed impossible, dominion of mind over matter, many bodies fell in this battle, but it allows me to hear you, your voice bringing me calm, relieving my fears, in trembling I protect myself, parallel lives, high and low tones, music fits everything in my material life, completes me and defines me, I can feel the universe, it is within me, I see its waves and its tide heals me, feeds me with raw fish, I travel through the stars, on polite stairs.

I no longer need thorns on my roses, if a simple sheep can eat them, I am completely imperfect on my own planet, my craters tell stories, I listen to everything that the darkness of the universe brings me, I kneel before its greatness, I am open, I am in tune, through the silence I can listen.

There's a well-to-do God in me, no pain, no loss, I promise you, 'cause I see for miles, I'm a thinker, I've been waiting and writing for a lifetime, and when there's no one else around, that's when I I'm free, the rain falling on the empty streets where they were, but I see them now, but I'll walk away, I have to leave., i ll walk away.

You can touch it, it's alive, you're your life, mr. Frankenstein, you stitch him up perfectly, he even gave you a brain, but how does it work without a soul, the strings of our puppet, how many characters will it take to make you happy.

I can touch the heavens, opening for me today, my destiny arrived in time to save me, no pain, no loss, no tears, the time is almost here, our dreams will all come true, because I can see my dreams through miles. In time, my love, you and I will know where we are. We dance all night, one movie scene, one heart, one soul, one life, our eyes will not be blinded, we can all be free. Thank you to the universe, lord of time, in time my love, all night.

Every rose has its thorns, every cowboy sings a sad song, just as every night has its end, open your heart to the universe, give yourself to this journey, with an open chest, without fear, trust and know your path, through the night you will walk, Sing your sad songs, beautify the sadness, make the beautiful one during the nights, may she comfort you, without words, just making love, it cuts me like a knife.

Words flow through my mind today, counting blue cars, the universe has shown me the path it is making for me, a door has opened to another dimension, it will save everyone around me, but I need to tell all my thoughts to God , in the clouds I walk, searching, asking questions, just like children do, what are your thoughts God, tell me if I'm too far away.

I count only blue cars, but it's getting cold, and my shoes make noise in this place, many questions, which we generally do.

Who we are, what is the meaning, I am very far away, I travel at such a great speed, let me know when we arrive.

That I can remember that day, when the universe sent me an all small things will work out, trust me, and so I do, I surrender to your strength, I prayed enough for my dreams, time to live them, new roads, old words, everything gains meaning in my life, the journey will be prosperous and peaceful, don't doubt anything from now on, everything is possible, everything is in your hands, you changed your words, this changed your thoughts and your attitudes take you home, walk without fear, you have acquired the key to all the doors.

You are the key maker of your destiny, there are many of us, but you don't need to prove anything else at the gates of heaven, you were worthy, your sign of the bull kept you on earth, your charm enchanted everything and everyone, your hunger for knowledge led you through the most beautiful streets, they were wonderful company, I just thank you, getting up and walking, every day, the stars and roads of the universe opened up to me.

May my guardian angels celebrate the victory, because the next battle will be one of peace, may it be love, and may it make you happy.

Smile until you cry, laugh, be the clown, playing hide and seek alone, a time bomb that will explode us along the way, in parallel lines, in string theories, like a child jumping ropes, taking time to get lost in time.

Keep it simple, a love song, because nothing can go wrong, he's falling for her, they have an invisible touch, when you know it, the moment comes to life, and the walls transform, it's a showroom of life, the other side , she feels this invisible touch, I didn't know what to say, so I kept quiet, but now I know. I'm tired, I need to breathe, stay silent, meditate, pray, and be grateful, I can only imagine...

The path of witchcraft, Santeria, the wizards of tomorrow, the stock exchange of the future, transforming copper into gold, a wizard, a Merlin, in the form of communication, the geniuses of imagination, those who have the gift of oratory, who practice leads you to silence, and thus build your home and follow your Sun.

What people are looking for is a way to smile, it's not difficult when you know how, just listen to the music, all the time. I don't lack inspiration, it's above sabotage, choose a plan that suits you, and dive into the universe.

Chapter six, Between six and nine...

I'm always looking for love, I'm always looking for life, don't get lost between six and nine, go back to three and start all over again, to pretend you never lost, the life he leads, while the world is sleeping, and If he reveals how sensitive he is, what would others say, for those who care, live while they are sleeping. All the energy that exists in good, meaning love, exists in evil, fear, strangers looking for the night, don't stop, hold on to this feeling, I believe, street lights, people, I hold on to this feeling.

An insane world, but there is sanity in it, the loyalty of old friends. Life is a collection of moments, the idea is to have as many good moments as possible, a mystery.

But today is a gift, that's why it's called the present. It is not easy to face the reality of life, the needs of the majority outweigh the needs of the few, we just want to feel something that we have forgotten or abandoned, beneath this chewing there is an idea, and ideas are bulletproof.

Knowing how to wait is a virtue, accepting without questioning that everything has its right time to happen, is having faith, because they will never take away our freedom, because I have always depended on the kindness of strangers, and the rule of the fight club is, you don't talk about fight club.

It takes a lot of audacity to face our enemies, but equal audacity to defend our friends. Either you die a hero, or you live long enough to become the villain. You saved me in all the ways that someone can be saved, they say that one of the two always loves more, I wish it weren't me.

The fears that once controlled me, don't even come close to me, never let anyone tell you that you can't do something, not even me. If you have a dream, you have to protect it, people who can't do it for themselves will say that you can't do it, if you want something, go and fight for it, period.

The most important thing you will learn is to love and be loved, life is like a box of chocolates, you never know what you will find.

I hate that I can't hate you, no matter how much I try and no matter how little you do. You are the answer to all my prayers, you are a song, a dream, a murmur, I don't know how I managed to live without you for so long.

So many bars, in so many cities, and she had to enter mine right away, her sex is on fire. I have the feeling of love, she is a woman, she will free me, i can't free anyone.

Believe what you want to believe, but don't live like a refugee, anyway, somehow, someone will kick you around, but you don't need to live like a refugee.

Sex between souls, a bed in the universe, a meeting in dreams, souls separated physically, and totally connected on a spiritual plane, the sex of the gods. It all starts with breathing, a meeting of breaths, a sensitive touch, a breath burning on the neck, eyes intertwined, colors mix, a meeting of energies, in a single vibration, at various frequencies, an anatomy of the soul implanted in your memories.

Light and easy movements, easy, easy. I talk so much about love, that talking about sex for me is sacred, preserving my energy I learned.

I'm happy in my solitude, but I can't do without a meeting of souls, ancient dormant spirits. Sex is like a gun, you aim, you shoot, you run.

I want it all, and I want it now, I don't ask for too much, I just ask for the truth, in a toast to the future, so much to do in so little time, that's why I live it all, I'm living it all, and I want it all, and I want it now.

Evolve your streaming, may it be an enlightening experience, the touch between souls is deafening, an explosion of energy, it's no wonder you'll wake up wet, heart beating fast, and a memory to keep in, preserve your body fluids for soul encounters , you will see where magic is created, I don't want to be friends, I just want your love, no revenge, no bad romance.

I just wish life was like us movies, and the hero always has his way, When they threw you to the lions, I remember it as if it were yesterday, these are real tears that I keep inside, because it can't be like on TV, and in the end you come to me, but this is real life, and these are real sorrows, but I will never dream of the end, these were real tears, these are real wounds, that I am healing, but in the meantime, I will be dancing with myself, I have nothing to prove, simply dancing with myself.

She whispered, blind and without any fear, he gave himself a guitar solo for you, love, you never abandoned me, I'm grateful, hallelujah he gave birth. In a dream I gave myself up, and I found you, because you only want me the same way.

Crazy life, life, take me, distill and relax, I'll only come back when I find myself, poems sitting in a tree, somewhere in the world, a deserted beach, me, the words and the universe, and it pushes me, there's no more signs of stopping, it calls me, and the lights tell me when it's love, my skin feels its presence, in praise I sing to you, in my place where I feel safe, so lead me through the darkness until it becomes day.

I hear your call, lights will not pass me, I can't stop, you showed me a life where we are both happy, I hold on to it every day, and nights too, when I understood the distance between us, I learned to be happy, happy alone, finding my self-love was fundamental, I lost my mind, I lost my ground, fish in the sea staring at me, I learned and ran, to a fortune that awaits me, an escape plan, my retirement.

But life is too short to care about everything, I found my fortune, I restored my life, I lost my control, I lost my mind, I gave myself to the sea and a new man came out, from the darkness I rise every day and walk my roads, leading love, restoring life, while this syrup runs down the dry throat, suffocates the throat, let me serve you right, in black and white, my love will serve you right, but redemption comes tonight.

I will be your confessor, tell me what you need, while you sink your heart in sorrows, open your eyes brother, see the sun, rise from the ground, from the tea, see the magic that is within you, let your love serve you, You can try it, I guarantee it will work properly.

Time to wait for tomorrow, to find, what you came looking for, when walking in the universe you stop asking yourself, it's all new, there's no need to show any surprise, because everything will be familiar to you, I believe in a thing called love, in my eyes carry the flames of the ashes of my soul, whatever your style, of a hello, be polite, education is a care, it is a curve that heals, in the distance of tomorrow, Far beyond yesterday, she waiting, that everything that you have said, is that you have learned to love as one.

Starlight, we will find a place where we belong, so your starlight won't shine alone, there is a place where you belong.

You will see over the mountains, I believe that everything that was said will return to where it came from, prophecies, words in the wind, the universe is a star of light, don't forget, let it shine in a place where it belongs.

Blessing in ignorance, Just like before, the answers aren't so clear, all these thoughts make sense, one step closer to Edge, shut up when I talk to you, I was breaking down, I just needed room to breathe.

But there was a time, I looked my father in the eyes, in a happy home, those days are gone, but everything changes, everything evolves, so child, don't worry, heaven has a plan for you, the universe belongs to you, he is walking with you, hand in hand towards the sunset. I still hear the songs reminds me of a friend, but everything changes, so children don't worry, don't worry now.

My imagination frees me, transformed me and transcends the world, I made my home in the sky, I feel safe there, my darkness keeps me company every night, when I pray I ask for peace, I ask for love, I thank you and I ask for forgiveness, the way I enter at night, I understand the day, living in a circle.

I see the portals, and inside there are pirates, I sail through calm seas, but at night rough, I carry the flag of peace, hoping for my resilience, only for the one who It matters, In the rain I drive, it's been so long, I can't remember the last time, I can't see the road in the rainy rearview, but I'm not stopping now.

She always takes me home, only she knows where it is, so I'm on my way. Her love guides me, calls me, she gives darkness to light, but she always rises, she is my road, only I know the way, and today I can see the road through the wet glass.

Foot over head, unconditional things, I hope 11:11, it's part of my planning, friends with benefits, I've never felt so healthy, I'm seeing it now, it's not been long since I fell with my feet on my head, it ran over me but inspired me, and I found love in everything, in everything you are.

The universe takes me, it's all his fault, I'm a Rolling Stone in its waters, he promised me he wouldn't hurt me, because there are no directions we can't change, let it lose, find itself, breathe and exhale, all the blues for Outside, open your eyes brother, see, your life is beautiful, enjoying it every day is your lesson, follow your line, don't go after anything, attract everything you want, and if it's not love, stop the lie and shut up, everything will go downhill, you know that, follow your line, the one on the side doesn't interest you, let it get lost, everything will go downhill, string theory, an instrument, a compass, a tool at your disposal, listen yourself, say goodbye to ads, all music goes with you wherever you go.

Where will you go until tomorrow, will you still care, I feel this, when will we go until tomorrow, where will you go with the mask that I found, Jesus knows me and he knows I'm right, you will see my face on television every Sunday, don't buy a piece of paradise, buy it for me, because he knows me, and he tells me that everything is going to be alright.

My life is beautiful, and full of magic, all with a very high quality sound, I'm sorry for the attitude I have when talking about you, I'm me, hey it's me, it's been a long day, all the way, I'm a artist, it's in my being, after midnight I let everything flow, I find my satisfaction, after midnight I let everything be peaches and cream, you will understand how to dance, freedom to your imagination, after midnight., you will swing your tambourines.

Life is on the fast lane, you will get lost, don't be scared brother, trust in your God, give the future to him, live now, bury the past and walk, with your eyes open, forget the phone for a second, all the information is there In you, knowing is not knowing, I can only imagine, an imagination that imagines, imagines. image and sound, what can I say, you have it all.

They are not spirits, they are astronauts, in high vibrations, contact would be painful, so they preserve us, it is just love, a universe of millions of songs without ads or interruptions, All this with very high quality sound. Oh if you could speak my language.

I come from a lineage of warriors and wizards, time magicians, Dr. Strange carrying the time stone, healing your hands so that it becomes magical, Visualizing the world is necessary, without time and space, just the world in which you live, the magic happens between your eyes, and certain days, they made it better, it is the fastest, much faster than us, and where it goes no one can know, while the world is sleeping. Nothing can stop my heart, it's been in the dark, I hope it never stops.

Every night, hold on tight, any way you want, this is the way you need it, my words, like an outburst they surprise me, thank you sir, I just want you to remember, a love like that can send us all the directions, the power of a child, the displaced chemicals, just remember, the walls that lie in this place, fall to the floor.

Number three, harmony and balance, number six, health and happiness, number nine spirituality and achievements, and I think I have been liberated, think and speak, buy and drink, use and be bold, no sir, yes sir. I even thought there was a heart beating here, but I'm going to reinstall the system, read, vote, don't forget. The words walk through me, I won't fall down, this isn't my home, if you feel anything. Keep me running, I'll run, I won't fall, I won't go down, this isn't my home.

Keep me wild, keep me alive, I would change little things, I had to change everything, this isn't my'home, if this feels at all.

And how do you feel, amen direction home, a complete nobody, like a rolling stone, I never understood that it's not good at all, for others to take a beating because of you, after they took from you, everything they could steal, as if feels, holding on alone, without direction, like a rolling stone.

You were once such a muse, you are invisible now, you have no more secrets, and how you feel is your own.

Money, hold it with both hands and make a pile, it's a hit, I need to pay the bills, know now, this is a work of fiction, it was created by my imagination, my mind, but... it was created with a lot of love, It's a love letter to the planets, to astronauts, the universe was written with a lot of love, I'm very proud of it, that it can lead you to reflect, judge less, and love more, we are ants in evolution, we are nothing more than insects, but everything was handmade, everything was sculpted, at the beginning I see Elvis, at the end I see Raul, and in the middle I see Belchior Cazuza, Gilberto Gil in life, I go slowly, so as not to lack love. Whatever your style, say goodbye to ads, go offline, you're just a click away.

And if I could describe to you everything I feel, you would be my poison, one look could kill me, I want to kiss you, but I want too much. I want to hold you but something tells me to stop, poison, inside my veins, I won't break the chains. All I can tell you is that my life is very plain, put tea for two, and explain my point of view, I'll be there when you wake up, and I sleep all day, complaining that it doesn't rain, that's an escape, guitar, if you don't like my point of view, you're not a saint.

You grow in me, or I grow in you, what we are now, with our eyes closed, we will fly through the stars, and when the children are old enough, we will teach them to fly, we can always go back to the beginning, we can do anything. Me and you together, two of us together, we can do anything baby.

We will go to the end of the world, I will sail the best beaches, I will take myself from coconut waters, on a crazy train I will deliver myself, millions of people, living like foes, wanting to learn how to love and forget how to hate, I go off the rails on this crazy train , there are priests and the drops out that make their own rules, you have to listen to my words, oh yes.

I can now walk between six and nine, hit me with the best shot, the light in the window is a crack in the sky, go back in the darkness and see what your mother said, don't talk to strangers, no more tears, I see the man, around the clock, and I see someone screaming, no more tears.

Universe I need you, you're my cure, no need to worry, I'll be home soon, to satisfy you, it feels so good inside, baby I love you, what more can I say, hey babe I need you , I miss you more every day.

I wake up early in the morning, and a feeling washes over me, you know I need you, and I guess I just want to tell you, that what you need is me. Babe, I love you, and I miss you more every day, what more can i say.

Closing a chapter, closing six and opening nine, it's good enough for me, poetry commands me, we are together side by side, nothing here is what it seems, there's a fear that I haven't left, in silence, we could come together reinvent, fill your head with common sense, climbing the walls with you, half awake and almost dead, in silence. We still have to bleed, all this energy, leaving empty beds out there.

When the vision comes in LED, the little things that take me back home, today I feel complete, I salute you, the vibe of the moment, in whatever order you want, it was a very big struggle, until today's peace, I no longer I remembered what I was fighting for, they spit you out, and leave you on a road, chewed up, left for dead, this game, throw your money away, two for one, one for nothing, you can't take it, walk away from the game, come back where did you come from.

Chapter Seven, seven deadly sins...

Greed, I never thought I was greedy, I drank champagne with kings and queens, but now I remember why all this was done, from now on, what starts tomorrow, will start today, from now on, and we will go home, home again. Greed still drives us, we need homes, the power to control, don't ask for too much, and so, we can return home, home again.

Gluttony, I'm a Taurus, I like to eat well, what can I do, when the world becomes a fantasy, and you can't go back to the world you lived in, no one lives in the shadows, it's in you, you get out alive , for you dream with your eyes wide open, I will eat and drink, I will find my way to freedom.

Envy, nothing that was real was left behind, I don't believe in envy, I don't see myself in anyone else but myself, I've been with narcissists long enough to learn, I wish my best to others, and I hope they understand my silence , in my peace I walk, a curve is ahead, I can only see so Far.

My anger, I bury it with my past, there is no anger left inside me, I see myself happy, I am happy, death doesn't catch my attention, I want calm days, light winds, and sunny weather, there is no anger in me brother, Just love, It's what I offer.

Lust, it never suited me, it didn't attract my eyes, and when the eye betrayed me, it didn't attract me, I got lost in my characters, I play everyone I can, I don't see sins, I don't see any evil, except myself, We will walk with daily lust, without fear, accompanies flight plan.

Laziness, what would I do without it, it is in my being, my planet, I am lazy, I love my moment of doing nothing, I am happy in my nothingness, I find myself in it and it satisfies my desires, I dream of laziness, only it You know what good it does me.

Pride, arrogance, pretension, blinded by the Sun, pride has to be the first to die in a good man, humility and perseverance will be necessary on the journey, everything returns to its position, be positive, creativity and inspiration, everything is good from within, Be humble on the outside and giant on the inside, self-love is not arrogance.

Love all, trust a few, do wrong to none, be able for thine enemy

Rather in power than use, and keep thy friend, under thy own life's key, be checked for silence, but never taxed for speech. William Shakespeare, All's Well That Ends Well.

I had to confess to enter heaven, I believed in sins, justice and punishment. Today I see it all as a big deception, the fear that was implanted in me, people telling me what was right and wrong.

I will always rebel against authorities, after all, we all have our weapons buried in a dark basement, full of gold coins, but if you don't go there, then down low, because everything in life is a composition, my words will be best sellers, they will be songs made with lots of love and gratitude.

One day we will die, but remember to look at all the others where we will be alive. Being happy for no reason is the most authentic form of happiness.

Life is like a book, only after reading it do we know what it contains. Everyone is capable of mastering pain, except those who feel it. I wasn't looking for anything but a good time, I needed time, they don't ask you for anything to enter the universe, no fees are charged, there is no sin that will not be forgiven, everyone is welcome, you won't find books to teach you what to do, through your forgiveness you will see the doors if they open, the moments of truth in your life, when you bleed just to know that you are alive, it all started with a photo, a capture of a moment, that made me whole again.

I started walking again, we never know what will end us once and for all, but believing that something will do you good, that will lift you up, it is essential, there are no sins in the path of the universe, what exists is high and low vibration, there is no right or wrong either, it is a question of the evolution of being, it can come Without fear, there will be no pain, no loss, no tears, in time, dear, in time everything will be alright.

Any love that destroys freedom, will turn to hate, sooner or later, Osho Gita, when you are chasing what was lost, change makes other plans, bringing shine to the moonlight, burying moments of the past, one day you wake up, and seven years have passed, sometimes a shadow shines a lot of light, artists and madmen dive into the same waters, but only one comes back from there.

When you find people who believe in the universe, it's wonderful, a light person, they don't charge themselves so much, so they won't charge you either, I see love today differently than yesterday, love for another person comes full of rules, detours and prisons.

Today I see free love, there is nothing that belongs to me in the material world, much less a person, the rate of people dying in a relationship between two is absurd, you want to control the other, and call this control love. These rules and customs that we have followed for generations, We cannot claim a being, and say that it belongs to us, when you hear the heart beating in your chest, and know the rhythm of your body, there are no possessions, our spirit leaves alone, We don't take land much less people, love comes to liberate, never arrest.

You can't stop the fire with a spark, everything in the universe comes to teach you, I'm cold, I'm the little dog, if it makes me feel everything, keep me running from sins, make it worth my time.

I'm not going down, I'm not going down, this isn't my home, if it feels all, Keep me wild, I don't feel pain 'cause I know it too well, I was going to change a little, but I had to change everything, walk through The universe will give you a vision, it will bring you death, but it will teach you how to create life. From within a child's imagination, the best stories can come out, a fantasy world, created to special order and waiting for you, a park for your mind and body, a bridge that connects you to your soul, and all of this works for you.

Because of the heart, everything is perfect, so stop for a minute, be grateful, have hope, hold on tight, the pain ends, hope is a waking dream, hope will give you courage, never lose hope.

Believe in tomorrow, even better, I believe in today, when I walk with my eyes open I understand my being, I make peace with myself, after all it's me, and no one is going to make me leave, those are my words, it's my dream, I had to wake up to dream again, so start the day with a soft voice, the universe will give you more than you expect, trust it, there is no dream too big, only minds too small.

You satisfy your greed, you leave everyone around you in misery, forever happy, envy leads you to hate, which led you to anger, don't be angry with me

I gave up everything to touch you, all I can bring is your life, and I don't want the world to see me, because I don't think they would understand, I can't fight the tears that come, I surrender and accept, I'm grateful, thank you , I will continue my life writing, photographing and loving, may the unconditional come to me, may I constantly draw it into my soul, I think they understand, when everything can break, I just want you to know who I am.

The number seven, a fiction that my self wants, I have the number seven tattooed, but I have a G clef, a rose and a compass, I hope that will take Me home one day, I gave in to my dreams, I woke up in a giant universe of possibilities, my imagination is my business card, I am polite, I know how to get in and out, seven protects me, heals me and let me go, seven plus seven, fourteen, what does that mean, only seven plus is twenty one , boom, with a blink of an eye, without remorse and without regret.

May I have the strength to let you go, I keep you in sight, and I'll be closer than I thought I would, I'll throw my chains off, forever, I have no more reason to fight this feeling anymore. I had to crawl across the floor, I fell through the door, they say misery loves company, we can make misery, I know what you pay to feel.

A factory that makes misery, we create the cure, we create the disease, my friend, we live on the tip of a spear, and a rope around our neck, getting out of your mind from time to time is necessary, incorporate yourself, get up, get out from misery, forever happy alone, good luck sir, may the universe treat you well, may you feel loved and welcome, stay cozy, enjoy your trip.

Tonight I don't want to sleep, I just want to continue loving you, without pain, without loss, our dreams will all come true, in time everything will be alright, in time we will dance in the streets all night long.

One heart, one soul, you'll see, that we can all break free. get up Maria, show me that Spanish dance, wake up Mister Jones, hand me that bottle, I can never be alone, these are my favorite colors, my new Picasso, he looks at me, right in the spot of light, I will never be alone , I will never be alone. We don't want to be big stars, we want something to believe in. And we will be happy, because we will be so free, sharing a smile, so far from home, making songs, making life, just astronauts, happy Alone.

You can change the world, you take good care of business every day, everything is fine, it works every time, one world you have already changed, yours.

I'm just a Latin American boy

No money in the bank

No important relatives

And coming from the inside

But I bring, from the top of my head, a song from the radio

In what an old composer from Bahia told me

Everything is divine, everything is wonderful... Belchior words.

We've reached the halfway point, I deserve a cold beer, this contact with the universe, without regret, read the warnings, read the signs, if you can't handle it, step away from the game, take your money and run. Walk like a free man, and no one cares. Just roll with the chances, go with the changes.

The road to nowhere leads to me, we meditate and we pray, you want the best, the best band in the world, kiss. Babe if you feel good, if you feel hot, you know your man works for two, stop crying all those tears, feel nice, sweet work rolling, a distorted guitar, an easy chorus, for me and you sing along, as we go so far, a rock and roll band will take control, all the songs go with you wherever you go, before you say goodbye, I'll say hello, How do you do. I see you in that chair, with perfect skin, when we are young we can feel the things you do, to say goodbye.

All that I can see, if I could change the world, like in a fairy tale, because love is love reflecting, come full circle, if there's a spell on you that I can take away, time, don't go away, I raise my glass, in your honor, to all my crazy dreams, it was just killing time.

System crash, someone distorted me, think, speak, buy and drink, read now and don't forget, use and be bold, may the good lord shine a light on you, like the end of the afternoon.

Come on get up now, let's go up, like the afternoon sun, come, just come, the doors open, the gift of perception, with your eyes on the road and your hands on the wheel, a good time, and back to the, I go slow, I let go, babe roll, all night long. I got the feeling, she's gonna set you free.

Chapter eight, rewrite the stars…

I'm the man on the mountain, with the mud on my feet, I'm the one who brings you roses, when you don't have any, I'll be so humble with you tonight, what a nice breeze, 'cause I know my car won't start, but give me a glass, from your jar of love. I believe in your music, you help me along, I want to get lost in your rock and roll and drift away. free my soul.

I can feel, like a little bird that chases the thunder in the wind, all in the dark of shadows, all in the stars, how you found me, what you came to look for. If everything were to stay like this forever, tonight I throw myself on you, down with me. And I wonder, will things stay this good forever.

Everyone's looking for a connection, a continuation, I look at my life and see the things I've done to myself. I still search for the answer, but the road to nowhere led to me, and I'll do it all again, living for today and not tomorrow. I hope the street to nowhere doesn't overtake me, I hope I never have to say goodbye.

Today I won't cry, print smiles in the newspaper, the hearts of the saints, fresh meat for the customer, meanwhile the city burns with fire. This time remember to make mommy happy, baby you don't want to make me happy. choose a plan and walk brother.

Crawling on my skin, are words that don't heal and confuse reality, control, I can't see, like wounds that don't heal, my own reflection, insecure and afraid, words that bring me down, fear is how we fall. But with open arms I will be waiting for you, because you and I together can do anything, we have the blue sky, you know better than me that we can do anything.

Photography, everything I have of you is a photograph, a memory, a smell of my memories, my days in the sun by your side, humming songs, serving our country, serving our king, before the white man comes and takes it all again . Know your customers, you don't need protection, we understand, the truth in your heart brother, no one can steal.

Dad's breeze, a dream, free will, is it a mistake, would it be great to be able to live in a world where everything is possible, a world of fantasy, a world of our own. I believe we can live in the world we design, all with very high quality sound.

If I go crazy, you'll still call me Superman, you'll be there to hold my hand, you know how I live my life, from coast to coast, in a dark room, lie to wound, in the name of the damned.

How can I continue in this hole, knowing all the truth that I know now, all this time, the smile of the doma, the salvation that comes to us. A dark room, that's where it all started, listening to the Doors, Mr. Jim talking about the other side, I was young, but my witchy side always accompanies me, wherever I go, it shows me the power of love, more than a feeling.

Don't accept money, don't get fame, just feel the power of love, you don't need a credit card to ride this train, Mama kin is waiting for you, because you were dreaming, and lost touch with everything that was real, lived like a gypsy , lived as you wanted, but the way I see it, just don't forget to turn off the light when you leave. I am a passenger, I go around and around, I see the skies, and they are so beautiful today, and everything was made just for me and you, we are passengers, astronauts, passing through this world, everything was made for us, why don't you take advantage , happiness is an imaginary state, see the stars come out tonight, say hello to the Moon, and see everything that is yours, and sing lá lá lá.

Let's rewrite the stars, a new world, one that makes you feel your soul, the other side, let it roll babe, let it roll, all night long. I'm high on the mountain, come on UP, just one sip, and you'll fall down drunk, in full sweet sunshine from the cup of love, I'm so humble with you, see the reflection of your face in a flame, what a beautiful buzz.

Give him a sip from your cup of love, just one sip, and he will fall down drunk. dance with yourself, when you have nothing left to prove, don't ask me why, but dance with yourself, if I had the chance, when you have nothing left to lose, invite the world to dance with itself, I'm waiting for the my vibrations of love, the truth is that they have always been here, so dance with me, dance with myself.

With your eyes wide open, I will show you everything, I will show you love, if it were just a request, come alive when I see your ghost, where they keep you low, if you come closer, and you have nothing left to hide, you'll love the taste, a lifetime of searching for something at the end of the road, always wanting more, more than I can give, it would keep bringing me down.

I needed to change my look, my hair and my face, a new world opened up, and you started the fire with just a spark, I just know that you are, you are starting something somewhere, and here I am dancing in the dark, stay hungry, a reaction of love, your world falling apart, and you dancing in the dark.

Life is a star, one day here, the next it goes, it is a road, of all cities, there is no road that is not worth your time, the lights, this distance between things, a previous disagreement, but now we look into each other's eyes.

Life is a road, I like to drive all night, a road and a collection of songs, something that always brings me peace, a safe place, where my heart guides me, and the sun and the moon are my directions, a compass, a notebook, the universe is a game, for those who seek adventure, it is full of mystery, love and gratitude, these are the weapons that I carry with me, only through forgiveness did I heal my wounds, I hope I can heal other soldiers , I came in peace, I bring a message of love, just a hello from my planet, in words of welcome and forgiveness. Be good to each other.

I see a woman sitting on the floor, with a baby in her hands, they are feeding from a trash can. I cried a lot because I saw this same scene so many times, over and over again.

My heart was loose, I rolled them sevens with nothing to lose, call all my old shots, and now I don't feel at home anymore, this is no place to lose your mind, take your crazy heart and give it one more try, your body hurts , playing guitar sweating all hate, whiskey was a thorn in his side, this is no place for the weary type, no place to be left behind.

There's no going back, young hearts die young, my white hair, I have it with pride, time to learn, young heart beats fast, and there's no going back now, my heroes who died at twenty-seven, soon tomorrow comes .

Light the fire, I also saw, for those who cling to the edge trapped in denial, enough of this skin, it's time to change, devour the tail and start over, soon tomorrow comes.

Parts and lubricants, have your workshop, keep your imagination in check, use all the tools that the material world gives you, the next step, is a curve, I can only see so far, so imagine, be optimistic, see the world through a pair of sunglasses, who doesn't have eye drops, delusions, five dimensions, five directions, the universe will guide you in whichever one you choose, cradle of love, rock the cradle of love. Mr. Idol, I'm no one's fool, it's easy, you can please me.

You don't have to live like a refugee, the prisons that surround you, are growing, through all the pieces, you're still falling, and every time you fall below, you break into pieces, a journal of memories, all your pieces , they are still falling, I knocked down the walls that held me, I fell out of love, where else would I find you, only by falling could I see you, and now I picked up my pieces from the ground, and every time I fall, I fall into pieces.

Say goodbye to the ads, tell me something girl, you're happy in this world, I just hope for change, and on the bad days I'm afraid of myself, do you need more, in all the good times we've had, you only feel yourself in bad times, we are far from shallow now, all I want, are your kisses and hugs too, blue shoes, Silk food, something normal, a universe of a million songs, life is too short to care about everything, follow the beat of the drums, let yourself get lost, let your heart guide, waste time, love yourself, get up now, forget the zombies in the park, distill and relax, breathe and exhale, restoring your life , loss of control, a leap is necessary, a leap into a new life, find a way for you to feel the way, drink this coffee syrup, and follow your journey.

People will tell you that you are in the loop, because you stay stoned in the morning and drunk in the afternoon, preachers who talk on TV about Jesus walking on water, if you don't like the way I live, just cut your long hair and leave me alone.

And every step I take is wrong for you, I got so tired, but I know you're just like me, I can feel you there, I've become this, I'm more me and less like you, everything I wanted to be , I'm ready to enjoy a lot of music, I'm my hero, certain days make me better, I always have a lot to do.

The age of man, I come from a lineage of Jedi's, a new day a new star, a new hope, at the round table I sat a while ago, I remember it as if it were today, the lands of death and snow, where nothing growing up, my friends in uniform, my brothers in arms, tell everyone that we are here, and that the end is near, time for us to return home, touching all souls, they had their turn, now it's our turn, it's ours voice, and let's be clear, you know when I'm here, I found you in myself, while I'm here.

I had to go high, there was no other way, home sweet home, I went to emotional rescue, it could be mine, tonight and every night.

My destiny, I surrender every day to the universe, I see your plan and how great it is, I see my dreams, my desires, I need to tell you what I feel inside, there is no denial when I look you in the eyes, there are no doubts in my Mind, now it's forever, I hear the echo of the promises I made, and I don't want to go alone, but everything about you, tells me it's forever, I'll love you forever.

A chapter, a line, words, a piece of paper, and a virtual keyboard, you workshop owner, writing my truths, in prophecies of tomorrow, but always looking at the now, will be better for sale, just my words, from my being to the document, words to Léo, something tangible, here I am, and you are a rocket queen, I opened my heart to the universe, it will pay my bills, take me to a world of adventures, give me the means to my ends, I may be a little young, but the universe is obscene.

Chapter nine, Wolfmother…

I told you the joker was a wanted man, you can see him flying, mother wolf, only humans let anyone free, you will never see a group of animals being led by a weak one, only the strongest and most agile, can command, I sleep with wolves, I walk in a pack, but I have no leaders, I am my own master, the sun guides me through my doubts and questions, there is no fear or past, but I trust in the now, I have patience, I know how to smile for no reason.

I like to dream between a sound machine, why don't you come with me on my flying carpet, close your eyes and let the sound take you, I look around, and I don't know what to think, fantasy will set you free.

Number nine, Wolfmother, find your spirit, embrace your soul, see the true love that exists within you, celebrate life, go on a red carpet, dancing the night away. I had good times from coast to coast, leaving a sad past behind, and the truth is not just one, there are several.

"The universe is not just stranger than we suppose, it is stranger than we can imagine." - J.B.S. Haldane

I hear angels bringing the news today, I close my eyes and started to pray, tears of joy came to me, and with my eyes wide open I can see, all the light that exists within me, and to be the man I have to be, we create life, I know this place, I will show you everything, I will show you love.

With eyes wide open, if I had just one request, that he not be like me, with arms wide open, I will show you everything, where everything has changed, with eyes wide open.

And now that everything goes away, I feel the sun burning me, it calls out your name, and it feels, like the sky goes away, follow me to the sea, dip your feet in salty water, throw a handful around your neck, cleanse yourself of negative energies, you walked with the dead.

Go for a swim in the sea and come back alive, you are on fire and burning to the core, set fire to me, until my feet no longer touch the floor, Take me high until my back can longer feel any more, don't burn me down.

I deserve to celebrate; I embark on a tour to hell, in the news media, am I medieval, look at me give me your hand, then a kiss, live in me that no one will throw empty hands or stones at you, but from drunk to drunk it is denying me, I think I'm such a current guy, celebrating life, guitar in hand, to go beyond, loud my friend, with a little help from my friends.

I can do no harm except myself, no harm except myself, I go deep into my feelings, I put out what I need, I try to show you, I knock on wood three times, on some corner, some alley, on the other side of the street.

I had perverse ideas, you getting closer and closer, my love, my accomplice, you haven't changed at all, neither have I. let's go against the grain, from Gilberto Gil to Caetano, I bring good news, balloons that fall from the sky, talent for madness and long speeches, death is alive brother, time to be reborn, plant to harvest, be your shaman, if you are not yours doctor, you have a terrible doctor, I saw the face of death, and she was alive, wake up brother, get up and walk, I saw your name on a poster, so I can then advise what is right or wrong, the rest leave it alone .

You listen to me but pretend, with your mouth shut now you get along fine, a lot of ass kissers, to pamper you, the rest leave it alone. Neon lyrics and everything, last year they would say I was crazy, I warn you, go to the fight, make your point precisely, the fans of today are the sanders of tomorrow, but never mind, go to the fight. The universe, love is an imaginary state, the bourgeoisie wants to get rich, and as long as there is a bourgeoisie there will be no poetry.

I who came from the middle of the bourgeoisie, I also smell bad, and they sleep peacefully, the bourgeoisie doesn't notice the pain, the bourgeoisie only looks at itself, the bourgeoisie stinks, and as long as there is a bourgeoisie there will be no poetry.

Let's take the stolen money, let's go to the street, to the street, I'm bourgeois but I'm an artist, I'm on the side of the people, I live off my work honestly, I'm interested in my people.

I'm an outcast, half anarchist, half sorcerer, we're going to run away, they'll never say it again, I'm an outcast for many, and a sorcerer for few, I made my days start happily, insomnia made everything infinite, every day there was section time owl, oh my love, we are on the verge of a happy day, every day is day, and all in the name of love, in the comings and goings of your hips, all the muscles you feel, give me your encore as a gift. This is the life I wanted, swimming against the current, just to exercise, oh my love, and that's how I make the day rise happily.

Have faith in God, have faith in life, nothing is over, try, raise your thirsty hand and start walking, dancing in the air. If you like, just be honest, you will be able to shake the world, victory is lost, try again

My baby, everything can change right now, you just have to believe, roll the dice, baby, I have no money, I'm six, sevens and nines, you have to roll me, in chapter ten we will march captain, my captain, poems are my maps and coordinates, in a submarine, where I only see the tip of the iceberg, ten percent, that's what my eyesight allows, that is, ninety percent imagination, there is a light in the dark, you don't need to close your eyes to see it, you can feel it , if delivered, thanks will be necessary, it will be yours open sesame, the forty thieves, all the pirate gold you will find, open doors.

Writing my entry into paradise, I deserve my rest, my mind flooded with feelings, the rock and roll that exists within me awake, complete and alive, singing a love song so divine, I know It is only rock and roll, but I like it, I like it. Can't you see that this soul was alone, healing its pain, solitude, I'm lonely, but I'm happy. I know I dream of you, a sin and a lie, wild horses, can take me away.

I know I dream of you, a sin and a lie, wild horses, can take me away, that I can always choose, and writing my way I find absolution, I waited for you all alone, my love, I miss you, mine lines, no easy exits, a lot of words, we've waited so long, come on.

I will take my time, the universe has taught me patience, I travel in its spiral circles, recognizing myself in parallel timelines, a Ronnie Wood, you always ask for more than I can give, I spend my life in honky tonks looking for you. my desires, my dreams, a deck of cards, on a dock I placed myself, this is not me, I am not the fortunate one, it is not me, son of a millionaire, I am not the one who is fortunate. I was born to be wild, sultan of swing, in the darkness in the meantime, a man blowing words, one step forward and everything can go down, competition knows its place, turning down the sound, check your guitar, if it's off you can give us follow, it will be a day job, sixth night will make you free, any crowd will be welcome, I don't care about those who play in bands, I call them rock and roll.

I am the fly that landed in your soup, I am the fly that arrived to abuse you, in the dark I see how blind we are, since you are gone, Let me protect you, I will make you happy again, because you try to understand what love is, my dear. What does love have to do with it, what is love if not a second hand of emotion, who needs a heart, when a heart can be broken.

Who needs a heart, when a heart can be broken, what does love have to do with it, and I take you in a new direction, what is love, if not a second hand of emotion. we may Lose, we may Win, take it easy, don't say maybe, your sweet love will save me. You are disappointed, I know what it's like to be just a shell of yourself.

But don't forget what lies ahead, soon your pains will be gone, sister run free, light and loose, this road will be tough, but we won in the end, so enjoy the view, keep pushing, we're almost home.

The crosses brought hell home, however fast we can, brother it won't be long, in all your strength, run free and wild, almost home, we're almost home.

The way I obey you at night, never take me, never leaders, never leave this place, let me breathe, you can see the dolphins crying, no matter who you are, all these words, they are finished. Come to me, never leave us, stay with me no matter who you are. I Will get by, I'll survive. The universe was made of Magic, we Will get by .

Chapter ten, Blues on Black and greens and blues ...

Jack on fire, BLUE on Black, blind now i see, truth, lies and between, tears on a River, Dead man's touch, Joker on Jack , doesn't bring you back. And if everything is a mirage, a lie that your vanity wants, when you wake up, what will happen, you don't want to know what mom said, time stops, stay in the moment, without limits, just this chapter, stay with me.

Funk the funky out, time keep circling in the future, I want you to fly like an eagle through the universe, love is the solution, let my spirit leave me, fly for the revolution, something new, Mr Anderson, don't shut up, you and I Smith, light and dark, positive and negative, in a circle of fire, in an infinite loop, an eight flying like an eagle, fly over the revolution.

I see you around me, let it go or lose it, if it were all so easy, to love and be loved, let it or lose it, but let it go, please, see everything around you, good love will come back, so look at what you have, or you will lose control, so hold on or let go, if not, you will lose control, but don't let go, you will lose control.

My life, thank you, I feel safe here with you, I don't ask for much, to live my own action story, rocking in a free world, between me and you, I can only honestly say that things can only get better, we are loud, and that's what they call the blues, laughing like children, rolling like thunder, through every second, without excitement, a simple I love you, my Michele, living like lovers, and that's what we call the blues.

Adri and Ana, Liu and Ana, Luciana, keep on going, oh yeah, you have to keep on going, my love, wishes of peace and success to you, souls who touched me, like a worm, I played my guitar solos, keep on going, love, how to explain it, is so normal for me, I go wherever it takes me.

Daddy will tell you, don't worry child, heaven has a plan for you, don't worry now, we rule the world, after the blue lake, where everything changed, see child, God has a plan for you, heaven has a plan for you. don't worry. The universe opened the doors of perception to me, since I was little, I've been observing, taking notes, taking it easy, going kayak, I need to delve deeper, talk about myself, a screen between the two of us, one crime at a time, a brand that I founded, the Now, where to start.

When the sharpest words come to cut you, I'll be there brother, I'll be waiting for you, I'm home alone, I'm out on the town, I've been at the bottom of the bottles I've been knocking over down, lying around, on a lonely day, I'm working tonight, Sharp words, I've been practicing a lot, that's what I found, a typewriter, lying there on the floor.

In the universe there is no right or wrong, each being will have its own form of contact, there is no correct position to start with, just close your eyes and empty your head, breathe in and out, feeling the air pass through your body, lighting up all the chakras , feel the energy rising up your back, to the back of your head, always controlling your breathing.

With your eyes closed, visualize a point of light in your mind, and push it upwards, as if it were a rocket leaving the earth's orbit, see it rising in your mind, and when it reaches the top, enter a spiral tunnel in your forehead, push the light through this wormhole, with an empty and open mind move forward, you will feel an energy accumulating in your forehead.

Let this energy take over you, it will be an explosion on your forehead, you will feel your third eye opening, and with your eyes closed you will be able to see, imagine yourself in the universe, without gravity, without direction or direction, you will feel some vertigo, it is yours soul detaching from your body, dizziness will be normal, don't be alarmed by them, just jump, if you have the opportunity jump, say goodbye to your body, enter the universe, see its formation and what it brings you. everything is at your disposal, you can take it all on your own, whatever your style or religion, contact with the divine is personal, there are no rules, no ways of saying what is right or wrong, everyone will have their own way of concentrating energy, and how to see your soul in space.

It all depends on what you are looking for, the path is individual, each one will have their own vision, and whatever way you arrive at the universe, it will be right.

The important thing in the universe is the journey, not the destination, but knowing what you are looking for can help, because in fact most of the time we have no idea what we are looking for, it is a journey to the other side, you must have heard this before, really It's a leap to the other side, it can be enlightening as it can be just another question on the pile, but if you know what to look for, the universe will help you find it. I was scared at first, I didn't know what to expect.

When this energy comes into contact it's scary, the universe talks to you constantly, it knows you like the back of its hand, there are no places to hide or run away, from then.

You can go back, what you saw cannot be unseen, things around you came to life, everything tells a story, everything has an energetic karma, everything is linked directly and indirectly, the answers are not clear, they are just new questions, clearing your mind won't last long, because the path is revealing, when you start talking to the universe, you see that many things from your past don't make sense, you learn to value your time, people who just want to talk are a wishing well, they throw words as if they were requests from a genie in a bottle, if you know the power that a word has, the universe will show you how great you are, in such a small bottle, I'm sorry you feel this way, but we all have a touch of gray.

The darkness of the universe is fascinating, when you feel free to explore, discover planets and stars, the milky way is so beautiful, the solar system is a quantum supercomputer, it feeds us with its sun rays, but there is so much information in the sun When I close my eyes to listen to you, it's always something extraordinary, maybe you won't forget me, I need you here with me.

Meditation was and is very important for me, a minute of silence is already a lot in the world we live in, we are always full of things to do, mouths talking, we need some time alone, just listen, to the voice of God that is within us. For us, clearing our mind is much more difficult than it seems.

Thinking about nothing is already thinking about something. Always pray and be grateful, the path to forgiveness is through gratitude, self-love comes after forgiveness, when we learn to be grateful.

When I was about eight years old, I took some guitar lessons, and the first thing the teacher wanted to teach me was the correct way to hold the guitar, the classic shape of the instrument, that for me was where he lost me.

Someone telling me how to hold the neck of the guitar, something that would be so personal for me, everyone will have their own way, their way, I have always rebelled against authorities, I can't listen to anyone tell me what is right and what is wrong, I find this so personal, I grew up with people telling you what you should do, I never accepted it, I was always against any form of authority.

I always found myself in my silence, the path of the thinker, it was as if my instruction manual was built in , somehow I felt, what I didn't know, music helped me a lot, there in those poems I found myself, the search for knowledge, mine wasn't in books but in a headphone, through music I understood my being , something that always called me, something unknown, something new, my soul was in contact with me from an early age, as a teenager.

I had experiences of leaving my body, of seeing myself lying in a bed, unable to move, not knowing what to do , I woke up screaming, the return of the soul to the body was a blow, it was as if I were light years away and simply returned to my body once and for all.

Only with an external vision could I learn to look inside, in silence I grew, without being able to share it with anyone, each one would have their journey to the universe, and mine had just begun, finding my happiness was a matter of life or death. , with my eyes closed I found my light, in the middle of total darkness, it was a walk through the shadows, the negative and the positive always together, the sun teaching, the moon to observe and when the dogs start to smell it, it's the time to wake up and think about tomorrow, to find it.

Being an only child was a gift, as well as a painful path, not having anyone to compare myself to, but I had a happy childhood, I liked being alone, I always had a sharp imagination, I was happy in my solitude, everyone wants everything, but they can't have it.

Sometimes it's in front of you but you can't grab it. It took me time to understand that the path was lonely, I valued my friendships a lot, I didn't know how to be alone at the beginning, as I didn't have a brother or sister, I learned to play alone, I was one for making castles and fortresses, I designed my world in my toys , I spent hours talking to them, I was very happy, he was my teacher, he was the good side of solitude, love, playing alone is loving yourself, getting to know yourself, exercising your mind, creating characters, stories, giving life to something that is dead , Name the bad guys and good guys, hide and tag with yourself, in your shoes walk and sleep, Black hole Sun, why don't you come, and wash all this rain away.

If you find it, what does that mean, haven't we already found ourselves, and living in the now, so that this eternity searching, and if it were just the now, without questions, just forgiveness, without words, just silence, lessons of a sunset, feet in nature, planted on the ground, mind clean and beautiful, thank you, I do see you every night, I do.

What can I say about myself, I am a sensitive, sensational guy, I am on my way, I learn daily from everyone who passes me, I have respect for the elderly and children, I am polite and formal, but I am also sincere and honest, no I don't think all truths should be told, I think silence is the best love we can give someone, the simple act of listening will open more doors for you than it closes, always have common sense with you, be it conscience, your mind is open, acceptance and affection towards the living being, be the type that takes the spider out of the house, and puts it in the forest, breathe it out, so that I can breathe you, and I wonder, when I will sing along with you.

So many words to describe the universe, I'm a dreamer, I always have been, an astronaut, a lover of the arts, a simple drop of rain, may the poetry that lives within me reach you, I'm no stranger to the dark, I've been rejected many times, I know what it's like to feel on the outside, I'm angry, I'm hurt, but I'm not afraid of being seen, because that's me.

We cross the barricades, and to the beat of the drums, we can walk, a solution for peace, may the sharpest words find their home in common sense, may it be pure consciousness, may it make you see, with the power of tea, make your imagination to shine, a conversation with oneself is necessary, peace agreements to be negotiated, a last appearance to the life you lived, stop and face it, you would do anything for what is fair, but you see what I see, firm feet, I run until I walk, I think I move, but I'm not going anywhere, I became what I couldn't be.

Forget the cage, because you already know how to get out, sit down for a while, and have a cigar, breath, by the way, what color is pink really, the name of the game is riding the gravy train, and everything has the same value, everything counts, and everything falls into place if we can form a team, and in the night where the cold wind blows, I don't want to be buried in a pet cemetery, and in the night when the moon is shining, I will howl, humming songs, I don't want to live my life again.

Be curious, I threw a coin in the river and jumped to the other side, they didn't even know who I was, miles and miles opening up to me, an old and familiar ghost of mine, I walked through the dark valley, I was told the truth would free myself, I didn't wait to see, in the darkness I made my nest, I learned to see in the dark, I searched until I found my switches, today I can turn on all the lights, and I know that there will always be a new light to turn on, I jumped into tomorrow, Before he comes back, we can get away from all this, darling, we are losing gravity, we will fly over the roofs of the houses, like a crow on a walk, I don't ask anyone for anything, if I can get it myself.

Where does all this information about the universe come from, will it be imagination, pure fiction of my head, I don't want to play ball with the law, I could use a break, they are memories in my mind, soon I will be on my way, they are words from my heart, fiction of my knowledge, when justice is a game, you sitting like a Buddha, you will be the champion of the world.

Chapter eleven, Money away…

Money is a hit, Thank God the universe, neither string theories nor parallel lines will ask you for money, but there will also be no excuses, without toll comes great responsibilities, in a dark sky you see the light, when nothing else is sacred, wash my eyes so that I can see, in an elevator I will raise my frequencies, positive vibrations of a conscious mind, I wish the best, waiting for hope to wait.

Money, this will keep you down for a long time, but you will overcome, you will survive, we will overcome, in you is all the power to control your physical state, mind over matter, it will be a fight in the jungle, a thunderdome, two enter and only one exit, your greatest enemy, a mirror, a copy, a spoon bending, a snake screaming, being crushed from its skin, you will have to see for yourself, money will take you down, so down, down.

But the power is in you, time has taught you that money is always welcome, may it bring peace wherever you make your bed, the universe has given me all the tools I need to fly, in my astronaut helmet, I breathe the air of the gods , woman, mama, let me be.

Listen to what I say, I don't want to see shadows ever again, my darkness is lightened daily, I make myself happy, I learn the imaginary state of love, a smile without a reason, a look of welcome, a silent word, I have to go, I want to fly away.

Polly always wants a cookie, it's not me, let me take you for a walk, cut you, want some help, Polly said, her back hurt, and she was bored just like me, I promise you heaven is true, cut you even in parts and see, oh madness, music is my aeroplane,

Sometimes I feel alone, in an icy and cold world, where words hurt, today's sincerity is in tomorrow's tears, all this anger stored inside a single person, all this negative energy accumulated in the middle of dark matter, we need to see in five dimensions, we are zeros and ones, never forget that, whatever tomorrow brings, be there, be yourself, even if it's bizarre, decorate your uniform, be all you can be, and be it now.

My name is never gone, money forgotten, when you wake up in your makeup, remember to pray, pretty god's, pretty dressed, I hope you make it, come to the other side, there is no distance between us, the sea is right there.

Law of attraction, many thoughts about money, show me where to find it, where to look for it, we are a reflection of ourselves, until you understand this you will not understand the law of attraction, if it were pure mathematics, it would be easier, x and y are different, but their sums are multipliers never divisors, if you want to attract money, be it money, be it abundance, it waits for you, and in the night comfort you, get lost with me, enter inside me, and wondering when we will sing together.

Music is all around us, all we have to do is listen to it, sixteen moons, beautiful creatures, too far from any Starbucks, believe in what you can't play, a musical note, a tuned organ, the sound of the universe, deafening for some, and a complete mystery for others, permission to take off Major Tom, flying by imagination, lunar airports, gas stations in the air, delicatessens in motion, feed the soul, illuminate all the darkness within the being, allow yourself the new, allow yourself and that's it, creations of a living mind, desires and professions of a heart in solitude, may my universe always embrace yours.

Waiting for a Saturday night, I find myself trapped in my desires, I still feel pleasures in the flesh, it's difficult to separate, sensation and feeling, passion and love, tug of the ear, it has to be done, wake up the child inside you, It's rejuvenation of the adult in you, high ground, keep rolling, world keep spinning. the universe without ads, without interruptions, with music of the highest quality.

I got lost a little in my chapters, I gave myself over to this feeling of passion, writing after all these years has been liberating, but no matter how much I give myself over to this wave of inspiration, my critical side comes, bringing all the insecurity that exists Inside me, I don't set up my office in the dark, but that's where a lot of my imagination comes from, I have quick thinking, that always helps me, but it makes my attention deficit run freely in what I wrote.

I need to fall in love with the words I choose, it taught me to appreciate the artist. Today I see how my life works on good and bad days, work must be done with love, whatever it may be, what we build when we are in love is a totally differential calculation, that I can always lose myself in my loves, may they be One way ticket to hell and back.

I need to write, let my demons off the leash, they need to get the sun, feeding them from time to time is essential, take your demons to the light, and bring your angels to the darkness, remember it's all a circle, running in an eternal now, the good and evil are one, man and woman are one, two heads are better than one, he gave me life and shows me how to live.

I know everyone likes a Good Guys and Bad Guys story, but we created heaven and hell simply as a unit to measure the height of frequencies, hell would be the lowest possible vibrate, and heaven would be the highest possible, nirvana, namaste. I know that I get lost in my words, I am a passionate being, talking to souls, be patient with my way of communicating, I am always under construction, always trying to be the best, I strive to vibrate higher every day, I see that my energy transforms and heals many, I speak in English because I want to share good things like humility and kindness in people, if we only look at hell, that's all we will find, and don't forget your mirror, when you look to hell, he will look back at you.

Listening to frequencies can help, raising the pitch whenever possible, brother and sister, let's talk more about love, look around you, how many wounded soldiers are on the ground, there is a lot to be done, if you are in a position where you can help, help. Many are in misery, if you find it brother, see the light that exists in you, no one will see it if you don't believe, be who you are, find yourself, what you are looking for, be polite with life, it will smile at you come back every day.

Life gets shorter, leave everything behind, and value the day, the moment, be grateful for everything and everyone, forgive yourself every morning, be it rain or shine, accompanied or in solitude, wake up and drink your coffee, look what you you can do it in 12 hours, live your life in cycles, celebrate all the beginnings and endings of circles, change your skin, renew yourself, let It Loose, babe everything goes down, everything is happening, at this exact moment, the planets align.

Money in the universe is just a click away, don't go out of your way to chase money, let it come after you, make your days as creative as possible, keep your software updated to the best possible version, see the world in zeros and some, or in matter and atoms, just see the world. I feel like I'm on a crusade for peace, I see a pilgrimage of people like me, shouting for peace and love.

There are many of us, an army of kisses, words of love are necessary, for that a positive thought and a happy mind does everything. Be good to each other, if one day you can learn to play an instrument, do it, we are one, I always wait for this moment, and now it's time to take my place, stand up for the human race, welcome , I've been here waiting to be your guy, no one leaves until the night is over, the amp is humming, welcome to the show. the show.

You did a good job boy, you'll go far, now dance, now you lead your way, with a thousand lies and a good disguise, it's always been just you, I see you writing your lines, I see the love in your eyes, oh sun , don't forget, I need you here, when you come everything becomes calmer, your shine is my shelter, and when you leave, whoever stays stays, whoever goes goes goes goes. who was. my shelter, the sun comes and warms my soul, and makes me calm.

I woke up optimistic, the sun was shining, I was grateful for four, five seconds.

I'm going to spend three days there. For the last three chapters, I salute myself brother, all this child, creativity inside me. I ask you, Tony can you fly, but Tony couldn't fly.

Tony is part of the wonderful people who die. On one side the photos, on the other a song, I opened my heart to you in photos and songs, it was how the astronaut in me learned to communicate, poker face, I play spades to start, then I'll show you what I have , they are my hearts, my poker face.

You can't read my poker face, When the second Sun arrives, and all the planets align, in the blink of an eye, everything changes, no one ever taught you how to play this game, and if you can't handle it, go back to where you came from , take your money and run, the frequency of hell is always open, like a radio station, or a subway station, take a walk in your darkness, if what you're looking for is just money, it's easy, don't kill anyone to put it on, but If you seek power, be a good King, treat your subjects in the best possible way imaginable.

My new life is exciting, I get lost in my ups and downs, tie your mother down, give me all your love tonight. Keep away this country that charges, he is not my friend, my father is and will always be love, that no lie is stronger than the truth, that there can be peace among the human race, we need time to heal and care for the spirit, the physical is in chaos, but only through the mind, we can lift the body, emotional health is necessary. It's a war between mind and body, together they work perfectly well, like brother and sister, it's a special place, that when I stay too long, I break down and cry.

Every day I wake up and tell the devil to get out of town, because he lost his job, come full circle, do your duties, I always thought everything I did was crazy, but time taught me to raise my glass, and toast yesterday, a crazy dream, killing time in my being.

Time doesn't let it slip away, raise your glass of drink, you don't need to pay the debts of hell, just don't anger him, come full circle, dive in brother, be free, so free that you can never hurt anyone. In time we will all travel away, get up and walk.

Twenty four hours ago I wanted to be sedated, breathing, nothing to do or home to go, I didn't control my fingers, I didn't count on my brain. Just take me to the show, quick, quick before I don't go.

May the universe always allow me to write, may it be my carpentry of life, in me I am a carpenter, making my art on street corners, may

I know other worlds, other moons, other galaxies, may it be the guardian of my life my captain, I have the soul of poets inside me.

I grew up with good music and good books, I was happy from one coast to another, I will reach a high ground. I try to do little by little, if we are new believers, but always be dressed for success, for your love.

What I'm going to tell you brother, what mom is going to say, I don't know, and what my dad is going to do, just let me go. I'm looking for a summer breeze in my life, I was born on the beach, that's where you'll find me, physically preparing me for your love.

Life, money isn't everything, love doesn't compare to fear, all that really matters is freedom, if you have an empty glass, it's enough for something more, keep going, come on, you can do it. I have a hangover, I certainly drank more than I could, I walk alone, to understand this feeling right, it's all a plan that matches you. So I live day by day, growing, sometimes happy, sometimes sad, letting the music take me, carrying its message of love, listening to the music all the time.

Believe in yourself, see the amount of blessings you have daily, tell a true story, that comes from the heart, that brings peace, that is Love, If you don't have a beautiful story, remember that you can embellish them, use your creativity, play like a child in kindergarten, everything is possible, everything is new, everything was necessary to create this moment in your physical reality, it was your choices that led you here, now lift your head and move on, keep rocking on, bring love to deafened ears, all music has a rhythm, just like us, listen to the rhythm of your heart, let it guide you through the universe, we can only find if it has been lost, what you are looking for, what your being wants .

Breathing and exhaling, no explanation needed, it's automatic, I reset my server, I started a new binary code, one that looks like me, writing lines every day, I travel in my imagination, I leave it free, light and loose. a needle and a spoon, the queen of the underworld, sending me dead flowers in my mail, a beer before lunch, it's too good to think better, little Suzy takes me down, sends me dead flowers every morning, and I, I won't forget to put roses on your grave. A minute or a second, let it be her secret, shine a light, horses that drag you away.

The child lives easy to do, the things she wants I buy for you, wild horses, could they take me away. A new day, a new cycle, I saw you suffer, a hard and painful pain, I saw you the same, I can make you feel bitter my love, because wild horses can take me away.

Sweet Virginia, California, I feel so breathless for you, my feet inside my shoe, leaves that fall, trees that grow, smiles without a reason, without fear, just smiling, I was born in the middle of carnival, even being alone in the streets was very Over time, I learned from my greens and blues, the sweet and bitter of life, is constantly present in our steps.

A smile opens doors, embraces the entire universe, the best way to give back is to smile, angel, my angel, when will all these clouds disappear, and where will It take us from now on, with no money in our coat, and no love in our souls, angel you are beautiful, but I see the sadness in your eyes, and all our dreams form on top of the smoke, but angel, where will it take us from here.

Angel, don't weaken yourself, everywhere I look I see your eyes, come on, love, dry your eyes, and be grateful for being alive. If there's one thing I've learned, it's not to talk badly about money, sometimes it goes away and takes a while to come back, I still want to live a long time, the universe will pay the bills, every day is an adventure, my credit card has always been a knife, never saved money for the sunset. Living in cycles and circles, always a train leaving the station, a sound of harmonica takes me, a soft sound of a saxophone, humming songs in my ears, protectors of my reality, vision beyond reach. I just can't let you slip through my hands. I have my freedom, but I don't have much time, let's make some life while we're alive. Let the water fall, let abundance come in your steps, wash your soul, get you drunk when necessary, let water run down the rocks, wash away your sorrows, and bring magic into your life.

It's hard work, being yourself all the time, getting lost in others is very easy, getting lost in yourself, so don't even talk, your convictions, your ideals, your ideology, I also want one to live by.

Many think that thinking is not work, I was always judged as a bum, I embodied the role in my life, the path of a thinker, always lost in a new love, always looking for unanswered questions, the life of a genie in a bottle, three wishes would be enough for your greed, would make you a happy man, while you're sitting in your silk chair, I hope you don't see me in your company, dead flowers inhabitants of your home, water the plants, they're alive, so like you and me, something that can take the pain away.

You can send me dead flowers every morning, I will never forget putting roses on your grave. Of course there is a crazy side to me, there's no doubt about that, I wouldn't know how to deal with sanity, I wouldn't know how to value it. In my madness there is light and darkness, just like my sanity, I am complete, a spiral circle, spinning in the universe, a universe that exists between my madness and my sanity. Let me exercise my madness in peace, that's where it all comes from, my sanity.

I am all in one, I am everything in the same place, the sun and the moon, the breath and the exhalation, I turn on and off, I am fire and water, earth and air, I walk in delicate steps, I enjoy the dawn of the day and the dawn of the night, I'm a good vivam, I don't like to complain, but I love compliments, I make my life with words in the wind, delicacies released in the air, simple man, I'm a Knight, I've always let my education speak louder, my peace always it was bigger than my wars, I became a son, I am a father, I thank my sisters and brothers, today I look them in the eyes, I feel your pain, I see your forgiveness, I smell your perfume, I wish you a good journey, may you find what went searching, may it bring you peace, whatever answers you found, good luck, I will be by your side, in darkness and in light, count on me, I will always be a healing soul, a pirate stealing hearts, and stretch out love, love love, let me be all that I can be, carry me and carry me in your arms, may my mind be a parachute, may it open as I fall, and find peace, may I find myself Even though it is the true path of love.

I grew up with money, and I know something was lost, at the sound of my voice I felt it, I came from a working family, they gave me everything they never had, I'm grateful, I'm grateful every day, but money in childhood brings back a lot of envy, a lot of pain, friends who are enemies, a life within another life. I grew up with people telling me that I had everything, but is money everything, we live in an unfair world, only a cold soul can't see the pain that spreads, every day people die, it's the balance of life, being born and dying.

Money opened many doors for me, I can't complain, I had the pleasure of meeting magnificent people, an eternal emptiness, words that never found the pleasure of flowing into a river, and then returning to the ocean, the lack of money is necessary for you to appreciate , and visualize everything you want, what you are looking for.

Money made me happy, of course it did, this song is for you brother, may the bottles of vodka and whiskey tell our stories, which contains a time that not even we ourselves remember, may this be the record of a life well lived, which from now on Forward, money only brings me what belongs to me, may it make me happy, may I distribute it in abundance in hearts searching for answers, may money clear the mind of your being.

May money be love, and may love always be abundantly abundant in your life. May it bring you peace, bring you light, may it make your journey easier, and may it make it easier for everyone around you to walk.

Global warming rising upwards, no one cares, if you can't take it, walk away from the game, there are no sides, only players, a purple rain is approaching, two knights are howling, they bring good news, they will turn the face of death , and she was alive, stay with me, this is not the first see that you get away, stay with me one more day.

Three plus nine equals twelve, that will be the next chapter, if you stay with me one more night, this is not the first time you have to run away, this is not a class, with teachers at the blackboard, if you pass one more night. Go or don't go, if you can manage to stay an extra night.

This is not a party where people know your name.

Chapter twelve, Keep on living, the coffee is on the table, ready for you to drink off, I'll be here when you're ready, Go with the changes, with the chances…

If you're tired of the sand, go to the sea, Keep on going, Go with the changes, you got, to get you, got.

The apple, I never bit it, I always wanted it, I dream about it every night, songs in my head, poetry on my tongue, words of love, in a note in a bottle, traveling through the universe, Keep on going, life Crazy life, short life, since I can't take you, I want you to take me. All my friends, millions of faces, but I have no one around, I had to leave, This is my life, a lonely city, that I control now, when there is no one around, all the rains that washed my street, I was falling, falling in the empty streets, where my friends are, they said they would return to eternity, I should have known they would return, and the rain would wash us down.

I will never go away. In time, everything will be fine, you and I will be fine, we will be in the streets singing and dancing, one heart, one soul, you will see your way, and you will know that we can all break free, you will go far, you and I, you know we are.

In time, all the little things will be fine, don't worry, be happy, and in time, dance the night away, go far, dancing all night, all night we'll be dancing, you'll see, believe, until it becomes real , be creative like a child, make your fantasies come true, this is the closest to heaven you will be, sooner or later you lose yourself, forgive yourself, learn self-love, totally unconditional, don't fight for the tears that will come.

Don't let the world see you, because they may not understand who you are, even if it's a bizarre, glass ceiling, just a stone.

I'm hard-headed, a crazy boy, with a pot on my head, I'm a weak trait and Ziraldo's sincere, will the world understand me, I don't want them to see, when everything's made to break, I just want you to know who I am. I thank you, all I can say, every line of the day, has a touch of gray, I will survive, it was a lesson for me, the ABC's that we have to face, I throw my ashes into the sea, I thank Yemanjá, I am the son of a saint

My name is Lucas, trying to maintain a little love, falling in love with you, I will pass, I will survive.

If you think that a kiss is only on the lips, and a dance is only with the ribs, my friend do the twist, and never try to touch with your fingers, because what lives in your soul are memories, all encoded in your DNA, the one we know about, but we don't know what or how.

Sitting and writing, something that transforms me, I must have done this a lot in other lives, because only I know how it makes me feel, being able to throw words to the wind, but always careful not to hurt them, always words of improvement.

There are people who think that being sincere all the time is beautiful, But even sincere words can cause pain, and a well-intentioned soul will not use words to hurt, sincerity cannot be used as a weapon for the weak, sincerity and truth are different things. If you can keep the words that will cause pain, that is not lying, it is being careful, words are very strong, so they must be used wisely, a word can heal someone, just as it can also kill one.

We live in a world of gossip, talking about other people's lives has become a game between families, an eternal comparison to see who is the most balanced, the strongest, the richest and healthiest, gossip, pure and simple gossip. Talking about other people's lives never opened my eyes, I always thought it was a waste of time to compare myself with others, because I never wanted to be like anyone, I hated the rule book, the playbook, I was well educated, and I make good use of my education , but I wasn't born to follow a line, I'm not going to be behind or in front of anyone, I'm going to do my line, without waiting for any number to be called, because I am the numbers and the letters, I have to find myself a future, and If you move my way, I want it all, and I want it now.

This has always been my game plan, so give me a sign, a toast to the future, and to the dreams of youth, nothing is lost, everything can manifest itself, so much to do in just one life, so I will live it all, and I will give all.

The life of others does not interest you, just as yours will not interest others either, preserving yourself in silence is necessary to manifest what you want, secret in your projects, talking too much is like letting the air out of the balloon, as less people know about you, but they could dream, and create something to remember you, don't open up so much, we learn in silence, your words have to be valued, because using them is always a great responsibility, use your With intelligence, it doesn't have to be a chess battle, or a war, every time you use them, but a little wisdom wouldn't hurt you.

Time will always be divided, between evil and good, we can only visualize the circle, when we understand that we are one, there is no good and evil, only the evil that man does, I see the earth getting right, just like a child, all our planet needs is time, time to understand better, how we can help, planet earth deserves our full attention, we have already thought about colonizing other planets, instead of trying to save what we are living, it is the human way of being, to end everything before the next generation arrives, it won't be our problem in a hundred years, politicians thinking every four days, when they think at all, we need less politics, and more love.

We still have several places in the world without basic sanitation, people growing up amidst garbage and violence, the power of demonstration could help these people, if you are in a condition that can help, all help is necessary.

We live under the fear that everything could end at any moment, prophets putting a date for the end of everything.

The truth is that nothing has ended, we are the ones who end it, the planet lives, and continues to turn, we are poisoned in our veins, poison, when we will break these chains, I don't know.

Living in fear is scary, not respecting human and animal life, letting your worries dominate your movements, as I said before, there is no good and evil, we are one. To have this vision of the world, you will have to close your eyes and learn to feel, everything here is connected, we have motherboards, and wireless, everything has its time and place, everything is moving in its time, so be patient, Life can surprise you, over and over again.

Tell me what it takes for you to let go, surrender to the magic of life, feel the power within yourself, release all the love trapped inside you, tell me that your body doesn't miss a touch, and how you do it sleep at night, thinking you may have lost everything to the roll of a dice, just tell me what you need to let go, because I don't want to burn in paradise, let go, let it heal, you've already let it bleed, embrace your scars , ask for forgiveness for having been hurt, healing is forgiving, and forgiving is loving.

Keep living, happiness is an imaginary state. I despise gray days, do everything for your desires, don't wait for life to pass so quickly, think and dance, think well, think and dance.

May it all be in the name of love, a feeling among many, but as strong as its name. In the name of love, once again in the name of love.

Staying alone for a while did me a lot of good, being without a human touch made me value human life, being able to identify good and bad days, without hearing my voice for a long period of time, made me understand sound and silence, so as good and evil, noise and silence do not exist alone, they are found along the way. Keep on going, what else can I say, life is an experience full of energy, our souls are constantly satisfied, moving forward is necessary, the now does not return to the past, nor does it jump to the future, so do your best in the future.

Now, only you are aware of this, there is no such thing as wasting time, everything is to teach you, patience will always be welcome. When what you want in your life begins to manifest, first remember to be grateful, and understand that this is the process, visualizing, feeling, touching, tasting and seeing.

To create manifestations in your reality you need to believe, before everyone else, the first to believe in you, must be yourself, only after you feel what you want, will it come to you.

Always with dreams the size of the world, you don't notice the little things that you manifest in your daily life, appreciating the little things is very important, it's the little things that make us believe that everything is possible, it's the little things that make us become big, the macro is the micro of tomorrow, always have dreams, and make them as big as possible in your mind, so that the least of all come true, see the way you look at the world, because that will be the way the world will look at you, don't be fooled, it's a mirror, a blackboard, full of equations and boxes, the universe and its darkness, how else would you notice the brightness of the stars.

Stay hungry, keep walking, never give up, never surrender, life will always be what we make of it, I believe in destiny, but I also believe in free will, it's choices, visions, it's all in the palm of your hand, all those lines and life points, we have all our organs in the palms of our hands and feet, everything flows towards the heart, touch each other, get to know each other, embrace each other, love each other.

Run for yourself, do the best in your days, it's not a competition, it's a unique simulation, made to order for you, finding your spirit will be the most important thing, separating the material from the spiritual, understanding what's around us, they are timelines that live in the now, we cannot see, but we can feel, there is something more, everyone feels this need to believe in a higher power, everyone wants to find the meaning of life, there is no point in suffering for anything, you don't cause a fire without a spark.

Turn on the radio, see how invisible waves travel across the planet, we are surrounded by energy, vibration and frequencies, whether it's the angel on your shoulder showing you the way, it's just a love reaction, feel like dancing in the dark.

Now that you know that anything is possible, what will you do, you will allow things around you to grow and flourish. I had to give up on my dreams, become an adult, pay the bills, bury myself trying to please society, I found myself a broken man, with no vision of a future, no perspective whatsoever on a life, my dreams were so buried that I didn't even remember them.

Waking up is not just getting up, it's thinking again, seeing again, breathing again, waking up is knowing that anything can be possible, you just need to believe, several Disney films teach you this, but in real life we call it fairy tale, is it so difficult to live your dreams, is all this internal struggle necessary, and love, where does it come into all of this, life is a blessing, only by valuing what has been given to us will we be able to escape this prison that we created for ourselves, this could be heaven for everyone, if I need to go a little crazy to see, stay, only crazy people know what it's like to lose something like sanity, in madness there is a lot of love for life, the act of rebelling to patterns, such as positive and negative, madness and sanity work together, it's a balance of the mind, the being that always wants to be right, can only be wrong, rules and customs, it's not possible to please everyone, that's why I do my rules, I have my customs, a premium level experience, just a click away.

Flash, everything goes by in the blink of an eye, count your time between breathing and exhaling, life is beautiful, you are beautiful, everything around you exists to make you happy, there are tools, utilities, everything is done for your comfort, but If you can't respect and value the material, you will be completely lost in the spiritual, if you see yourself, it can be very painful, it can surprise you, the question that doesn't want to be silenced, do you think you are a good person, who are you? .

It's easy to point the finger at others, walk without knowing yourself, pointing out flaws like a photo book, a game of mistakes, there is no right or wrong when your heart is in the right place, the power to judge is only useful if we can judge ourselves before anyone else, the things that bother you are messages for you to learn, it's us mistakes that get everything right, falling and getting up, sleeping and waking up, the end and beginning, everything tangled up in the middle, insisting on patience, that's how it is I do my days, trying to understand before judging, seeing pain in others and respecting it, learning to heal, giving meaning to everything we experience, A soul that learns to heal itself, it will heal everyone around it, that every the violence of the world brings you hope, that you can feel and see all the love that exists around you, that you can always help, create bridges and beds, learn about loving, the bitter and the sweet of life, every day.

Sometimes a shadow makes a lot of light, a change is necessary, but sometimes change has other plans, to change you need to be willing, it is a process of great patience, creating a new being, within a single body, dying and being born they will always be new, say goodbye and hello at the same time, kill and give life to something new. To develop we need to know what we want, what we are looking for, it will be necessary to get lost millions of times until you find your way, know how to apologize, learning from mistakes will be of great value, always observe in silence, seek peace within yourself , and so find peace in the other just by looking, be it peace, be positive, the other option is negative, so let's go, let's meet, if we allow it, the third eye is the mind, when we talk about opening it, I mean open your mind, wake up, that is, see more than your eyes allow, take you high, to a place where you can see.

Maybe the good lord will shine a light on you, he has collected all the flies from your life and for that I am grateful, come on UP. May all the songs be in your favorite tone, I have a feeling of great duty with these twelve chapters that I describe to you, I'm going to take a few days and think about the last chapter, the thirteenth, remember that I always need to be grateful, I have a wonderful life daily, I have nothing to complain about, just a boy from south Detroit, I took the train going nowhere, the book of I don't know my brothers and sisters, for a smile we can share the night, strangers on the Boulevard, looking for the nights, living just to find an emotion, I love music, I'm grateful for it every day. Some will win, others will lose, the film never ends, who knows, maybe you were born to sing the blues. Don't hide in your darkness, bask in the sun, don't stop believing, hold on to that feeling, believe.

Chapter thirteen, The end, the beginning and the middle between them...

Keep on living, keep on loving, go with the changes, go to help. The universe is happy alone, we are all inside it, the true love way, we will be so happy alone, making a song, sharing a smile, so far from home. If there's one thing I make clear here, it's that patience will be necessary. Exit room four, one seven. Your lucky numbers are, 04 08 15 16 23 42. Expect the unexpected. Things end for something else to begin, if you have the chance, invite the world to dance, smell things, create magnificent memories of colors, give a name to each perfume, so that just like your questions they can disappear into the air, that they fade away, May the universe open your mind, and wake you up, it's not complicated, just believe, and you will see, how alive. One thing that is in all the sacred books is the phrase, do not be afraid, it is repeated several times, fear will hold you back, knowing how to deal with death is as important as dealing with life, make your departures and arrivals In the best way possible, walk with light steps, on comings and goings, make your way without fear, be peace and be love. Dylan Thomas said, when one burns one's bridges, what very nice fire it makes. Share the adventure that is living, affection seeking affection, making love with life, follow your journey. I found my conscience, and I wish with all my heart that you find yours, that it brings you peace, that you see the divine that exists within you, that you can change your words, and thus change your life, magic happens when you walk . Remember to follow the gold bricks, go for crystal shoes, but I wouldn't give up my blue all star for anything, blue is my favorite. Be kind, be polite, be all the love there is in this life, tell blender secrets. May your conscience bring you satisfaction, make your days pure magic, remember that a day in bed, a good book and good music with a hot coffee can be your most productive day, use your imagination, be a child and creative at the same time, live constantly in the now, value the family you chose is extremely important and special, be the one who brings smiles, be flirtatious, but don't be inconvenient, treat everything and everyone with respect, the respect you want for yourself, give to others, always give before asking, dress for success and dance alone, without anyone around, even without music, always dance. I wish life was like the movies, and the hero always came out of the darkness at the end. But this is real life, real love, old wounds that are healing, dreams in the air, real pain, feelings that I can't hide, this is real. May I be judged by what I know, not by what I do. May I be saved the way no one has been saved before, may I gain my wings of freedom, and may I be free. Sometimes all you need is a Robin Williams hugging you and telling you that it's not your fault, but would I have to be a good will hunter, some kind of genius to have some forgiveness around here. Maybe you just need to cry, cry until without realizing it you are laughing, laugh at sadness, be positive in life's setbacks. Be reasonable. Don't let anyone take you out of your normal state, don't allow any energy to destabilize you, walk like a warrior, be a samurai in times of peace, a soldier returning home, always carry peace in your heart. Pay attention to the numbers in your daily life, they can be coordinates or messages, morse codes are still widely used for communication, pay attention to the sounds around you, everything is making contact, everything has a beginning and an end, I watch the pigeons , I love birds, they make my imagination light up like a Christmas tree. The door to the universe is at the door of perception, see with your eyes closed, use all your senses, improve them at all times, use both sides of your brain, do mental and relaxation exercises, your mind is your best electronic accessory, Learning the codes of the mind will be important, create new codes, install the most current version and run your antivirus, life is increasingly just a click away.

But let's talk about the universe, after all that's why I'm here now, to tell you that it's out there, you can believe in several truths, or you can believe in nothing, there's no toll to heaven, if you have patience , you will raise your frequency, but to go up, I need to see that I am below.

Vibrate loudly, bigger than you can imagine, the wind blows messages into my ear, and just tells me to go ahead, make myself happy, without fear, without doing any harm, not even to myself, get up and walk, that's what my heart tells me, play your guitar, get lost in the city streets, make someone smile, drying the tears of those who cry. It's a constant fight between mind and body, take time just for yourself, alone with no one else, take me on, I'll be gone in a day or two. Take your soul for a walk, finding yourself in your darkness will be eternity in your life , remember that with our eyes closed we see more than with our eyes open, the imagination has no amount of data, it is at your disposal to take you wherever you want to go, know how to build your castles, create a reign of peace, without flags, one love, one soul, several lives, many truths and many lies. But I'm here to see you bloom, something I can't refuse. I know the Universe will tell you, you can't touch what you don't have yet, but you have to want it, and you have to want it now, to be happy alone. Your heart is on the loose, this is not the place for weary kind, this is not the place to lose your mind, pick UP crazy heart and give it one more try.

I want you to get down from that ladder my friend, the angry boy still lives there on the couch, everyone has to face their demons, maybe today you can put your past behind you, and if you don't want to see me again, I'll understand.

My love, remember that hard times come easy, times get crazy, complications keep coming, all of this can eat you up inside, but remember the heart always finds a reason, and love always finds its way, even when it hurts. , it's just another day knocking on your door, even when it hurts.

I walk on the sunshine, and my love it's time to feel good.

The universe will tell you yes, it is not a question of if, but a question of when, the impossible is a matter of opinion. When you talk to yourself, and there's no one home, you might try to fool yourself, but then no one told you how it was going to be girl, what happens to you my love, you'll just have to wait and see. With all the changing seasons of my life, I've had my nose to the ground, but I've jumped into the river many times, to make it my home, I knew the storm was coming, and everyone thought I was high, I had to Going through this alone, the only thing I know is that I never wanted it to die.

Sometimes you just know, and what you don't know you don't need right now. A beautiful day, everything we need, a day of peace, there is no right or wrong, wake up on the right foot in life, don't forget to say your prayers and be grateful, I'm grateful for everything, see how your body works, what your way of thinking is. produce, the functioning of your body, there are no rules, each cycle is a circle, let it go, learn your patterns, customize your body, Bruce Lee said something beautiful, be like water, always malleable, be all forms. The universe teaches you to be malleable, to have resilience and patience, as long as you still have love, there will always be passion, I can be a lonely fool out in the Sun, free is a lonely word, we are under control.

"Do you come from a land down under

Where women glow and men plunder?

Can't you hear, can't you hear the thunder?

You better run, you better take cover" Men ar Work.

“ Hey

Well, my temperature's rising, and my feet on the floor

Crazy people knocking 'cause they're wanting some more

Let me in, baby, I don't know what you got

But you better take it easy, this place is hot

And I'm so glad we made it

So glad we made it, you gotta

Gimme some loving " Spencer Davis Group.

" Chances thrown

Nothing's free

Longing for, used to be

Still it's hard, hard to see

Fragile lives

Shattered dreams (go!) " The Offspring.

And the world can be a fantasy, for anyone with a dream, for everyone who wants a way to free themselves, dream with your eyes wide open, eat Alive. Whatever your style, all your music goes with you wherever you go. All I can tell you is that my life is quite plain, I can make tea for two, and I'll be there when you wake up, so stay with me and I'll take you, it'll be a nice getaway. But all I can say is that my life is pretty plain, you don't like my point of view, okay. Sanity, only those who have lost it can find it. When you come home and all the lights are out, you will never be alone, I will be there for you.

The middle between them, let it loose and everything comes down, as John said, I'm here watching the wheels roll. When they ask me children's questions, I just say everything will be fine, they shake their heads and say I'm crazy. I see the bright and empty nothingness, in total darkness is where I see the whole ocean running, and it all belongs to me, and I see what is mine.

The truth is, everyone is going to hurt you. You just got to find the ones worth suffering for.,

Bob Marley, I feel that.

In the middle of the story we meet, come with me on the path and I'll explain, I already told you I love you today. The universe takes me on adventures through all the seasons, the heat and the cold, the earth and the air, good and evil, light and dark, everything becomes one, together we are, we can build more than we can destroy, let's go heal instead of getting sick, positive before negative, everything is a circle, in a square, when opened there is a triangle, everything is spinning, like small parts of a clock, time doesn't stop, not in dark matter, just jumping in dimensions you will have the feeling, the mechanical energy remains constant for any trajectory, it only depends on friction, the energy before is equal to the kinetic energy after Simplify life, the kinetic energy plus the potential, it can be heat or sound, but they are energies, good ones, let them spin. I threw a stone into the sea, and I saw the waves steady themselves, in circular points this energy turns into waves, and they go to the slopes, life needs to be simple, the less you possess, the more you let go, empty your mind, the better meditation, empty mind, open heart and ears, pray and be grateful. The net force is equal to zero, the impulse is equal to zero, continue at your constant speed.

“I'm a real rebel with a cause, I tell you what freedom is to me: no fear.” Nina Simone

"Live each day like it's your last, 'cause one day you gonna be right." Ray Charles

" I'm happy to be alive, I'm happy to be who I am, I'm just like anyone. " Michael Jackson

"The important thing is not to stop questioning." - ...

"The greatest enemy of knowledge is not ignorance, it is the illusion of knowledge." - ...

"In science, there are no shortcuts to truth." - ...

"Science is not only a disciple of reason but also one of romance and passion." Four reminders of science in the universe.

We travel in energy waves, radio waves, life and its magic, give me peace on earth, give me life, give me your love, let me come and go, don't let me get lost in you, have the key to my home, but know how to take care of it, come in my dreams, tell me your secrets, wake me up in the morning with your breath, I promise that for me it will always be fragrant, it will always be something new and as old as our souls.

" Dear Prudence, won't you open up your eyes?

Look around, round (round, round, round, round, round, round, round)

Look around, round, round (round, round, round, round, round, round, round)

Look around " The Beatles.

" Some things get better with age, I'm not getting old, I'm evolving, Music is a necessity, Everybody's got a different way of telling a story, and has different stories to tell. " Keith Richards.

Touch of gray, we will all come and go one day, we will and we have seen, boy don't you know, if you lie feelings will show. I feel evolving, not aging, I carry a thousand years of information, billions are submerged, we only see a tenth of everything, so never abuse, don't let go, evolve, and be evolution for everyone around, be it love, be it forgiveness.

" The object of life is not to be on the side of the majority, but to escape finding oneself in the ranks of the insane. "

Marcus Aurelius, Meditations.

"So I say to you, Ask and it will be

given to you; search, and you will

find; knock, and the door will be

opened for you." Jesus Christ.

" How do we change the world? One random act of kindness at a time. " Morgan Freeman.

The universe gave me a vision of the world, of human beings and their nature, to feel again, to empty the mind, to stop the heart for seconds, life calls for calm, delicacies, like birds flying, in the blue until the path to the end of world, I'm learning to fly, slowly I take myself, so as not to lack love. Use your imagination, open your mind, you and I can do anything. The universe is a tool, use it wisely, make a beautiful and sincere story, be true to the viewers, I know how much it costs to feel something. The universe has its own music, its unique and universal silence, we will survive, it's all right, we will get by, we Will survive.

" When you've seen beyond yourself, then you may find, peace of mind is waiting there " George Harrison.

The universe is the sum total of everything that exists, dark matter and dark energy, and we learn to feel it in the void, in nothingness, just like the universe we are in constant change, we are in constant expansion, the universe is full of mysteries, and One of them is dark energy, a negative force, but the truth is that we still don't know anything about it and the universe, and as Einstein said, if you can't explain it in a simple way, it's because you don't understand it very well. There are things in life that we just feel, and when we believe in this strength, it becomes real, sometimes I wonder, does everything need an answer, that way we only find more questions, I know that I got here doubting everything , but isn't it time to dock the ship, and just look at the stars, every answer will bring you 3 or more questions, this search for answers is endless, and what I've learned so far is, that every story has several truths, If you focus on just one, you will find several lies, it's complicated. In the end it only depends on you and me, what truth will we tell ourselves, what to share, when everything is so personal, everything is a great mystery, and each being will find the answers only to the questions he asks, So there is no right formula, a little notebook giving you tips, the universe is a huge mystery, and to tell you that I spend my nights and days thinking about it, I feel closer to the galaxy than to the neighboring city, this feeling is strange, but it's just that I feel part of a whole, I see myself connected with everything and everyone around me, I feel the invisible energy that circulates between us, I feel an enormous force that takes us forward, the universe feeds me, sends me information, the Sometimes I don't even know what they mean, but then everything falls into place, like a sum total done little by little. Love, where does it come into all of this, I see love as fuel, something that fills our voids, and gives us strength to move forward, a passionate heart is something beautiful to see, how silly we become, attentive, fear of losing what you don't have yet, the love between two souls is something magnificent, that whole chemical equation that takes place in the bodies and in the mind, various hormones and fragrances being expelled, the physical count, the touch of fingers, simply an explosion of energy, everything is magic, everything is a fantasy, close your eyes girl, look inside, let the sound take you away.

Love, how to talk about the universe and not talk about love, I had great loves in my life, I met beautiful souls, I was always attracted by intelligence, an intelligent soul captured me, conquered me. I threw myself headlong into my relationships, I fell in love until I lost myself, and that was the case for a long time. I was very immature, so I ended up becoming the person, giving up on my dreams and leaving my goals aside, I don't blame anyone but myself, today I understand that love and relationships are different things. Nothing that imprisons us is good for your soul, love sets you free, it never holds you back. I was very possessive in my relationships, I came from a sexist society and was blinded by pain, I hurt myself a lot until I learned. If you love someone or something, let it go, give freedom to the person you love, and be that freedom in yourself, respect is love, affection needs care. I am a fool, I am in love with life, I gave myself too much to know that today I need to preserve myself, somewhere to lay my head in winter, a hand to shake in summer, a breath to remember every day. Love takes care of you, there is no charge, there is no right or wrong, love is normal. Before you can possess another soul, you need to learn to control yourself, how you think gods are created, the pain you feel, confess, don't let anyone get the best of you. Self-love, unconditional love, an eternal lesson, freedom of souls, through forgiveness, gratitude and silence.

May the universe protect me from the evil of good people, and from the kindness of bad people, protect me from myself.

"It doesn't hurt to feel sad from time to time. We create our own unhappiness. "

" Once you replace negative thoughts with positive ones, you'll start having positive results. " Willie Nelson

I drank all the whiskey I could, I literally looked at the bottoms of bottles, I was a drugged, and I was left for dead in action, I was never a bad person, I gave love whenever I could, but I lived high in the morning, and drinking in the afternoon , I learned that what you love, has to take you high, but it wasn't just pain, there was a lot of love on my roads, and I'm grateful to everyone we shared moments with, I learned a lot from all the souls I recognized, even I learn, I was happy, I buried my past and made a toast to the future, the universe educates me. I'm happy in my universe, life forced me to build, a make-believe world that my imagination created, I see the child in me, more alive than ever, funny how lucky I am, I'm learning the magic of the universe every day, my school, my partner, I thank you. Life is short, live your dreams, don't harm anything that breathes, don't harm yourself. Finding love is essential, but remember, love is internal, the divine is within you, never outside, be it love, be it light.

It's been a long day without you my friend, and I'll tell you ALL about when I see you again.

The end, the beginning and the middle, here I am, and you are a rocket queen. I let my imagination take me, I don't worry about the end, I made peace with death, I learned that later comes life, I also made peace with the beginning, I took my stumbles, but I got up and was able to walk, and the middle, where we are, now. My now is one of pure gratitude, I opened my heart to the Universe, I gave myself to life, the path to nowhere, it led to me, I was able to make peace with myself and say goodbye to myself, I injected my soul with freedom, as the song said , salvation, salvation, salvation is free. I had to die and be born, clear my head, I'm happy with who I became, I learned from my cycles, and I know that we live in a circle, the path forward is a curve, you can only see so far, so live in the now , turn on your headlights, always be prepared for bad weather, rain is welcome, you live what you give, never forget to be grateful.

In time you won't have to sell your soul, you won't need to jump for Joy. Remember, patience, hope and resilience, three things that without them you can't believe in something, that's subjective, when in doubt, I believe in myself, the book of I don't know, did I write all this. My heart is delivered on a silver platter, the universe guides me, and on radio waves I am inspired, it transformed me into words of affection, of love, of God for me.

" You know I want you

It's not a secret I try to hide

But I can't have you

We're bound to break and my hands are tied "

Don't forget to breathe with each comma, they are words of love, made with affection, by my hands for yours. All I seek is my peace of mind. look ahead, a new world waiting for you, with open arms and closed eyes, what more could you want, a universe of your own, made to order just for you, good luck friend, may your journey be one of peace and love, between ups and downs, go with faith, walk in your footsteps and make your own story, tell a happy story.

A LIFE LESSON FROM JIMI

by Fiona Sinclair

Tom first heard about it crouching over an illicit transistor built by an enterprising boy in tech class. It was break -time, he and his mates were tucked behind the outer wall of the gym; their 'secret' hiding place teachers turned a blind eye to.

Each band Radio Caroline announced was met with a choric wail by the boys, because most knew attending the festival was a fantasy.

Except for Tom. 'I could go' he thought to himself, tallying in his mind his not inconsiderable savings account, product of multiple money-making schemes including digging up lug worms, 5 paper rounds and washing cars. Keeping the idea to himself, in history the Plantagenets were cold shouldered as he planned not an essay but an expedition. A train to Victoria then one down to Southampton. Radio Caroline had helpfully informed that tickets could be bought on the gate.

Tom was not a reckless boy. He had a healthy balance of curiosity and caution. However, his previous his ventures had been small scale and pecuniary. This was more ambitious but satisfying himself of the slim chances of jeopardy, for the first time and not the last Tom shook hands with opportunity.

His cover story for mum was a last minute 'I'm staying at Mark's, Friday to Monday. We're camping in his garden." 'Alright dear, have fun 'she had called from the kitchen. Content that her son was more worldly -wise than other boys his age, sharing the raising of younger siblings whilst she worked in London and Dad skippered the pub. 'Only a white lie' he thought to himself. 'I 'll tell her everything when I get back. '

Tom had deftly deployed his knowledge of geometry to make the best use of his backpack. Tent, sleeping bag, Calor gas stove, were stashed or attached. 'Food' Caroline claimed would be abundant at the site nevertheless he lifted a small frying pan from a cupboard, bought bacon, sausages and chocolate. Heaving on the bulging rucksack he resembled a miniature solider on manoeuvres.

The trains were positively in cahoots with the boy, delivering him to Southampton without a problem. But at the ferry port, an adamant sign 'No unaccompanied minors. 'Bugger 'he thought. Tom knew that he was handicapped by looking young for his age. Slight of stature, and skinny, his thick dark hair was worn long in an effort to obscure his boyish features. Nevertheless, he had never even managed to blag his way into an X rated film.

Letting his backpack slide to the ground, he leaned against some railings, to ponder the problem. 'I need to adopt a family' he decided and began scanning the groups queuing for tickets like a small-time conman looking for a mark. One family with a brood of kids caught his eye, particularly a boy of his own age wearing an England cricket shirt.

At school, Tom was gifted at cricket but awful at art. Each lesson his art master gave him a free pass out of the rear door of the studio to join an informal cricket practice. Consequently, the boy knew that fellow cricketers could chew on the subject for hours.

'What do you reckon about our chances in the Ashes?' he enquired of the boy who surrounded by younger siblings noisy as starlings, was grateful for the distraction. The parents abstracted by luggage, demands for crisps, and finding cash, did not notice this supernumerary addition to their family.

When his turn came, with a knot in his stomach large as a cricket ball, he informed the girl in the ticket booth 'I'm with them' gesturing with his head. The girl was clearly suffering the effects of a heavy night out, she slid the ticket to him with a yawn. 'Result' he inwardly cheered.

Hordes of festival goers overwhelmed the ferry. Accustomed to 'nice' families off on camping holidays, the staff shook their heads at the girls with flowers in their locks and young men apostle like with their long hair and long beards that had some older passengers murmuring about 'national service.' But this exotic crowd was blind to disapproval as they chatted and laughed in a lexis foreign to their observers 'Hey man, dude, right on ' bounded about the boat as they leant against the railings in pimped jeans and cheesecloth. Tom fizzed inside like a shaken cola. These were properly 'cool 'and made the efforts of his 6th formers to join the counterculture seem ridiculous.

At Hythe, He ditched his new chum with a cheery' Have a good holiday 'leaving the boy open mouthed as he struck off in the direction of the festival.

Ramshackle signs, daubed in white paint, posted the way to the site. Tom hitched up his backpack and joined the cavalcade making for the entrance. Many were on foot also bearing knapsacks or hastily rolled sleeping bags like messy roulades 'Hope it doesn't rain 'he chuckled to himself. Others, more fortunate, had borrowed dad's Bedford van and of course the posh kids swanked in their jaunty VWs. But it was the motor bikes he ogled as they growled up the corridor created for them by wary pedestrians. Their sound stirring him like a wild drum groove.

The same tightening in his stomach as he approached the entrance. But the chaotic organisation went in his favour. A group of students were red faced and frowning as they tried to calculate change in their minds or on their fingers. Hands were rubber stamped without glancing up at their owners. Tom was processed like the others and high on relief he jubilantly strolled into the site.

'Let's get settled first 'he decided, grinning to himself ' I sound like mum' . The pitch he selected was not too close to the toilets but not too far from the stage. His tent was erected ably. The backpack stashed within. Around him grown men struggled with the puzzle of ropes, poles and canvas. Some tents immediately swooned; others leant tipsily. Laughter accompanied their slapstick antics peppered by the occasional 'Bastard thing' 'Blood hell'.

Tom tried not to appear smug but envious looks were thrown at the boy and his more biddable tent. 'How did you do that so fast kid?'

'Scouts' he explained, grateful now that his mum had cajoled him to join. He began to lend a hand 'Put the poles here, hammer the pegs there' his experience passed from pitch to pitch like the wisdom of a tent guru.

Tom had always been self-sufficient. He often sought solitary pursuits such as fishing. If other kids pitched up, he could easily strike up a casual acquaintance. Being good at sport guaranteed he was a popular boy. He did not know it then but this ability to be alone without feeling lonely was a gift. In contrast, his classmates always went everywhere accompanied by siblings or mates so that compromise often led to inaction. Answerable to no-one Tom's horizons would always be far less inhibited.

Nevertheless, the group of 4 in the adjacent tent were marking his solo status with nudges and whispers. 'You on your own?' one young man barely 20 himself inquired incredulously.

'Yep, he nodded'.

A girl parted her curtain of blonde hair to stare at him with green eyes that despite her youth showed nascent maternal concern. 'Any trouble and you tell us.'

Thrust into the adult world early, what with his micro businesses and helping dad in the pub, by his teens, he had learned to read faces like a palmist read palms. His neighbours seemed genuine. Suspecting that in fact, he had more life experience at 14 than these students on their first holiday without parents. Names were exchanged and the boys immediately cadged a can opener.

'Look after my tent whilst I go for a wander?'

'Will do 'they answered as the youths set about opening a can of Watney's party pack seven.

Treading warily over sneaky guy ropes that tried to ambush, he weaved around groups strumming guitars, lads spread out on the ground like rugs with beers cooling in buckets of water. He caught the rank smell of weed. Billy Johnson had once pinched a spliff from a snoring brother's pocket, presented it to the kabala behind the gym. His mate Brian had been sick, and he had been immune to its active properties.

Clear of the campsite, he examined the stalls selling crystals, flimsy dream catchers and joss sticks that competed with the weed for stench, all of which he dismissed as 'Hippie tat'.

But the aromas from the hot dog and burger vendors did beckon to him. Tom had not eaten for hours. Often when he was absorbed, he simply forgot to eat until his body suddenly screamed out for fuel. Now he bought a ridiculously large hot dog.

The festival's stage was a no-frills affair. Organisers were clearly gambling on good weather since there was little cover for the acts. Marshall amps clustered like heavies guarding the mics and jumble of cables. Arc lights made the best of their situation.

With his usual uncanny timing, Tom was at the front when the event came to life. The first acts attracted only a threadbare audience. Scribblers of one hit wonders, which like a perfect ace in tennis would never be repeated. Nevertheless, good musicians who had learned their craft the honest way scurrying up motorways in dodge vans from venue to venue. Meeting other groups in cafes with bleary eyes and a grunted greeting. Now they belted out their numbers hardly able to believe their luck at being on the same bill as Bolan and Dylan. Their sounds bounced around the festival fields between loudspeakers attached to trees like giant bird boxes.

The following morning, his neighbours traded eggs for bacon. One of those spontaneous friendships sprung up between them, a camaraderie born of a common interest. Conversation played easily, especially between the boys, music and sport, mostly.

Beside their tent, a Norton motorbike dozed like a cat in the sun. Tom's dream bike. The objective behind all his money-making schemes. Two years' time he would start on a lighter bike until his body caught up with his ambition. The motorcycle's owner, a leather jacketed lad called Pete, had observed the way the boy's looks were magnetically drawn to it.

'Like the Norton?'

'Love it 'the boy replied in a tone of pure yearning. 'One day… '

As the conversation side tracked to motorcycles, roll ups were handed around. Pete hesitated at the boy' Want one? 'The girls gasped. But Tom's smirk suggested a seasoned smoker. Another extracurricular activity behind the gym. His mates frequently pooling their pocket money and sending in the biggest lad to buy from local newsagents.

Over the following 2 days a dizzying zoetrope of bands passed before his eyes. But the musician most lads had come to see would close the show. Tom and his new mates had dug in and defended their position at the front for hours. Hendrix kept them waiting but there was no hard feeling amongst the crowd who seemed to accept that genius works to its own timetable.

The guitarist strolled on around midnight. A mumbled 'Hi' and lopsided grin greeted the audience. Tom got the sense he never hurried anywhere. 'Please be brilliant' he repeated to himself like a mantra.

A signature riff shrieked like a harpy around the site. Followers roared, the unwitting were open mouthed. Tears in Tom's eyes as with heart rate ramped up by the music, he watched the long, elegant fingers rip up and down the guitar's neck.

A familiar melody was the springboard for extravagant freestyling, hints of the song reappearing to reassure that the musician had not abandoned it entirely, dissolving again into more improvisation. Dissonance that somehow made sense. More than virtuoso, there was something preternatural about this playing. Every now and then lyrics were added to the mix. Counterculture words that were parables for the times yet somehow secondary to the music that was where the real revolution was taking place. Pure showmanship at times plucking with his teeth, complicit with the crowd pleasing in what mums would universally have called 'Showing off'. Occasionally, a look no hands trick as the guitar worked to a frenzy seemed to play itself. But at other moments Tom noticed the musician achieved a kind of ecstasy in his playing, a sublimation of sound as if he played only for himself and the audience ceased to be present. The last cord came too soon. He bowed like a troubadour, left the stage with an air of finality.

The lads turned and aimed for their tents. Shuffling as the crowd slowly decanted. A little dazed by the dazzling spectacle just witnessed they were reduced to a few words.

'Genius'

'The best'

'Going to stop trying to play.'

Almost at their camp, Tom sighed 'Oh bugger, I've left my jacket '. He made his way back to the flotsam of cans, bottles, bags, t shirts strew across the grass. Searched the ground with his torch, turning over items with his foot. Not a hope.

'Lost something kid?'

The soft voice issued from the side of the stage. In the dusk left by the subdued super troupers he made out the outline of a figure perched on a small marshal amp, smoking. Peering at the gold braid on the loosened hussar jacket, Tom recognised the gentle drawl at odds with the raucous voice of the musician's playing. He suddenly felt very young indeed. 'My jacket 'he managed to mumble. 'Bummer 'came the reply.

Previously Tom would never have considered himself as starstruck but now, all coherent thoughts seemed to have evacuated his brain. Not sure if the exchange was over, he hazarded a 'Great set 'hoping he did not sound too sycophantic. But the musician received the compliment with grace 'Thank you, good to hear' and with that he gestured to another amp that might serve as a perch for the boy. Taking the seat Tom barely breathed.

'Was it a good jacket?' the musician inquired?'

'Not as good as yours 'the boy replied'.

The man grinned. 'Got it in the King's Road' he patted the front frogging. Tom's curiosity began to override his initial shyness now. Enough for him to inquire why the musician was sitting there alone. The man exhaled a column of smoke but wafted it away from the boy in a courteous fashion. 'Gets a bit intense up there. Always need some space afterwards. '

The man certainly looked spent compared to the vital force of some 30 minutes ago. Crumpled on the makeshift stool, his face was drained of expression. Under cover of the half-light, Tom studied the musician. He seemed younger than his stage persona, humanised somehow by the scattering of acne across his face. His hair was a charcoal smudge. It appeared to Tom that he was at the same time, just another young man, yet there was also an uncanny air of difference about him.

'You a musician?' the man inquired. Assuming every boy now attempted to strum a guitar with the ambition of becoming a rockstar. However Tom shook his head adamantly 'No'. A pause then 'I prefer sport '

The guitarist's turn to stare with curiosity at the boy. It was clearly a long while since someone had spoken so honestly to him. 'What kind of sports?

'Cricket mostly' the boy responded. The man looked bewildered 'What's cricket? Tom laughed and was at a loss to explain this game that seemed unintelligible to many in his own country.

'It's a bit like baseball 'was the nearest analogy he could come up with.

'Never cared for sports' the musician chuckled. 'Too lazy '. They both laughed.

'Here with your folks?' the man inquired. The boy shook his head. 'On my own '

A conspiratorial look crept into the man's eyes 'A maverick eh'

Tom went a little red at what was obviously meant as praise. Fortunately, the half-light concealed. The musician appeared to relish the temporary distraction, a chance to turn away from the crucible of his own life.

'What are your dreams for the future kid?'

Tom found himself explaining the dilemma of being the first child in his working-class family to win a place at grammar school. How his mum was ambitious for him, expecting university and a white-collar profession.

The man lit another cigarette from the embers of the previous one, and considered as he did so, 'My ma was fierce, 'specially when I dropped out of school, but 'he nodded to the guitar propped up against a makeshift stand.' My mistress over there had other ideas 'he chuckled at the memory 'and my ma sort of gets it now '. The young man was clearly thinking back to that time, recalling his own predicament. 'It's tricky though 'he admitted 'you don't want to hurt your folks but on the other hand… 'he paused -

'You don't want to end up working in a bank' Tom concluded with an emphatic smack of his lips. The pair burst out laughing, sharing the same sentiments concerning a life cooped up in an office.

Suddenly looking at the boy squarely, 'But what do you want?' No one had really asked Tom this but without missing a beat he replied 'I want to stick a pin in the map of the world and go visit '

'Like an explorer, eh? Well strikes me you've made the first step '

The man's tone was wistful as if he envied the boy's freedom. The blank sheet of his future. Of course, Tom had read about the tangle of the man's existence. How although only in his mid-20s, his life was already stuffed with experience, good and bad. His genius creating chaos rather than contentment. The guitar had become a demanding mistress who seemed to have the upper hand.

The musician signed and shook his head 'No point in me giving advice 'he said 'but right now, your life's your own -you're not obligated to anyone . ' Tom had never thought of it in those terms. 'No point in ordinary' the man added. 'I don't think it would suit you anymore than it's suited me'.

His cigarette was extinguished, and he ground the butt under his boot heel. This seemed to act as a timer for the man. He rose, picked up his lighter 'That's my cue 'he said 'back to reality -and that's a whole different discussion' he grinned.

The boy rose too and spontaneously extended his hand. They shook. The musician smiled at the formality. He took a few steps then turned and looked over his shoulder,

' You have a good life you hear?'

'And you too Jimi.' It was the first time he had dared to use the man's name.

The last Tom heard was a chuckle and 'I'm trying to kid 'as he disappeared into the darkness beyond the lights.

Tom did not career back to his tent, words spilling from his mouth. Instead, he said nothing of the encounter. 'Find your jacket 'Sally asked, he shook his head 'bad luck 'she tutted. This was the only time he could have shared his story without it being received as a tall tale. He was never sure why he kept quiet. A sense of betrayal perhaps blabbing about this man in an off-duty moment, who had given this boy his time. He knew too It would take on a life of its own, being passed around the site becoming grubbier with each gossipy retelling. When he returned to school, he knew his mates would listen with sceptical 'Yea right '. And as the years went by, the occurrence began to seem more like a vision than a fact.

It was however an influential meeting. Certainly, did more for Tom than the school's career officer. Whereas Jimi burnt out like a super nova, Tom had an instinct for self-preservation that made him avoid prolonged excess in the years to come. He remained also pragmatic, got a profession, not white collar but one that opened up the world to him. Learnt that saying 'Yes' to everything but the downright reckless lead to opportunities. Knew that his genius, was being in the right place at the right time.

Fiona Sinclair *has had a number of poetry collections published by small presses. She is now trying to write prose.*

SEMI-ORDERED IMPORTANCE

by Trever Sims

There was a man, he wore a nam coat and had a long posting beard, past chest often tucked behind buttons, maybe a wage in the acid wars or even their ammo box lunch money counterpart, or maybe speaking on it too long or late. He sold, or handed out but I only ever bought, a pamphlet, less than ten pages printed and folded toward a magazine, different authors or artists and the few times I found, paid, the insides were words I had never amidst others compiling whispers into greater sense than none. Albeit, approximates apodictic comprehension their, angles, often couldn't amidst their construction, jagged scissors or blotchy margins between thought bubbles of paragraphs. Nor can I recall if he answered with the price spoken or held fingers toward the amount. Its date was the day printed without any predictable sequentiality and most of what sensed was months if not years feedback delayed. Sometimes when without bills I'd diverge, wide concrete arc, unknowing his readership, if my purchase, present inability, would be missed. Others he'd sight in a passing aisle of the campus library, white beard amongst olive else, silent, finger active searching. Thought waves would link back, first the last exogenous creations read then further determinative randomness - sometimes the probabilities concluded greater that contents were assimilated without knowledge, contact, only cut then copy singles, eluded quarters dimes, probably nothing to care; others he was the maestro, directing topics or denying hasty scrawl, 'this, elucidate them, just a bit more.'

She sighted in him, a bit enough, as much as could within an opposite of. But she did in all, then and after through long enough.

We talked nonsense and the more outlandish, the wider the borders, the better the laughs the goal, surprise, took you far out there. Far, there, wherever away from the logic of, they were breaks after all. First in college apartments then obsidian obtuse paycheck digs she was finding things, and building ideas from questions, at work and then to else, of undeclared technology, unspeakable knowledge, dangerous inputs to apply the Socratic process in public or private, borders within borders and, if any of those thoughts to be even tangible fractions of hidden realities … "Deeper." I took it as her mantra, she repeated it enough.

Then she died, or disappeared, was grabbed or took herself. They let me into the space she was renting, a day after I was notified, maybe to gauge my reaction or simply as the detective asked, "Does anything look amiss?" I searched unsolved for years in volatile routines, weekends in a row for months, after flap with the current flap naked that subtle tilt of phone screen, away, maximize the parallax haze fog which seems to waft spew at particular angles, solidify the betweens.

There was a period of time they wanted me to brag, then mourn, then brag to get over it, over it to humble because you won't be us, they said, never but what you could be enough. The double reflexive, see it bounces if then if, but don't forget, never as.

They took to warning me while I began circulating intercompany applications, canvassing distant offices some in countries I couldn't guess continent, others were exercises against placing myself aside projections of decades cultural familiarity; Spain, another language promising the float within deciphering abstraction the sight to letters the sounds within a word. Would there still be Dali shirts? I placed myself finding talaverda murals every direction by day by night enough others wandering like me, not so certain. 'You must be happy,' some would tell me, 'You must visualize the fear and follow it through to the point exhaustion sleeps,' others, and I'd swill decanters of ancient improvement and vacillate senseless degrees honoring one then, next, those places my ignorance indistincts some for weeks one guessed and nodded, a retreated archipelago seat, former estuary of the Jade Road find a Magellan plaque, learn to bob and weave rainforest fringe, Brunei, baru nah, that's it, there could lose myself in its unknowns and differences as she had within somewhere, else, a system of governance I couldn't truly understand because none of the texts did either, or any, were they ever written as are and even then, outdated.

From amongst all scored a dual interview for those two backdropped degrees a haughtier skyrise than my local office, company regional and city honchos prefaced Spain, less a considered exam nearer foreplay to the second; after every enthusiastic answer I was further acclimated via things which could be subtly said and those never at all. There were others, ahead of me for these.

The regional, tweed sport pinch arounding a tie glossy mauve; the local coatless, shirt default button up, tie enhanced in the clambering sun, 3d foil or even by that then flimsiscreen, was it some holiday to excuse decorum, those years they approached and passed like highway exits; Rucker Sprott's three hundred-plus ligament tense a Ted Williams root staged up rhythm coil bloww a wallop a second the ball flew at you, me, on stare mouth novocained, syllables fought creation lost in its seams growing supersized threads shot toward me then reset huh-bloww, again and again.

"You were involved with a disappearing woman–"

The local cut the regional off, "Have you forgotten her yet?"

I stammered some plea, this, anywhere could help,

The local, "Hm,"

The regional, "There's still time."

If the opportunities weren't available and I was surplusage, anywhere… my enthusiasm waned, the news told me I'd be lucky to find a stable area of the world.

Clicking, modifying template attaching; a placement within Azerbaijan, a billion dollar deal they got those, worked those there yes some of its points we could swivel and after a hefty spreadsheet girder adjust cooldown sweat on the coast, a tavern notching Byzantine flags, smile at the waitress who liked the cufflinks measuring a roll to bicep not because, but their where, and I'd have only questions to hers. The allure held through nights before I cancelled the day of the interview. That and each place began to only see ephemerally, a jot to jot left what, eventually, rate of raffle ticket feeds dwindled then Turkmenistan; they emailed me the option, considering our past impress regarding your interviews, burgeoning supply chain pivot investment ratings, antifragility assessments, objective objectives despite, what it was, vague, fit you in or confidential. Research envisioned arid steppes of drained lakes, redirected to configure others amidst a desert geysering greenhouse gas from a limitless vein beneath the earth finish line fires secondary icing a crater the gate to hell with yerts singing, laughing just out of its methane range through the night lute, dutar, ghijack, improvisational sandstorms eroding archaeological reclamations from bronze age dynasties, find a way secure a weekened within Gonur Depe's mud-brick circuit board labyrinth reborn mornings with some woman origins so far apart her entirety abstract impossibilizing assume, with each twenty question response then next she builds herself across campfire crepes wondering, were we even allowed to be out there, or out there together, away from those hundred piece grand studs never rode never planned on horses and the notepad was thick of the not-to-do's and inverse of the can's; I saw myself developing a conqueror's patience, not being of there but amidst and across land, sea shadow leans of others, collecting, proliferating excess laughing off her absence with a force not within my essence yet still held seeming every man could see or should wary at least. That worst case began to particularize, acute not of the armchair dictator instead feared distinct frustration parenthesizing a comment gruff, shirk read off not me, to you, but us to it. Plus I wanted a house.

I order. The role used to be management but now has elevated to only of things, arranging, sense from dissolute.

I wanted a house, to not have to see others, the sight sound imposes. With her it had been an input, refracting between us until disappearing. Without, for years, it began to seem the cling of junk. Either or, that or maybe else would be cleaner. I chose the house.

Sometime therein I was contacted by a reporter, found my name in the missing report. He wrote "presence obituaries," double page sprawls of everything he could gather on "those absent, to hopefully fill the void." He was the cleanest, definitional professional I had ever met. I told him to never contact me again, and he never did.

My placement hasn't seen me anywhere outside of days to drive but vacations find warmth and everything around is replete with distance, at the most I just type and it's there, here into other plus I have a steady another she has her eyes, shape then into probably now, a few similar interests and even greater with me. Together we've done else, far longer and, by through until here, seems assured the longest at least for each. We find things to attend, some sparsely others just undershading infrequent. The rest we pass with friends casual enough ourselves the else, vis of or actually venturing there, wherever stacks.

This won't be read, I have written it understanding the dictum shut up and, accordingly, categorized it such while celebrating the unanimity of my eyes and only, the freedom in independent self glutton font even only this day I've had free to type it and the less before, inspired lightbulb sentences of loosely twined else, drops which approached this spill line; only for me, read, remember, see, sense.

There are times, volatile routines, I sit the kitchenette table it catches the light of night a curtain stood aside and I sit and stare grass, deck then grass then diminishing returns her, not her careless night mode turned the rest off, none of that, specifically. Only her else, what, where, since. I think, if this is done, it could be, I'll write all that, next, and maybe via wave output rather than these keys. As she would say,.

***Trever Sims** is the author of a forthcoming debut novel somewhere between literary and speculative slow burn science fiction. Try and follow along through the haze at, on, Twitter/X/whatever: @realytreversims .*

ESSAYS

DARK OR NOT DARK

by Carole Greenfield

There is a young boy I've been working with recently. He is different from any other student I've taught. His use of language, the way he focuses on things, the direction his train of thought takes, is fascinating and unusual in my experience. Our times together are an adventure.

During our first lesson, he discovered a flashlight in my drawer and wanted to turn it on and off, on and off. "Is it dark or not dark?" he asked. He proceeded to place it in the closet, carefully shut the door, opened it to find the flashlight still on, then shut the door once more, asking over and over, "Is it dark or not dark?" This routine repeated itself several times. He sought out other dark spaces, such as a filing cabinet drawer, in which to hide the flashlight, opening and shutting the drawer as many times as I would permit before attempting to redirect his attention. At some point during each succeeding lesson, he has taken and hidden the flashlight.

Today he surprised me. Instead of seeking the flashlight, he asked, "Where is my heart?" then touched his chest. "Is this my heart?" "Yes," I replied. I tapped the table. "You can feel it go bump-bump, bump-bump." "Is my heart dark or not dark?" he wanted to know. I paused for a moment, then said, "Dark." "Where is my brain?" He put his small hands to his head. "Is my brain dark or not dark?" "It's dark," I said. "Inside or outside?" he questioned. "Inside," I said. He opened a picture dictionary we use to the last page, where astronauts are floating in space around the earth. "Are they inside or outside?" he queried. "Outside," I said. "Dark or not dark?" "Very dark," I said. He pointed to the stars. "It's a little bit dark," he remarked. It's more than a little bit, I wanted to say, but did not.

I thought about how I've been feeling about my upcoming journey. My husband and I are about to embark on a year on leave, spending half of it in Denmark, the other in Holland. I often get the impression that everyone expects me to be over the moon with excitement -- the thrill of it, the incredible opportunity to not work for a whole year and simply have the time and space to explore two new cultures! Who wouldn't be happy about such a chance? Who wouldn't be thankful to the core to have been given such a gift?

Don't get me wrong -- I am thankful. I am happy. I am also feeling trepidation, some fear and, at the moment, a good deal of sadness. I am leaving a job that I love, people I have come to care for deeply, a school where I have made connections and a place for myself. And I may not return. When you take a year's leave, you are promised a job in the district, but not necessarily in the same school. You must accept this when you go.

I have been doing my best to come to terms with this truth, to balance gratitude with sorrow. Each day, each encounter, with colleagues and students, brings with it a blend of emotions. I am trying to maintain my equilibrium and appreciate it all. When you work with young children, you get many chances to bring yourself back into the present, and it is frequently marvelous.

"Is my heart dark or not dark?" the child asked yet again. "It's dark," I repeated. He took my fingers and pressed them. "Dark or not dark?" "Dark," I said. "Where is my heart?" he wanted to know.

"Inside or outside?" "It's inside," I told him. "You can't see it." He looked at me directly -- itself a rare occurrence -- touched the picture of outer space and stars, and said, "The moon is a light in my heart." "Yes," I replied. "Not dark."

Carole Greenfield *grew up in Colombia and lives in New England, where she teaches multilingual learners at a public elementary school. She takes inspiration from her students and enjoys writing about what she learns from her time with them. In the previous century, her work appeared in such places as Red Dancefloor, Gulfstream and The Sow's Ear. More recently, it can be found online at Dodging the Rain, Sky Island Journal, Stone Poetry Quarterly and Autumn Sky Poetry Daily, among others. Her first collection of poetry, Weathering Agents, was released by Beltway Editions last year.*

MAN IN THE MIDWEST

by Dusty Hayes

From a young age, I knew I wanted to be a machinist like my father and his father before him. It came as a shock to me when once I had fulfilled that dream I found myself ready to swerve into oncoming traffic to avoid going to work in the morning. I worked at a job shop in Porter County Indiana which has since shut down due to incomprehensible mismanagement. While there I programmed two CNC lathes primarily making parts for the steel mills up on the lake. The shifts were grueling, ten hours a day sometimes as much as seven days a week. Our foreman picked fights with anyone he thought he could provoke. At one point his instigation was so severe he incited a mutiny. His entire night shift up and quit on him leaving the shop only able to operate during the day. This was reflected in the workload, jobs piled up on his desk as we scrambled out on the floor trying to get them done. When I was told I was being forced to take more hours one Friday afternoon, I finally snapped. The next day I quit, never looking back despite their pleading for me to stay. This left me in an odd position.

Suddenly at eighteen years old, I had no job, no school to go to, and no direction in life. I had wanted to be a machinist since middle school. Never had I considered another career path, leaving me adrift with no clear direction to head in. What I did have was a 97 Lincoln town car, five thousand dollars, and all the free time I could burn. If I didn't have a road to follow I would simply have to go out and find one. This started a four-month journey around the Midwest in search of something to do with my life. From December 2018 to March 2019 I drifted aimlessly, not settling in place again until I figured out what I was doing with myself.

I spent most of my first weeks as a free man hanging around Chicago. My time was spent wherever I could find the ins on the local music scene. During the day this was the guitar stores and record shops. I would make a lap around the city each day starting near the lake at Chicago Music Exchange and not stopping until I hit the Reckless Records on North Milwaukee. Even though the trip only took me around a three-mile wide area I would spend the whole day chatting up musicians and trying out gear I would never consider buying. In the evening I steered towards the seedy spots where you could catch a desperate musician trying to replace some hardware before his set began, pawn shops. The stench of pot hung over the dingy stores. Seventies hits leaked out of decrepit speakers and reverberated off the cracked tile floors. The merchandise they sold was usually crumbling from decades of hard love. Occasionally you could find something in stellar condition but these items were almost certainly hot. No doubt one meaty bass line would send a cloud of cocaine and glitter bursting out of the cabinet on sale for a fifth of its retail value. The atmosphere around the pawn shops was half as lively as the music stores and three times as hostile. After the fifth shootout happened just outside the doors of my go-to pawn I decided the scene wasn't worth the hassle. Chicago had all the music culture a guy could want. At any point in the day, a show was only a few blocks away. You could lose entire weeks hunting boutique instruments to test drive with the highest quality amps and pedals never having to lay down a dime on any of it. Local musicians filled the streets looking for anyone who would talk shop with them. Despite all this, the city wasn't the kind of place I could hunker down for any considerable length of time. The basic costs of living were astronomical, sometimes a meal would cost double what it would if I had gotten it on the other side of the state line. The streets were impossible to traverse, at times it would take as much as a half hour to drive five miles. The people outside of my picked subculture were anything but welcoming. Head down and moving forward was the only way to get around the city without getting into it with some bored geek looking for something to do. After only a few weeks of hanging around Illinois, I decided it was time to take my search elsewhere. I put the Chicago skyline in my rearview mirror hopefully for the last time.

In January I crossed the now arctic plains of Ohio. I skid along an iced-over I-90 until I reached Toledo. Here I had the last of Ohio I could stomach. From the sex shops that dot every street corner to the strip club buffets in every outlet mall, Toledo was one of the filthiest towns I ever set foot in. The city was a concrete hellscape devoid of a single square foot of greenery. On street corners, people lurked glaring at me as I rolled through black ice-coated intersections. Icicles hung from roofs like the tops of inverted fences warning all who passed from wandering too near. I had made the trip to look at a used car but unfortunately, that turned out to be a bust. The vehicle, which I was assured was in outstanding condition, failed to turn over when I came to see it. I assumed the thing to be a lemon despite the five-toothed owner's assurance that the weather was the only thing keeping the engine from firing up. I cruised the streets awhile looking for somewhere to settle in for a few hours to regroup. Every parking lot seemed to be manned by at least one crowbar-wielding gentleman waiting for some sap to park and walk away so he could make off with a stolen set of wheels. I decided to grab a pizza at a drive-thru and eat it in the parking lot. I pounded several slices of my dinner before two cars came into a head-on collision in the street in front of me. The owners both lept out of their totaled sedans to begin screaming at each other. That was all I needed to see of Toledo, or Ohio in general. I shut the pizza box, zipped back to I-90, and got out of that state.

In February I decided to take a day trip to a small central Indiana town called Monticello. The snow had receded leaving muddy dead grass in its wake. I pulled into town around one in the afternoon. I parked in a public lot, a free amenity that too many small-town citizens take for granted. I sat here for an hour watching people walk by. Townspeople coming back from lunch hurried to escape the frigid air. When I got bored of watching I decided to join in on the action. I left my car, walking blindly down the street towards nothing in particular. I ended up inside a gas station that seemed to have been stuck in its exact position since 1982. White laminated peg board walls with advertisements hung up that were decades out of date. I asked the guy behind the counter what was going on in the area today. He looked at me bewildered as though it was entirely absurd that a young man would come into his store and ask him, another young guy most likely in his early twenties, what was happening around town. I paid for my drink and got out of the place before I rattled his world any further. A stroll around the area I was in told me what the clerk's reaction should have. Nothing was happening. Small-town America had lived up to its reputation, outside of the chain bar and grill currently hosting happy hour the town was dead. I walked to a grotto near where I drove into town. I was able to sit down by the edge of a river and watch cars roll in and out of town. For the entire hour I sat there less than ten cars drove by. How people make it through their days in a city like this I have no idea. The town seemed plenty hospitable with friendly locals and clean establishments. The culture however was nonexistent. This was the kind of place where you only went out to go to work or the store. You spent your free time at home with the wife and kids only occasionally splitting off for date night at the town's only Italian restaurant. A perfectly comfortable place to live but not a particularly enriching one. Entirely the wrong scene for me so once again I packed up my Lincoln and went back out on the highway looking for a path.

March came and with it the occasional warm day that would give you a taste of what summer was soon to bring. I wandered to the freshly melted shores of Lake Michigan where I bummed around the city of New Buffalo. Vibrant streets full of clean-looking people snaked along the pristine beachfront. I walked around the streets near the water where bars and business fronts had opened up their shops letting the new spring air blow in. The scent of a dozen kitchens floated around making the area smell like fried meat and spices. Everywhere I went people were cheerful, enjoying the splendor of the town with their neighbors. The only issue weighing on anybody's mind seemed to be me. No matter where I was, happy faces stiffened as they watched me pass. Men in pastel polo shirts diverted their manicured families from my path. Even at the bars where faux motorcycle clubs gathered to show off their sparkly Harleys, I was watched hesitantly. Maybe my dirty long hair and unshaven face had spooked the locals. It could have been that my flannel and third-hand jeans didn't fit in with their strict gap-bought uniform. Whatever the issue was, it was clear I was not welcome among these well-to-do citizens. I had found a place with the culture I wanted, no matter which street I turned down a band was laying down a heavy beat in some dining or drinking establishment. Plenty of people were hanging out enjoying the city instead of rushing to hide from it. No one was getting stuck up in rank alleyways. If only I could have met the criteria to hang around there I probably would have. I didn't stick around New Buffalo for long. I got a chicken sandwich at a bar and grill a few blocks from the beach then beat it.

At this point, I had begun wondering what exactly it was I was doing floating around from town to town. I had learned quite a bit about myself and even more about the place I wanted to live but not so much about what I wanted to do with my life. No grand calling had presented itself to me nor had I had a revelation calling me to study any particular topic. For a week I remained idle back home trying to find some reason to have done all this traveling. A sizable chunk of my savings were spent and I seemed no better for it. It came to me finally that maybe I didn't have a calling in the usual sense. I didn't lust to fill some position working day and night for my boss. The thing I wanted out of life was what I had been indulging in this entire time, freedom. I didn't want some inflated title or a corner office. I wanted to do the things I enjoy. Go see shows, hang out in happening bars, and see new places. No salary can match freedom like that. I would need income to have this kind of freedom, good times aren't always free. I found myself a position driving a forklift in a lumber yard. Just enough work to pad my wallet and sustain a living. After that, the good times were back on. I ended up living in Indianapolis, a quiet bohemian borough of the city where music culture thrives. The days go by peacefully as I indulge in the fruits of my travels. The scene of Chicago and the serenity of New Buffalo with just enough of that Toledo grit to keep things interesting. I may not have found a career but I found a life.

***Dusty Hayes** is an indigenous writer and psychedelic advocate living in Indianapolis, Indiana. He spends his days there engaging in Broad Ripple's bohemian culture. He never pursued a higher education in writing, choosing instead to hone his writing style independently. He writes about social injustice, mindful living, and psychedelia. Recently he has published his first book Rock and Terror : A Psychonomic Look at the Effects of Psilocybin. A gonzo journalistic documentation of a mushroom trip that gives the reader a full rundown on the substance and its effects. You can find him and his work on Twitter and anywhere ebooks are sold.*

BARBARITY AND BANALITY

by Les Jones

The barbarity and downright wickedness of the Nazis has posed millions of questions and will pose millions more. The normal thinking person's utter revulsion is characterised by questions as to why any human being could act to others in that bestial way. Hannah Arendt wrote The Banality of Evil after viewing the Eichmann trial. Arendt, rather than condemning out of hand, as most would, tried to elicit a degree of understanding from a trial that would disgust most, and as a Jew her views command attention. Arendt's use of the phrase 'banality of evil' has caused much discussion. What does it actually mean? Arendt died in 1976, so she had little time to explain or to ruminate on her phrase.

The dictionary definition of 'banality' centres around a lack of originality, and perhaps this goes some way to understanding Arendt. Kant's writing considered spontaneity to be inextricably linked, indeed the basis of, freedom. In fact in the Critique of Pure Reason the idea of 'understanding' is said to be spontaneous, which Kant defined initially as bringing forth representations from itself. Both theoretical and practical knowledge are, for Kant, denoted by spontaneity. It is self evident that spontaneity and freedom are intrinsically linked. McDowell writes that spontaneity or conceptual activity takes place in the realm of freedom. For Kant spontaneity 'brings forth representations from itself', it is the ultimate freedom machine.

It follows that to deny spontaneity is to deny freedom. Total domination, which strives to organize the infinite plurality and differentiations of human beings as if all of humanity were just one individual is possible only if each and every person can be reduced to a never-changing identity of reactions, so that each of these bundles of reaction can be exchanged at random for any other. (The Origins of Totalitarianism 1966 (438)). According to Arendt totalitarianism is about domination of the individual to such an extent that the individual, certainly in the Kantian sense as outlined earlier, ceases to exist. In a perfect totalitarian state each individual would be, to large extent, a copy of the next, and so on and so on. The state becomes the family, in fact more than the family. In losing one's individuality one gains this all powerful (as far as that country is concerned) totality, similar in many ways to a deity, but so powerful that it permeates all lives.

Eichmann, according to Arendt, is a classic case. Arendt found Eichmann 'thoughtless', which she defined as 'the heedless recklessness or hopeless confusion or complacent repetition of' truths, which have become trivial and empty'. Eichmann's concern was both selfish and empty, in the sense that empathy seemed to have been dug out of him. Eichmann could not answer this central question of Kantian ethics 'Could I live with myself if I did this deed', and yet he could recite Kant's categorical imperative. This tells us much e.g. certain words mean nothing, he is not engaging, words need to be shown in action. What is to be made of that? This question must haunt the compassionate human being, for it can be levelled at all Nazis and those with similar views, just as much as at Eichmann.

Now it will be self evident to the average person that a chasm exists between Eichmann's parroting off of Kant's categorical imperative and Eichmann's behaviour. In fact parroting off is a good description, since it invokes the image of a parrot repeating sounds that mean absolutely nothing to the bird. The words have no meaning for Eichmann, they are a delusion. And not just any old delusion either. These meaningless words cover up a monster on a monumental scale that any right thinking human being would find repulsive. A man who can allude to Kant's imperative in this way, and presumably not see how utterly devoid of humanity it shows him to be, may indeed be called banal in the Arendt sense. It also shows deep wickedness.

Eichmann, in his trial, used a number of contrived arguments to excuse his wickedness. One of these arguments was that ' if he hadn't done it then someone else would'. But Eichmann has, apparently, read Kant. Even a cursory reading of Kant would reveal that acting both with regard to moral imperatives and doing so autonomously is at the centre of his moral philosophy. Putting the notion that 'if he hadn't done it then someone else would' is not even a serious attempt at defence, indeed it is risible, in Kantian terms. The defendant is an autonomous agent. Here he is seeking to defend himself by denying his own autonomy. Using the 'someone else' argument throws the idea of morality through the window. Now the argument ceases to be about right or wrong and bccomes a discussion about self seeking, personal ambition and ego. What the business is actually about seems to matter little, the major concern is what will this position do for me in the hierarchy I have chosen to belong to. It is a grotesque and disturbing form of argument in these circumstances, and says much about the 'thoughtlessness' that Arendt says is Eichmann's hallmark.

For the truly moral being, whether they have considered Kant's Categorical Imperative or not, the notion of legacy is all important. Arguably this is the most important impact on humanity that an individual human being has. We need only think of Bonhoeffer, or Lawrence "Titus" Oates, Violette Szabo and many others to realise the importance of moral legacy, it is, perhaps, what humanity is all about. Eichmann's complete lack of perspective in these matters leads one to support the idea of his 'thoughtlessness' in the way outlined above.

Les Jones *is a retired educational professional having been Head of Department in Secondary Schools and Colleges, as well as GCSE and A level examiner and senior examiner. He has a long standing interest in writing, literature and philosophy. He had always tried to base his writing interests in the community, at one time chairing Lancashire Writers, contributing to local radio and drama.*

DISCUSSION ON THE DISADVANTAGES OF EXAM ORIENTED EDUCATION

by Alex Liao

1. Introduction

Exam-oriented education is spread all over East Asia like influenza. Some students have been hopeless about the strict and old-school education systems, and almost every day, there are students' suicide due to stressed feelings.

But unbelievably, the government and the education bureau didn't care at all, once another student jumped from a building, what they did was not help stop similar events happen again, instead, they utilized their authority and influence to decrease the popularity of those negative news about them.

To discuss the disadvantages of "exam-oriented education", we need to know what is an "exam-oriented education" first, this is a recent type of education in certain Eastern Asian countries that emphasizes the importance of "exams", or in other words, tests. Failure in the exams will make students think that they will be blocked in future learning, which could lead to depression, anxiety, and other emotions. (M. Liu, 2023). In this essay, I am going to talk about the cause and effect of this weird but current education system.

2. The cause of nowadays' exam-oriented education

To analyze exam-oriented education, we need to look at the imperial examination system in ancient China, as it did somehow impact the education system today.

The imperial examination system was once the strictest education style in the whole of China, it was invented in AD587, by the emperor Wen of the Sui dynasty. He promoted this educational system as the only way to be an official and work for the government, The imperial examination system developed in the Tang Dynasty and lasted for more than 1,300 years until it was abolished in 1905.

The imperial examination system focused on recollection and recitation, emphasizing the exertion and understanding of classical documents. Although this education system indeed caused plenty of great literature works and many poets, it also caused the ossification of thinking and the lack of creativity.

With the arrival of the Industrial Revolution, the demand for education had been altered, the industrial society required new technology, workers, and professional talents. The traditional imperial examination was unable to satisfy the circumstances. In this situation, the system of modern "school" had been built by using a standardized test system, which is exam-oriented education, that pays attention to the transmission of specific knowledge. The system pursues the competition of high grades and rank.

3. The disadvantage of this education style

Despite the motivation for students to have competitiveness, the problems appeared at the same time. Firstly, the excessive desire for rank decreased students' interest in subjects, examination-oriented education mostly revolves around examination-oriented requirements, and teachers will tell them how to learn. Under such a system, students lack their own independent interests, this system is an incomplete educational system.

(Wang, 2021), which declined the motivation to learn, but also because of the excessive pursuit of scores and ranks, students had no longer interest in the subject.

Then, exam-oriented education demands prominent outstanding memory and the practice of test skills, the student must memorize every single word of the knowledge and the skill of solving questions, which limits the ability to apply, Lastly, in the psychomotor domain, students reported a reduced ability to demonstrate and apply practical knowledge. This study emphasized the need to reassess the effectiveness of exam-oriented education systems to develop alternative approaches that could promote a more holistic development of undergraduate students' competencies. (Yasmin et al., 2023).

In this case, most students might only concentrate on their subject and the questions in the textbooks but ignore the comprehensive abilities to deal with real phenomena in reality, which leads to a deficiency of experiences. Furthermore, Examinations can encourage cheating among students. Some students may resort to cheating to improve their performance, which can compromise the integrity of the examination process.

Meanwhile, examinations can cause stress and anxiety among students. The pressure to perform well can be overwhelming, and some students may become anxious or even experience panic attacks during examinations.it damages the mental health of the students under the educational system, due to facing the environment of competition's high stress, several psychological illnesses could be discovered obviously. (Dekho, n.d.)

3.1. the graph of experiencing worry or stress

" " (Liu, 2023)

According to the graph above, we can see that more Chinese students are "stressed" instead of being" worried", this shows that the mental pressure most students in China hold is even tragically underestimated by people.

Moreover, it is short of individuation and diversity. unlike exam-oriented education, the creative education system makes each student have their interest and strong suit. On the other hand, exam-oriented education only emphasizes the unified answer and foundation and overlooks personal development, which leads to the stifling of the inborn talent of children, curiosity.

With curiosity, kids can be interested in anything around them, and then they start to learn, and study, this is the first step of education, however, exam-oriented education lets this disappear.

Finally, its educational resources are allocated unevenly, in certain regions students from wealthy family, they can get better education opportunities and resources, while some disadvantaged groups are facing the problems of unfair educational resource allocation.

The most serious part of this education system is that due to the fixed teaching foundation and the competition of ranks, students' minds could be easily rigidified by the strict standard, in this case, students are not people who gain knowledge for improving themselves anymore, they are robot or zombie of reciting test skills and unitive answers that won't influence their future.

So, education was gradually doubted by folk and people needed a rethink of exam-oriented education if it is still necessary for the contemporary generation.

4. Methods to solve the circumstance

The reformation is a necessary option now, by the development of society and the rethink of educational concepts, exam-oriented education is transforming its form, and surely it will turn into an educational system with more practices of comprehensive quality and evaluation diversity.

The schools will also focus on training the experience of students, encourage students to innovate and motivate them to service the society or community. At the same time, teacher training must be enhanced.

For this system itself, the government should plan it in a brand-new way, after the renewal, certainly the general teaching environment is going to scale new heights, and the quality of teaching will be better.

Furthermore, the government had invested more in education and resources, trying to allocate the resources as fairly as possible. On the other side, the traditional idea is still tough to change, a couple of parents and students themselves toughly consider grades and ranks as the only standard to judge an individual's ability and choose to ignore personal progress. Innovation requires support from the whole society, both public and private sectors, to encourage more students who excel in knowledge acquisition and their character and morals.

5.Conclusion

The modern examination system of China has a long history, evolving indirectly from the old imperial examination system which dates back over two millennia. This ancient system was instrumental in selecting the best administrative officials and maintaining peace within the country. However, as times have changed, there is a growing recognition that China's approach to education needs reform in order to remain relevant in today's world.

One key aspect that requires attention is the college entrance exams, which are often seen as the only fair way for students to gain access to higher education. However, it is important to consider alternative methods of assessment that can better reflect a student's overall abilities and potential. Educators should focus on promoting a more holistic development for teenagers, taking into account their emotional well-being, social skills, and creativity alongside academic achievements.

In order to achieve this goal, it is essential for the education system in China to gradually open up and embrace new approaches. By allowing for greater flexibility and diversity in teaching methods and assessment criteria, educators can better cater to the individual needs of students and foster a more inclusive learning environment.

Overall, while acknowledging the historical significance of China's traditional examination system, it is crucial for educators and policymakers to work towards implementing reforms that will ensure its continued effectiveness in preparing young people for success in an ever-changing global landscape.

Reference

Liu, B. L. L. a. D. (2023, March 4). Worry and stress rise in China. Gallup.com.

https://news.gallup.com/poll/189077/worry-stress-rise-china.aspx

Liu, M. (2023). An overview on the impact of the exam-oriented education in China. SHS

Web of Conferences, 180, 02036. https://doi.org/10.1051/shsconf/202318002036

Dekho, S. (n.d.). School Dekho - India's first search engine for school admissions. Schooldekho. https://www.schooldekho.org/school/blog/details/Advantages-and-Disadvantages-of-Examinations-345

Wang, L. (2021). The Development Trend of Examination-oriented Education and Quality Education in China: Learning from British and America Educational System. Lecture Notes in Education

Psychology and Public Media, 1(1), 128–133. https://doi.org/10.54254/lnep.iceipi.2021184

Yasmin, F., Farooq, N. M. U., & Shah, N. S. K. (2023). Impact of Exam-Oriented education system on undergraduate students' cognitive, affective and psychomotor competencies. International Journal of Linguistics and Culture, 4(1), 109–125. https://doi.org/10.52700/ijlc.v4i1.180

NOT A FAIRY TALE

by Sharman Ober Reynolds

I grew up in a family of strong women on the lookout for calamity. My grandmother, nicknamed Ensie because she was tiny, was a natural storyteller-both the main character and narrator of her life. Ordinary events triggered memories that were more present for her than the present, so while Grandma endured many losses in her long life, she was never at a loss for words. Born in 1885, she grew up in Salt Lake City, the oldest daughter of a physician and the first woman state senator in the United States, a suffragist who defeated her polygamous husband running for the same office. When I was eighteen, Grandma gave me $15 to register as a member of her mother's political party. Her father, my grandfather, belonged to the other one. There was always drama and sometimes violence in my grandmother's unexpected revelations, or so it seemed to me as a young child. I also came to understand certain truths about language and intimacy. Having been told about events that shaped and sometimes shattered lives, there was a current under the surface that percolated like a potent brew.

My dad bought a used green and white Chevy camper when I was eight and when Los Angeles was hot and so smoggy in hurt to breathe, we slept in our clothes and left before dawn for our annual two-week vacation. My sister and I held onto Grandma, who rolled like a cork on the bunk above the cab, the spot which offered the best view of what lay ahead. Our destination was Lake Tahoe, a crystalline lake surrounded by pungent Jeffrey Pines and meadows bright with wild daffodils. My dad, usually a slow driver, took Route 89's steep curves with reckless abandon, and the tiny burners on the camper stove bounced up and onto the floor. Our laughing became screaming, so great was our pleasure in the unexpected chaos. Eventually, the road lengthened to unending, hypnotic lines, and Grandma told us about the world populated by the living and "her" dead. The precarity of lives ran through her stories like quicksilver. We were her captive audience; she was our colorful fabulist. Her hair was a wispy halo of bluish-white curls; she wore a tropical muumuu, white oxfords, and a purple sweater, the color of royalty.

I remember the first glimpse of the fade-proof lake in the summer twilight, the deep woods, the meadow with its purple lupines, and the smell of pine-laden air. The air was close, and our voices softly reverberated in the camper. Outside, the sky was choked with stars, and time seemed infinite. I was a fidgety girl, worried about all sorts of real and imaginary things. At eight, I also stated paying attention. Sprawled beside my sister on our narrow bunk, I asked Grandma, "Where did you go on vacation?" It was a long moment before she spoke. When she did, her face changed from powdery-smiling softness to sorrowful resignation. "Oh my…there were no vacations. Roy died when your mom was a baby." Raising myself on my elbows, I peered over the bunk and swallowed hard, pushing the rock in my throat into my heart. I managed, "What happened?"

"Roy had a headache; lay down, and died. God is big on burdens. He makes sure everyone gets one." The incandescent light was harsh on Grandma's face, and her gaze shifted to something out the window that wasn't there. After a few moments of immovable gravity, she looked directly at me and added with a tragedian's sense of drama, "The undertaker said, 'Roy was the most beautiful corpse he'd ever seen.'" Yes, Grandma knew how to turn a phrase, and I conjured up a naked man with a cleft in his chin under a white sheet on a cold slab in the mortuary. Grandpa Roy never lost his muscular physique or wavy brown hair. But after seven years of marriage, Grandma lost her cheerful husband, brawny and smart, the bliss, the difficulties, the infinite distractions of human love, and the hoped-for things even she couldn't imagine. All that beautiful life!

Without Roy, and armed only with a degree in literature, Grandma was ill-prepared to run a 100 acre ranch. She once told me, "The steers were warm and breathy, and had melting eyes." For five years she managed her affairs through stopgaps and improvisions, then followed her brilliant mother and difficult brother to California for the promise of steady work and decent housing all bathed in abundant warm sunshine. But first, she made arrangements for her eight-year-old daughter, my aunt, to stay temporarily with her dead husband's parents in Mill Creek, Utah in a nice house close to a good school. After seeing their daughter-in-law struggle, grieving, and buried by the endless work at the ranch as entirely as their only son was buried in the family plot, Roy's parents told Grandma they could provide everything Martha needed while she was getting settled in Los Angeles. And since they were getting older, she could be of help to them as well. "Children's children are a crown to the aged...." they said. Scripture was truer than life for them and providing a home for their granddaughter would be a blessing for everyone. This temporary arrangement lasted years, and the blessing became a heartache because no matter how nice the house was or how good the school was, my aunt was the daughter left behind.

Grandma and my mother settled into a crooked bungalow on a minute lot on Griffin Avenue in Central LA. This was a far cry from "The Oasis." The foundation sloped and it's questionable whether the house was decent or not. Still, Grandma named their new cottage "The Doll's House" and planted hardy, weed-like flowers that survived for years: purple morning glories by the front porch, rainbow hollyhocks next to a weathered fence, yellow sunflowers, and orange trumpet vines that eventually took over the yard. She rented out the ranch, which wasn't easy in 1925 from 700 miles away. A year later, Grandma received an unwelcome letter from one of her thirty-plus cousins (her mother was the fourth of six wives) disclosing that her tenant was injured after falling into the irrigation ditch, drunk on moonshine he brewed in the barn. She decided to sell, severing her tether to Utah. For the first time in years, she gazed fully into her future, the one she would make.

As a young widow, she planned to be eternally loyal to my grandfather, and after a while, it may have been her loyalty she was loyal to. Perhaps she even felt some pride in her devotion.

Still, she was amusing and though not a beauty, had petal-soft skin, a commanding nose, and waist-length auburn hair she twisted, looped, and secured on the top of her head with a copper comb. Grandma had weathered the long years of her widowhood, but they call it weathering for a reason. It erodes. And she was lonely. Slowly, she turned her attention to all the beautiful, small things she hoped to understand since eternity wasn't one of them.

My mother was lonesome, too, and of all the needs a solitary child has, the one that must be satisfied if there is any hope of wholeness is the unshakable need for an unshakable parent. Grandma was, by nature, interesting and interested, a provocative combination. She wanted to be steady, but sometimes her life swerved a little out of control. At times like that, my mother tried to provide, even enforce, some stability. So, while Grandma served dinner to one of her beaus, my seven-year-old mother, determined to put the kybosh on this gentleman's unwelcomed advances, slipped out the kitchen door and hammered nails into the tires of his Model-T. I suspect dinner wasn't great either. Grandma probably served the only meal I'd ever seen her make, a chicken stewed with thick noodles she rolled by hand, flour to her elbows, powdering her bright cheeks she rouged with lipstick.

Grandma married two more times. There was a short-lived marriage she called her "misadventure." Her divorced husband, sleeping on the flat roof of his desert adobe house in Yuma to escape the heat, rolled off the edge to his death. My mother was not sorry she did not like this man more, but his death was shocking all the same.

Grandma's next husband was a large Irishman who worked for the railroad. He had a lively temper, was utterly devoted to her, and developed a winning strategy. Mac took over the kitchen and befriended my mother. He looked amused in all his pictures confirming that he never took anything in life seriously, including himself. He called Grandma Babe, and she loved him dearly. She was widowed again at 67.

Husbands die, and children leave home. Thank goodness there were books, and Grandma always had more than could be read. Stacks towered around her as if she were a librarian on strike, refusing to process returns. She devoured them. When she felt the stiffness of a book's cover, she knew what it was to have a spine. Rows of words were like heartbeats. Pages fluttered like a beckoning hand. In return, literature gave her a voice. As a young woman, Grandma taught at the Mormon Colonies in Mexico and came to realize that what she knew about Cortez was distorted by the suspect motives, sensibilities, and scruples of colonial interpreters. There was another reality to the Conquistador; he was sly and cruel as he appropriated land for Spain and plundered the Aztec empire for gold. So, she wrote a novel to set the record straight. He would have failed if not for the help of his ambivalent interpreter, guide, and consort, Donna Marina. Sold to the Spaniards as a young girl, La Malinche, is now remembered as the embodiment of treachery, the quintessential victim, and, having given birth to one of the first Mestizos in New Spain, the symbolic mother of the new Mexican people. If trouble is the backbone of all great literature, Grandma's life story, like that of this conflicted Native American Princess, was a tragic novel, not a fairy tale.

Grandma missed Utah, so when I was eleven, our family packed the camper and headed for Salt Lake. We drove between the Angeles and San Bernardino National Forests, rolling down our windows so there was nothing between us and the fragrance of chaparral shrubs, thickets of Douglas-fir, and massive oaks resting their irregular limbs, like elbows, on the ground. The strata of the Grand Canyon blushed golden and orange in the afternoon sun, and I stayed well clear of the edge, remembering the fate of Grandma's second husband.

My father set up walkie-talkies so we could hear my parents in the cab when they yelled, "Someone is going to get hurt!" This wasn't a threat, only the expected outcome of our roughhousing. Grandma was in the truck's cab with our parents, and we heard her warble off-key about her "Beautiful and Beloved Mexico."

"To my Mexican land

I sing of its volcanos,

Of its meadows and flowers.

They are like talismans,

Of the love of my lovers."

Southwest of Salt Lake, Grandma directed us to an undeveloped area near the city's landfill and decided a broken slab of concrete was a remnant of the Oasis's foundation. The blue grama grass was brittle and cracked beneath our feet. This land, an 18,000-year-old lakebed was like iron, and the encircling Wasatch, Uinta, and Oquirrh Mountains were so sharp against the bright blue sky they would cut your hand if you touched them. In this empty place that once held so much coming and going, working, laughing, talking, and loving, my grandmother was reminded of who she once was.

She leaned on her cane, the weight of age upon her, and looked beyond silver sagebrush into the distance. It was hot. Green and yellow grasshoppers filled the air, popping up like corn. Grandma shaded her eyes and said, "The land was so flat, I could see Baldy a day away, circling the cattle." My mother never knew her father, but she knew and loved her sheepdog, a protector and friend with velvet ears and wind-rushed, silky fur. He was left behind with the tenant rancher, and when nipping at a calf's heel separated from the herd, Baldy was mistaken for a coyote, shot, and killed. His bones were here, buried in an unmarked grave. But where?

"There was a window that looked south over the vegetable garden," Grandma's busy hand gestured where the farmhouse would have been as if the scenes of her Oasis were continually before her. "In the winter, we lived in the kitchen." She sounded apologetic when she added, "...and ate a lot of fried hominy. And every Saturday night, we took a bath in the same tub." Grandma stepped over the broken ground and told my mother, her bedrock. "I was first, then Martha, and then you." She stumbled. Mom caught her, and they laughed. A helpless infant, a mourning widow. In truth, they saved each other in 1919.

I wondered what else Grandma felt, saw, and heard in this intimate, abandoned place: maybe Roy's embrace, her laughing babies, pink roses on a wooden trellis, the marks of hooves between splotches of dried, flaky manure instead of asphalt. I hope the undertaker's foul parlor, with its severed flowers and bleached curtains billowing like cartoon ghosts, had faded, and the thought of Roy's muscular physique conjured remembered pleasures, not the terrible image of his beautiful corpse. I'm sure Grandma left something behind besides a few grains of corn between the planks of the hardwood floor. Something in the walls of the Oasis, sweet and pervasive, like freshly cut summer straw, would have lingered. There is sponginess about plaster, which absorbs love.

My mother and Aunt took turns caring for Grandma after a stroke left her an invalid. In my mind, however, she was always quick-witted, quick-moving, and generous. Every visit, every holiday, every vacation was an event, and she nourished me with her ranch, art, and life with its volcanos, flowers, and lovers. Her hardships warned me about rough weather ahead, and I've had my share. It is hard to trust the self-inflicted and random cosmos. Grandma once said, "Life is a mystery. People who try and plan it surely end up disappointed." Knowing how to live well, not afraid, not performative, not a shrunken life, is a conundrum. Each of us is more than the tragedies that befall us, what we've done, or the best things either. So, we write our own novel, and each word follows the one before because it is that book and not another.

Sharman Ober-Reynolds *was born in Los Angeles and completed a master's in fine arts at Arizona State University. For over thirty years, she worked in health care as a family nurse practitioner, primarily in autism research. She is primary author of The FRIEND Program for Creating Supportive Peer Networks for Students with Social Challenges, including Autism. In 2023, Sharman was the first-place recipient of the Olive Woolley Bert Awards and has published creative non-fiction in bioStories. Sharman now lives and writes in an old house in Salt Lake City with her family and Cadoodle.*

EIGHT THOUSAND MILES FROM QATAR

by Zachary D. Shell

Eight thousand miles from Ecuador's Chota Valley, where a gringo and his girlfriend sit in the November moonlight, watching a dozen boys kick a soccer ball on a concrete court and looking for a face neither has seen in five years, the Ecuadorian national team takes the field in Qatar, preparing for their second World Cup match against the Netherlands.

"Charley is out there somewhere," I say, surveying the concrete swarm in front of me.

"Would you even recognize him? He's a teenager now."

I nod slowly, not confident enough to answer out loud. Alexis repeats the question, and the slight irritation in her voice pulls my attention from the game. She's staring straight ahead, cradling her backpack to ward off the evening's chill, fighting fatigue after the six-hour ride from Quito. I skip the nod this time; yes, I would recognize him.

Noise erupts from the court, and I turn back to watch one of the teams celebrating a goal. A group farther down the bleachers begins an elaborate cheer, but my focus lingers on the scene in front of me — scanning the faces, looking for Charley. Suddenly, a voice speaks from my left: "¿De dónde eres?"

The question goes unanswered as play resumes. The action is raw, unrefined, just like when Charley and I sat here five years ago, cheering for his older brother Eddy. The voice speaks again, asking where we're from, and Alexis, who understands Spanish but only knows how to say the colors, answers her in English.

A halting response: "You are… from… United States?"

Alexis smacks my leg, and I turn away from the game. "Yes, we're from the States," I explain in Spanish, "but we're visiting Santiago."

The girl cuts me off to shout toward her friends. "They are American! I told you!" She looks back slowly. "Wait, did you say 'Santiago'? You know Santiago?"

I hesitate before responding, unsure how many qualifiers the answer requires. That I only met him on the bus? That I only stayed here for a week? That I haven't spoken to him or his family in years? I decide to keep it simple. "Of course I know Santiago, but we're just here for — "

The girl cuts me off again to relay this new information, but the rest of the group has already arrived. A small boy wearing the bright yellow of the national team's jersey jumps in. "Santiago Mendez? From here?"

"From right here in Chalguayacu."

Soccer Jersey is incredulous. "Imagine Santiago actually knowing an American," he begins, but I lose track of the banter that follows. I turn to check in on Alexis. A gaggle of younger children has emerged from who-knows-where, bombarding her with questions and, from the braver ones, requests to teach them bad words in English.

I put my hand on her shoulder. "Look at you. You're a star."

"I can't communicate anything," Alexis counters sharply. "And listen, I think we should figure things out before it gets much later."

The girl doesn't give me a chance to respond, snapping her fingers to get my attention. "You really came all this way just to see Santiago?"

"Yes," I say, omitting the fact that I never got a response on Facebook when I told him I wanted to visit, or from any of the four Charley Mendezes he's friends with; omitting, too, that Alexis is absolutely certain the family doesn't even live here anymore. "To see Santiago, and also to watch the World Cup tomorrow."

"¡Vamos, Ecuador!" Soccer Jersey shouts, grabbing the front of his shirt and holding it out proudly.

"¡Arriba la Tri!" I respond, but the girl is shaking her head in disbelief.

"All this way just to see Santiago. How long are you staying?"

"Long enough to watch the match, that's it. And not just Santiago, of course, but Blanca too, and Eddy and Charley — "

"Oh, Charley's out there now. Hey, Charley!" she calls toward the court. "Charley Mendez!"

I give Alexis a wry smile: See, I told you. She smiles back. Barely.

The girl keeps calling, but I cut her off. "No, don't do that. But we need to find the house. Can you remind me where they live?"

"Just up the street," she responds. We're on our way.

****

"How many gringos do you think Santiago brings home for a week?"

The question stops me about fifty feet from the house. From where I stand, I can see Blanca in the front yard. She's clearing off the clothesline, folding items one by one and filling her hamper. The view is familiar; my confidence, on the other hand, is wavering.

I close my eyes and search for the smell of detergent. Over the past five years, particular sensations, including the floral scent I imagine filling Blanca's hamper, have brought me back to the Chota Valley. Despite my fond memories, though, I have no idea if the family feels the same, or if they'll even remember me. Alexis is unconcerned; after our complete inability to contact Santiago, she seems satisfied just knowing the family still lives here at all. She repeats her question — surely, I concede, I'm the only one — and nudges me toward the house.

Blanca faces away from us as we enter the yard, gently moving her hips to the music coming through the doorway. At our approach, she turns around; a few hesitant steps in our direction, and we're face-to-face. As she pauses to consider the specter in front of her, I fumble with a greeting: "I don't know if you remember me, but —"

I cut myself off to look through the open door behind her. The light is on in the front room, the table set for a late meal just as it was the night I showed up. He sat next to me on the bus, Santiago explained then. I thought I would show him around. I remember Blanca shaking her head, laughing at Santiago's impulsivity. She filled my plate first.

Blanca leans over now to set down the hamper, and the couch comes into view, beneath family photographs on the wall and a framed portrait of Jesus. I joined Charley there that first night and asked him questions through his stuffed monkey, Pedrito. We returned every evening, reading separate books while Charley paused occasionally to ask for translations of his favorite words. He created his own English-Spanish dictionary that week, but I have no idea if Blanca remembers our lessons — or, as I've just begun saying, if she remembers me at all. Suddenly, my confidence falters again, the home no longer feeling as familiar, the laundry line less reminiscent of the —

"Zachariah!"

Alexis will tell me later that Blanca threw her hands into the air and pulled me in for a hug. She'll claim that, when Blanca let go, I just spun around in circles because my words had failed me. I won't be able to confirm any of this, having blacked out from delight, but once I regain self-awareness, after my first thought of Thank god she's here, I blurt out an explanation.

"We came for the World Cup! I want my girlfriend to meet Santiago and —"

Blanca interrupts me, nervously explaining that Santiago is away working.

"And you and the boys," I finish, and she beams. "We thought we could find somewhere to watch the match tomorrow, somewhere with la gente, with everyone."

"Here," she replies simply. "You'll come here."

****

The taxi drops us off the next morning, one hour before the match begins.

The first time I visited Chalguayacu, I had come from Loja, a provincial capitol in the southern highlands. I was finishing a year teaching English and wanted to explore the country. I had already visited many of the smaller Black communities up and down the coast. Before I left, I wanted to see the Chota Valley.

Nestled in the Andes just south of the Colombian border, the Chota Valley's history of resilience intrigued me. Jesuit missionaries first arrived in the area in the 16th century, establishing haciendas on indigenous land. African slaves were brought from the coast to work the cotton and sugar fields, and their descendants remained in bondage until 1852. Following abolition, communities of freed individuals settled in the valley. The area has been the heart of the inland, Afro-Ecuadorian population ever since.

My colleagues in Loja didn't understand my interest in the region. They had no connections for me, either, so I was lucky to meet Santiago on the bus. He had just finished his work week in Ibarra, the nearest city to the Chota Valley. I told him how excited I was to be visiting this part of the country. When we reached the turn-off for Chalguayacu, he invited me to stay with him.

Five years later, as Alexis and I walk the cobbled streets, I point out some of the signposts of that previous visit: here, the corner shop where I got beer before watching pick-up soccer games, and where the owner teased me, reminding me every time to bring the bottle back even though I had never forgotten; there, the street corner where three abuelas taught me to salsa dance and tried to set me up with every young lady who walked past; up ahead, the concrete card hall where the old men gathered, and where they pulled me in one night to teach me a local game whose rules and name I've long since forgotten.

On either side of us, a near-continuous stretch of clotheslines runs in front of the houses. Charley and I played volleyball every afternoon that week, smacking a soccer ball over Blanca's laundry and recruiting other kids to be our opponents. When he wanted to play football, we'd move into the street. I always insisted on playing with Didier, the smallest boy in the group. Our offense consisted of one play: me chucking the soccer ball into the air and, if Didier caught it, running down and carrying him into the end zone.

Farther down the street lives Santiago's brother Marco. He visited one evening with his twin daughters, Katy and Nedy, while I was working with Charley on his translations. The girls wanted a lesson of their own, so I came over the next day and taught them the days of the week and how to count to ten, how to say "Hello, teacher" and "Good morning, teacher." The girls' enthusiasm delighted me. I wanted more. Before I left, I told Marco I would come back one day and open an ESL school.

It took half a decade to return, but I'm hopeful people still remember me — the gringo who broke the rules by being interested, who left his mark in the short time he was here. And yet, though wandering eyes follow me and Alexis through town, these are stares of disbelief rather than of recognition. With time remaining before the match begins, I suggest we continue walking, but my perspective has shifted. The filter of hospitality has vanished. I see my surroundings instead with the markings of despair that my former colleagues must have imagined: broken tiles under our feet, barren yards and crumbling brick walls. A heritage of neglect on the community that bore its burden.

We turn a corner and pass a plot of cinder blocks, some construction that looks unmistakably familiar from the last time I was here. Two children emerge from the site, passing a soccer ball back and forth. One kicks it off the wall, and the other heads it back; another pass from the first, but a broken tile redirects the ball toward me. I put out my foot and kick it back. The boys hardly notice.

Encouraged by this burst of activity, I turn to Alexis with a flourish. "Here we have the famous construction project of Chalguayacu. It was just as impressive five years ago, when —"

Alexis interrupts me with the question I suspect she's been wondering since we arrived. "What did you do here for a week?"

It was the same question I heard the first time once word had spread of the gringo staying at the Mendez house. The same question asked at the start of another sunset soccer game, when I showed up to cheer for whoever was playing; when I left early to help Blanca prepare dinner; when the next day arrived and I was still in Chalguayacu, wandering through town and chatting with everyone I met. What are you doing here?

The simple truth was that I liked being part of the community. I liked the feeling that my presence here mattered — the conversations I had on the street and the time I spent with the children, that ESL school I was determined to come back and open. That had been enough for me, but I wish there was something more to offer Alexis. Something to show the spirit of the town. A street party for the match, perhaps, or a bomba circle.

I had bugged Rodolfo, Santiago's other brother, all week before he finally introduced me to bomba, the fast-paced, rhythmic music of the Afro-Ecuadorian highlands. He showed up at the house one afternoon with some friends on the street. He led me outside and pointed to two of them. They stepped back. I took my spot in between.

Bomba traditionally features the guitar but, on the streets of Chalguayacu, can be played with virtually anything; in this case, that meant one guy strumming on a cheese grater, another blowing on a granadilla leaf, and two more banging on buckets. Rodolfo handed me a couple of claves to knock together — easily the most traditional instrument in the bunch — and a Fanta bottle filled with puro, the fermented-sugar moonshine of the Chota Valley. I took a swig as he returned to his own bucket opposite me. Then I passed the bottle to the left, and the music began.

As the bottle made its way around the circle, one singer after another improvised lyrics over the rhythm and the high-pitched wailing of the granadilla leaf, producing a combination of storytelling, freestyle rap battle, and insult comic roast that ranged in topic from some people's girlfriends to other people's wives, and from those same people's sisters to — well, that was mostly it. I banged the claves while the music filled the air. I had been accepted by the community for a week, but this circle was their most precious gift: sharing the spirit of the street as though I were one of their own.

Now, as Alexis and I make our fourth right turn around the soccer court, I struggle to remember what I sang in my clumsy Spanish when the Fanta bottle returned to me — only Rodolfo's gentle encouragement and the good-natured goading from the crowd. Out of the corner of my eye, I see the children from before running toward us. One of them comes to a halt, raising his hand in a half-wave, and Alexis points at his shoes. The laces have come undone. She makes a motion of tying a knot, and the boy bends over to fasten them. He scampers off, leaving the whisper of a "gracias" behind him.

These children are too young to remember me, but this is what I'm looking for: validation from a familiar or not-so-familiar face, some trace of the welcome I received here and the relationships that remain. I visited five years ago searching for a secret slice of the country that I could keep for myself. The Chota Valley never left me; I hope part of me never left here, either.

****

"Hey, it's James Madison! We got Madison!"

Alexis shoves the dollar coin in my face and shuffles through the rest in her hand. "Sacajawea… Sacajawea… Monroe!"

She lets out a small whoop and shows me the handful of change. Ever since learning that Ecuador uses American currency, Alexis has been on the hunt for presidential coins. With my own arms swimming with halftime beers from the shop, she pulls two more coins from her pocket and adds them to the collection. "This means we've got 1, 3, 4, and 5!"

Washington. Jefferson. Madison. Monroe. Not too shabby.

Alexis takes a little leap and nearly loses her balance. She gives her head a quick shake. "Man, that moonshine went right to my brain!"

As if on cue, a voice calls out from the side of the road: "¿Toma otra copita?" I look over, and one of the three men we passed going the other way extends a bottle of puro in our direction. He gestures for us to come over and take another swig.

Like a moth drawn to the flame of the peeling Fanta label, I veer straight toward the curb. Alexis, however, lets out a groan. "I don't know," she says, "that last shot burnt everything going down." I don't disagree, but with Ecuador losing 1 - 0, we need all the good mojo we can get. I shift the bottles in my arms and throw back the shot.

Slightly wobblier now, I lead the way. "Up ahead," I say, gesturing to the far side of the street. "That's where Santiago's brother Marco lives, the one with the twin daughters."

My thoughts turn once again to the girls. I imagine them inside the house, using the English they've learned since our time together — reading a book on the couch, perhaps, and practicing their favorite phrases. The scene immediately transforms into the school I never got around to starting, the one I thought would've drawn me back by now. In my mind, I see a classroom filled with students from all over the Chota Valley. The girls are there. Charley, too. Learning the language they first spoke when I arrived.

I don't notice Marco standing outside until Alexis elbows me. I call out to him, but he shows no recognition as he approaches the fence. I try to break the ice, joking about finally returning to open the school. Nothing. I explain that I visited Santiago years ago, but his face remains blank. Suddenly, I'm worried that I've misidentified him.

"You're Santiago's brother, right?"

“Yes.”

“So you're Marco?”

“Yes.”

“I’m Zachariah! Do you remember me?”

“Yes.”

He finally says something substantial, but his speech is nearly incomprehensible; the local dialect was hard to understand even after a week the first time, and Marco’s accent was the most challenging. He continues talking, but his tone doesn’t get much friendlier. His words don't become even remotely more intelligible.

Marco looks at me when he finishes, apparently expecting a response, but I’m speechless — he could just as easily have invited me back this afternoon as told me never to return again. After a moment, he simply pats me on the shoulder and walks into his house.

Stupefied, I turn to Alexis. "Don't look at me,” she says, “I’m not the one who speaks Spanish. Let alone whatever that was.”

I follow her away, trying to reconstruct what Marco said. Something about that first lesson with the girls, maybe? His frustration that I never returned? I want to go back and explain that I left with good intentions. I want to point to Katy and Nedy and the book I know is in their hands. I want to remind him of all the other students that would’ve benefitted from the school, but another thought stops me in my tracks: What if he's forgotten?

I try to conjure the fantasy again, but the image has disappeared from my mind: the children gone and the school vanished, my name scrubbed from the facade. All trace of my influence —

Suddenly, shouting erupts behind us. The men with the puro are cheering, and one calls out that Ecuador has scored.

The game is tied and Alexis has four-fifths of the Virginia Dynasty in her pocket. Things are looking up.

****

I was awake before the sun rose the morning after the bomba circle. The music and puro had gone long into the night, and my head throbbed as I stumbled to the breakfast Blanca prepared for me: a cup of sweet coffee, cold from sitting out all night, and an humita — a corn-and-cheese paste baked in a corn husk, similar to a tamale. Rodolfo had invited me to his plot of land in the mountains that morning. I was still eating when he burst into the house.

"Zachariah, you're awake!"

I winced as Rodolfo bounded over. He reached out and touched my cup, shaking his head mournfully at the temperature and replacing it with the one he had brought for himself. "You're welcome," he said. "Let's go."

Rodolfo hadn't told me much about his work, but the first task, I discovered, was finding a ride. He suggested we try his friend Eduardo, a late arrival to the bomba circle who had brought an entire bottle of puro for himself. I wasn't surprised when no one answered the door; to his credit, Rodolfo didn't appear to be, either. He raised his hand and mimed the quick throwback of a shot of alcohol. I followed him away.

Three houses later, I was beginning to suspect the entire town was still recovering from the previous night. "Rodolfo, look," I began, "maybe we should just — "

"No, no. Don't worry. I'll go this way, you knock over there."

I looked doubtfully up the empty street, hoping Rodolfo had a backup plan — something other than waking strangers up to ask for a ride in a language I couldn't reliably speak. Instead, he placed his hand on my shoulder and stifled a mischievous grin. "Trust me," he said unconvincingly. "You'll be fine."

He walked away to continue canvassing, and I discovered a sudden interest in watching the grass grow. Luckily, it didn't take long for a truck to pull up from behind. Rodolfo was standing in the back, calling to me: "Zachariah! Zachariah! I told you not to worry!"

As I climbed in, a bottle of puro hit me square in the chest and fell to the flatbed.

"Everything good now?"

"Sí, claaaaro," he said. Of course. "Let's go!"

It's five years later when Rodolfo reminds me of that adventure. There are four of us watching the second half of the match in Eddy's room — Rodolfo and Eddy on the bed, Alexis and I in chairs next to it — and the announcer's rapid-fire Spanish calling the 1 - 1 tie is giving me a conniption. Punctuating his story with a gentle "tranquilo, tranquilo," Rodolfo urges me to stay calm. Just like that morning, everything will be fine.

Suddenly, in the 59th minute, Ecuador threatens to score again. From the corner, Angelo Preciado crosses the ball in front of the Dutch goal. The ensuing shot is deflected by a defender, and Gonzalo Plata secures the ricochet. He launches the ball from just inside the box. It clanks off the crossbar and bounces feebly to the side.

As the defense sends the ball the opposite way, the announcer goes absolutely ballistic and Rodolfo prostrates himself on the bed. "No, no, no!" he cries, pounding his fists. "How could he miss that!"

I can't help chuckling to see Rodolfo's unshakable calmness finally shaken. Before I can remind him to stay tranquilo, though, he's recovered. "Todo bien," he assures me with a grin. Everything is good. He taps me on the chest, patting the #13 of my Enner Valencia jersey, Ecuador's star player who scored the lone goal earlier in the half. "Just get us one more, okay?"

In the commotion, Charley has come running from the kitchen with the last of the halftime beers. Rodolfo gesticulates toward the doorway — "Charley, my boy, it was this close!" — before changing track, signaling for the bottle instead. Charley holds it out. The cap is still on. Rodolfo tells him to toss it anyway.

As Rodolfo raises the bottle to his teeth, Alexis leaps up and frantically pantomimes using an opener. With a wink, Rodolfo displays the cap already in his palm. He motions for her to sit back down and hands over a cup. "To Enner Valencia!" Alexis exclaims. I pound my jersey in agreement.

"Sí, claaaaro," Rodolfo responds, but then he points at a poster of Agustin Delgado on the wall behind me. As the national team's second-highest all-time scorer, Delgado is a legend of Ecuadorian soccer. Most notably, he netted the opening goal in the country's 2002 World Cup debut, a campaign which began an unprecedented tally of four World Cup qualifications in the 21st century.

For the men sitting in this room, 'Tin' is also something like the patron saint of the Chota Valley. Born and raised in Ambuqui, just a few miles from Chalguayacu, he was one of the first recognizable Afro-Ecuadorian players on the national team. His success opened new opportunities for Black players — while fewer than 10% of Ecuadorians are of African descent, they compose three-quarters of the team at the 2022 World Cup — and turned soccer into a unifying force, helping combat Ecuador's history of anti-Black racism.

Delgado is a worthy honorary, and Alexis and I echo the others' praise: "To 'Tin' Delgado!" Turning back to the game, we catch a hard tackle being made on an Ecuadorian player. Rodolfo erupts at the no-call, but Alexis is already on her feet, shaking her fists at the screen. "Give him a yellow card!" she shouts. "GIVE HIM A YELLOW CARD!" She looks at the stunned faces around the room. "Amarillo," she adds quietly, finally making use of her limited Spanish vocabulary. The room nods in admiration.

Over the final stretch of the game, Ecuador will outplay the more celebrated Dutch squad, coming away with a tie and never looking like the lesser team. This is a result Agustin Delgado and the entire Chota Valley can be proud of, a declaration of existence in the face of invisibility, and I'm grateful to be included in the small celebration that follows: a gift so much more generous than the ones I've been offering in return.

As we watch the team walk off the field, I imagine my former colleagues in Loja doing the same. Taking notice at last.

****

When we reached our destination that morning, Rodolfo tossed his backpack off the flatbed and hopped out. I followed, struggling for balance after the bumpy ride. As we walked to the field, he gave me the run-down. "Right in front is sugarcane. On both sides, also sugarcane. Farther back?"

"Potatoes?"

"Good guess," he groaned. "Well, this is it, and now you've seen it. Go explore." Rodolfo gestured to the open space around us and reached into his shed for a shovel. When I said I wanted to help, he looked at me doubtfully; when I insisted, his face turned almost apologetic. "Just enjoy the view before you leave."

I walked to the ridge of the plateau. Down below, at the end of the path that would lead us back to town that afternoon, people had begun to emerge for the routines of another day. I looked for Santiago's house, but the only distinctive mark amongst the cobbled streets was the construction that would still await completion half a decade into the future.

From the edge of Chalguayacu, my eyes followed the winding road to the larger town of El Juncal and the trickle of the Chota River. I gazed at the mountains beyond, jagged rock rising into a cloudless blue, and the ghosts from the valley's history stared back — watching Rodolfo toil in his field, just as he had in the weeks and years before, just like his ancestors when they first arrived in chains. In my periphery, a bus came into view: traveling from Colombia and heading toward Quito, people leaving the valley or simply passing through. Moving forward while the work in the mountains remained.

Five years later, after the match has ended, Alexis and I board that same bus in El Juncal.

"Caña, dos por un dólar," a voice calls out as we settle into our seats. An old woman is selling sugarcane up front. "Dos por un dolarito."

The woman walks down the aisle, repeating her offer — two for a dollar — until she reaches our row. I hold up two fingers and gesture between me and Alexis. The bus lurches forward, and the woman steadies herself, digging around in her basket with her free hand. She gives me two choice pieces — "Gracias, abuela" — and I hand back a five-dollar bill.

While the woman counts the change, I pass one piece to Alexis and bite into the other: fresh from the ground, just like Rodolfo grows above. Here, she's telling me, take this; here, like a bomba circle or a soccer celebration, like a shot of puro on the sidewalk, take that, too. I tried to leave my mark on Chalguayacu, imagining my reflection everywhere I looked. I came back searching for evidence that my time here had mattered, but it turns out the only legacy was the one left on me instead.

Here, take this; here, have that. Something to keep, even if just a memory.

The bus picks up speed as it leaves town, passing children on barren fields kicking soccer balls and clouds of dust. When the woman gets off at the next stop, I realize I'm still clutching the change from the five-dollar bill. I open my fist and look through the coins with Alexis.

Sacajawea. Sacajawea. Sacajawea. Rutherford B. Hayes. Here, take this.

Eight thousand miles from Qatar, where the Ecuadorian national team vies for World Cup glory, life continues in the Chota Valley and a bus travels farther down the road.

Zachary D. Shell *lives in Denver, Colorado, where he teaches seventh grade Language Arts and constantly dreams of going back to Ecuador. If he's not singing with his barbershop chorus, you can find him writing as his favorite local coffee shop. Now. You can find him there right now.*

INVERTED REALITY QUICK REFERENCE GUIDE

by John Califano

We live in a time of rapidly shifting political and cultural landscapes. Norms and beliefs of less than a decade ago are now defunct. Long gone are the trusted voices in mainstream media like Walter Cronkite. Today, people are incessantly bombarded with propaganda 24/7 and don't know whom to trust or what to believe.

This phenomenon is particularly troubling for older generations struggling to acclimate to entirely new dystopian words and phrases along with their ever-evolving meanings. The situation has gotten so out of control, people who were taught that 2+2=4 and grew up believing that biological men and women are actually real men and women, have now begun to question their own sanity. Admittedly, I was one of them.

For me, the tipping point came when I witnessed an angry mob of about three hundred young people flood the streets of Lower Manhattan. They were mostly dressed in black, wearing dark face coverings and T-shirts identifying themselves as "Anti-Fascists."

Having attended a number of peaceful protests over the years, my first impulse was to reserve judgment. But then I noticed something peculiar. These civic-minded citizens weren't just exercising their First Amendment right to free speech. They were indiscriminately shattering storefronts, jumping up and down on the roofs of cars, smashing windshields, and—even more alarming—they were hurling rocks and bottles at helmeted police and counter-protesters.

I immediately thought, is it just me, or is something terribly askew here? Are these young folks really protesting against fascism or are they promoting it?

I retreated to my humble abode riddled with doubt. I thought that perhaps I had been missing something, and that, maybe, there was a new way of . . . you know, perceiving reality that I somehow wasn't quite getting. I mean, hey, nobody wants to feel left out. I certainly don't.

After doing a little research I discovered a godsend: the INVERTED REALITY QUICK REFERENCE GUIDE.

I must say, this handy tool has rescued me from countless moments of self-doubt, confusion, and frustration. Not to mention saving me thousands in talk therapy.

Here's how it works: Say you're watching CNN, MSNBC, or some other bought-and-paid-for mainstream news network, and you suddenly find yourself in a cultural and political quandary. You're not quite sure, but you suspect what you're being fed is the inverted opposite of what you know to be true, sane, and rational. You whip out this nifty quick-reference guide, look up the word or phrase in question, and Bam! —your sanity is affirmed. Now you can dismiss all your paranoid, politically correct fears of being caught on the wrong side of history.

One minor precaution: If you're inclined to buy into any of this delusional, dystopian, hate-filled nonsense, it might be a good idea to ensure that you're armed to the teeth, have prescription drug

INVERTED REALITY QUICK REFERENCE GUIDE

NORMIE LINGUISTIC FORMS	INVERTED TRANSLATIONS
Tyrants	Liberators
Barbarians	Humanitarians
Self-Defense	Genocide
Fascism	Anti-Fascism
Oppressors	The Oppressed
Guilt / Shame / Self-Loathing	Cultural Merit Badges
Genital Mutilation	Gender Affirming Healthcare
Morbidly Obese	Healthy / Sexy
Memory Loss / Cognitively Impaired / Unfit	Sharp / Focused / Capable
Untested / Unsafe / Lethal	Proven / Safe / Effective
Biological Men	Toxic Masculinity
Biological Male Declaring Pregnancy	Birthing Person
Pedophiles	Minor-Attracted Persons
English / Math / Science	Racist Tools of Oppression
Attempting Civil Discourse	Triggering Emotional Distress
Racial Hierarchy / Power Transfer / Enforcement	Diversity, Equity, & Inclusion
Dissolution of State Sovereignty / Cultural & Personal Autonomy	Free and Open Boarders
Open Season on Law Abiding Citizens	Defund the Police
Politically Motivated "Get Out of Jail Free" Cards	Criminal Justice Reforms
Apathy / Corruption / Malfeasance	Free, Fair & Legitimate Elections
Intolerance / Revenge / Violence	Radical Justice
Free Speech	Hate Speech
Questioning Official Narratives	Treason / Domestic Terrorism
Highly Paid Stenographers	Award-Winning Mainstream Journalist
Truth / Facts	Lies / Misinformation
Truth Seekers / Critical Thinkers	Crackpots / Conspiracy Theorists

coverage, and that your kids and grandkids are attending school on another planet because—in case you haven't noticed—this insidious weaponization of language is helping to both fuel and obfuscate the global shitstorm currently brewing on the horizon. Not a good look for future generations; not a good look for humanity.

For some, this may sound like a stale throwback to the 60's, but what's needed now more than ever is a megadose of genuine peace, love, and understating.

John Califano *lives in New York City where he contemplates his existence and works helping at-risk parolees transition back into the workforce. He's worked as a writer, actor, visual artist, and musician, and has performed in clubs, art galleries, feature films, and Off-Broadway productions. His work is featured in The Broadkill Review, The Willesden Herald's New Short Stories Series (UK), Adelaide Literary Magazine, The Writing Disorder, Poetry Super Highway, Embark, Dream Noir, Spank the Carp, Across the Margin, and Literary Yard (India).*

LUCKY DUCK

by Amanda Klarsfeld

Six of the seven deadly sins can be attractive, pure eye candy. Greed is a handsome Wall Street mogul in an expensive suit, hair slicked back, holding a cigar. Pride is those Lululemon-clad soccer parents, sipping Starbucks while watching their son score the winning goal. Lust is the glossy pages of the Victoria's Secret catalog you stole from your older sister. Gluttony is taking your buddy out for sushi, steak and back room bottle service in Vegas for his bachelor party. Wrath is road rage, a sleek sports car swerving then speeding away after flicking off the texter-driver in the next lane. Even Sloth can be sexy, lovers lying in late on an unmade hotel bed, feeding each other from last night's room service tray.

But Jealousy? Jealousy is ugly. Jealousy is embarrassing, unwanted, unloved, unlovable. Pimple-faced. Jealousy is standing out in the rain, looking inside at the party you weren't invited to. Jealousy is a big fat loser.

1980

My first memory of feeling jealous is from when I was five or six. My mom and I went to Sara Walker's apartment for a play date. She lived on the Upper East Side, as did we, in a large but not fancy apartment, similar to ours. She had two married parents, just like I did. She had an older brother and I had an older sister. We went to the same private school, The Town School, on East Seventy-Sixth Street, with only twenty-five kids per grade. Neither one of us had pets. We both had skinny legs but were good at running. Her room was pink, mine, yellow. At the start of this play date, we were on an even playing field. I did not want anything that she had, as I already had it, or something similar.

The polite thing to do when you have someone over is to ask them if they want a drink and, when you are a kid, it is the polite thing for your mom to do. So it was Elaine Walker who asked me what I wanted to drink. Elaine was Sara's soft-spoken, somewhat spacey mother with squinting, smiling eyes who, looking back, may have been stoned all of the time.

Growing up, there were orange juice households and apple juice households. Apple juice homes usually had a drooly baby somewhere on premises and they served all kid guests in plastic cups that still tasted like apple juice, even when there was water inside. I hated apple juice. Thankfully, Sara's was an orange juice house, like mine.

Out came the Tropicana carton which, in those days, featured a barefoot young girl with oranges on her head, wearing a grass skirt. "Can you pour?" was a question my friends and I had been throwing around lately. Some of us could, some of us couldn't. Sara's mom didn't wait for us to have this discussion. She got out two mugs from a high cabinet and Sara and I watched her do the pouring; this was not a serve-yourself kitchen.

"I want the ducky cup," Sara announced, gleefully.

The ducky cup?

Sara's mom lifted one of the mugs to show me what was inside: a ceramic, three dimensional yellow duck. It was the kind of thing that a child might love as a toddler and perhaps retain an attachment to when she was a little too old for it. The duck itself looked ready to retire, its tiny black eye dots partially flecked off after one too many washes. Not that this bothered me then, at least not consciously, but it was also a germaphobe's nightmare – so many nooks and crannies for bacteria to multiply in. In summary, it was babyish and a little gross and I no more wanted that ducky cup than I did someone else's undies or their old teddy-bear with a drool stain next to the remnants of its bitten off ear.

"Are you OK if Sara gets the ducky cup?" Elaine asked. She pronounced her name Saaaaaara like the first syllable was way more important than the second.

"Yes," I replied.

Of course. Ew.

Elaine poured us our orange juice, Sara's into the ducky cup and mine into a regular mug – nondescript, no ducky inside.

As we reached for our drinks, I noticed the satisfied smile on Sara's face, like she had won a game I didn't realize we were playing. Why was she excited about this cup? I certainly wasn't. What was so great about it? It wasn't like you could even see the ducky. He was completely covered by the juice. Was there something wrong with me for not caring about the ducky cup? No, more likely, there was something wrong with her. What a baby!

I supposed that as you drank the juice, the duck would show himself, little by little. But still, was that really something to get excited about? It's not like you could take him out and play with him. He wasn't a toy. He wasn't fun.

Yet now, Sara was jumping up and down, squealing with excitement, like she was waiting to go on a carnival ride. What was she so hyped up about? The slow reveal of a silly little duck? First his tiny yellow head, then his ugly little bill, then, after your juice was gone, his entire glued-down, non-removable body? Was it really so fabulous to have him there while you drank, a visible indicator that you had, eventually, finished all of your juice? Like he was some kind of all-important juice-drinking finish line? Some kind of…. prize?

I wanted the ducky cup.

"Wait!" I said as Elaine handed us the drinks. "I do want it. I want the ducky cup."

Oh, and I did. I wanted it, more than I wanted the juice, or this playdate, or anything else in the world. I wanted to drink from that cup. I wanted that ducky to hang in there with me as I sipped my orange juice. I wanted to see the top of his head, then his bill, and then more of him and more of him until he was ready to come out fully, show his whole ducky body, and celebrate with me, for me. I wanted him to be my prize.

Sara turned to me, stunned, her lips quivering, her stare cutting through me, irises like two dark frisbees, filled with hatred. "No! No! I want the ducky cup!" she screamed. "That's my cup!" Tears formed.

"But Saaaara, she's your guest," Elaine offered. "Don't you want to share your cup?"

"No!"

It was my turn to tear up. "I want the cup."

The more insistent I became about wanting to drink out of the cup, the more resistant Sara became to sharing it. Our respective tantrums escalated until my mother and I went home, the moms agreeing that "we'll have to try this again another time."

"It made no sense to continue," my mom said when I asked her if she remembered this incident. My mother did not remember that the fight was about a cup, only that there had been crying and that she and I had "high-tailed" it out of there. And that's exactly what I remember too, leaving in a teary blur with barely a goodbye.

"And Elaine didn't handle it well," my mom continued, when I asked her what else she remembered. "She must have wanted to ring Saaaara's neck. The child was being obnoxious." My mother has never been one to see it from both sides. She would have been a great prosecuting attorney. "But she just kept cleaning her sink, passing the rag back and forth, like she needed to to get it shinier and shinier. She probably was just trying to get rid of tension!" My mother may have also missed a calling as a behavioral psychologist.

Sara and I still talk occasionally and I have seen her from time to time over the years. She lives in Brooklyn, works in marketing and has two girls of her own.

I texted her to see if she remembered the ducky cup incident. She didn't remember our fight, but she remembered the cup.

"It was a mug, like a coffee mug, and it said 'Who lives in this cup?' on it, with a little ceramic yellow duck inside." As soon as she said it, I remembered the words on the outside of the cup. But I'm not sure if I could read at the time. So maybe someone had had to tell me that this was what the words said, which may have made the cup even more mysterious, more exciting.

"I definitely drank out of the cup a lot," Sara continued. "I'm not sure where it came from. It was old. It might have been my parents' at some point. But I really loved the mug and always wanted it."

"Yes, you did!!" I texted back.

"I'm sure if we were young I wouldn't have shared. Probably after that, I wouldn't have cared," she replied. Perhaps.

I asked Sara to talk to Elaine and see what she remembered from that day but Sara was not in the mood to "engage" with her mom at the moment because they were currently dealing with some other issues. "Old people things," Sara said. This brought to mind an image of Sara, passing her own rag back and forth inside her own stainless steel sink, trying not to engage with her mother.

Sara and I spent a while catching up. Afterwards, I went onto Amazon where I found a modern version of the ducky cup and ordered one for her. I thought about buying two, one for each daughter, to prevent a potential argument. But then I thought that sending just one might inspire a story of its own.

I have learned how to hide my jealousy whenever I feel it bubble up. That's what adults do. When I want what you have, I bury it like an animal buries its poop in the woods lest you detect the scent. Best to keep that sort of thing to oneself, I reason.

Sometimes I wonder, though. What if I didn't hide it but, instead, shouted it out, let everyone know when I wanted what you had? What if we all did this? "I'd kill to make as much money as you do! I feel poor when I'm around you." "Why do so many people like your Facebook posts when almost nobody likes mine? Am I that unlikeable?" "Your kids are so much more well adjusted than mine are. Where did I go wrong?" We'd be seen as pathetic, right? "I want your goddam ducky cup!"

Or perhaps not. Perhaps we'd be thanked, because maybe the person we were envious of hadn't realized how good their lives actually were.

Or maybe we'd see that we were wrong, that the things we thought they had were simply smoke and mirrors, that these people we envied were just as incomplete and lacking as we believed ourselves to be?

Or what if we were lucky enough to have someone who loved us – who knew us better than we knew ourselves – whisk us away, before our tantrum escalated? What if they "high-tailed" us out of there, brought us home, dried our eyes and forced us to take a look around? What if then, for the first time, we could actually see the things we still wanted but no longer thought about? Not because they weren't important, but because they were already ours.

2023

I am forty-eight. I get divorced and move back to New York and start reconnecting with old friends. Sara is one of them. One night, we meet for dinner in Brooklyn.

I ask about her brother.

"Paul's divorced," she tells me. She says that he lives on the Upper East Side, where we all grew up, where I'm living now.

"You should give me his number!" I say.

Paul is seven years older than we are so we never hung out when we were kids, though I was aware of his existence. I think I found him good looking when I was younger, but he never seemed interested in talking to his much younger sister and her friends so I rarely got close enough to him to really evaluate.

Sara had worshiped him.

"Don't call Paul," Sara says.

"Why not?"

A sigh and a pause.

"Paul is going through a hard time."

I love people who are going through a hard time.

"I'm sorry to hear that. Maybe he needs a friend," I say.

"Yeah, I would stay away if I were you," she repeats.

I can't decide whether to be offended because she doesn't think he'd benefit from knowing me or flattered that she's somehow protecting me.

Months later, I'm scrolling through a dating app, and someone named Paul likes my picture. He writes me a message:

"Are you friends with my sister, Sara?'

The only way to reply is to like the person back. He doesn't look nearly as cute as he did when I was eight.

I like him back, but I say this:

"Oh, wow. Hi! Yes [smiley face]. I'm matching with you to continue this conversation, not because I think we should date. How are you, Paul?"

"Hi Amanda - Sara had asked me a couple of months ago if I remember you and told me you moved back to NYC. I think that Town School was so small that everyone knew everyone…." He goes on to tell me about his life. He doesn't seem to be as much of a mess as Sara had intimated. I suggest that I get his phone number and respond by text, which is always easier.

"I only give my number to women who want to date me," he says. He is funny. I am a sucker for funny.

For the next few days, Paul and I text constantly. I text him from my desk at work, pretending to look at an Excel sheet, while crossing the street, dodging people and cars and Citi bikes using only my peripheral vision, while on the subway, waiting for the 5G bars to appear each time the train stops so I can hit "send." Something is happening, but I am not sure what. What I do know is that I am enjoying this and I know that he is too. I rarely if ever use "lol" in texts, so I don't, but I am legitimately laughing out loud because he is witty and sarcastic and unpretentious. I like him.

I tell him that I once wrote about his sister and I text him the story about the ducky cup. He says he likes the story but that I should have written more about how handsome Sara's brother had been.

We decide to meet for a drink. We go to Dorrian's Red Hand, the Upper East Side bar that we New York City kids used to go to in high school. This bar had become famous in 1986 as the bar that Robert Chambers and Jennifer Levin went to before Chambers killed Levin in Central Park. This story, dubbed The Preppy Murder by the papers and on TV, scared the shit out of all of us but didn't stop us from frequenting one of the only bars we knew that routinely didn't card.

When Paul shows up, I give him a hug and a kiss which is what you do when you haven't seen someone in forty years but he seems surprised by it and a little stiff. He is not bad looking but he is not my type. Well, I don't really have a type but if I did, this would not be it. Maybe it's because he's short — my height. He's muscular, not fat, but because of his stature, I think you'd describe him as "stocky". He also has a bit of a New York accent. Well, maybe not, but he says things like "yuge" instead of "huge" and a few other things – I can't recall exactly what – that New Yorkers with accents say, older New Yorkers. Even so, he looks much younger than his fifty-six years. He is nice looking, actually. He has a sweet smile. But he really resembles Sara and for some reason the idea of romance with him seems incestuous.

But that's not why I'm here. I'm here to have a drink with someone I have things in common with. We are both single and recently divorced and have kids and live on the Upper East Side and went to the same elementary school. This is not a date, this is just a drink. Anyway, it's a no. He's a no.

He orders me a Tito's up with olives, which is the only thing I ever want, and he orders a vodka on the rocks for himself, I think. We get a table away from the bar. It's loud and crowded but we're far enough away from the action that we can still hear one another.

"I have a surprise for you," he says. "You are not going to believe this." Paul puts a cloth Morton Williams grocery bag on the table. I stare at it. Paul's eyes get wider and he smiles. Dimples form. He looks handsome. Whatever the surprise is, he seems very excited to give it to me.

"Oh my God," I say when I realize what it is going to be. "No way."

I reach into the bag, and there it is. Exactly how I remember it.

"Did part of you think it didn't really exist?" He asks.

"Absolutely. Yes," I say. "Memory can be so unreliable. How did you get this?"

"My mom is a hoarder. She keeps everything."

"Does she know you took it?"

"No," he says. "I snuck in."

"Paul."

"Yes?"

"This is the most romantic thing anyone has ever done for me," I say this because it feels true, even though I don't exactly know what I mean.

We talk about the ducky cup and then we talk about other things. We laugh.

"We have a connection," he says. "And it feels good."

We do and it does.

After I finish my martini, and I'm halfway through the next, I decide that he is no longer a no. He is a yes. For a moment, he's talking and I'm not even listening. "Yes, yes," I say to myself. "I am changing the no to a yes. He is a yes."

He kisses me once in the bar, and once when we're out on the street.

We go our separate ways. He doesn't even suggest otherwise. Which is good, because after my "yes" light goes on, I have no boundaries. Maybe it's a result of having been married for twenty years. I still have a vague idea of the bases which I'm assuming are the same as they were before I was married but, frankly, I don't really see the point.

Paul texts me a picture of the tulips he sees on his way home, but I don't get it until the morning because I pass out as soon as I get back to my apartment. Literally, I fall asleep with my coat and shoes on, which is something I have never done before. I realize in the morning that I hadn't had dinner, and so I'd been drunker than I normally am after two martinis.

In the morning, I take the ducky cup out of the Morton Williams bag and wash it. I hadn't realized this at Dorrian's but it's dirty. Very dirty. I'm not sure why or how it got this way, as I imagine it's been sitting in a cabinet for at least forty-five years. I scrub a little too hard and some of the yellow paint comes off of the ceramic duck. I decide to let it soak for a while in the sink.

Who Lives In This Cup? Sara was right. That's exactly what it says on the outside. The duck itself is in worse shape than I'd remembered. In fact, the body is lumpy and slightly misshapen. I understand how, as a young child, I was initially unimpressed.

I let it soak for several hours, towel it to dry. It's still a little dirty but I don't want to push my luck. Paul and I text about it. I tell him that I think a spray of bleach will do the trick but that I'm afraid to apply harsh chemicals. I tell him that the Task Rabbit who comes to assemble my IKEA cabinet is thirsty but I don't have any clean glasses so I might have to give him the ducky cup.

"No. Ducky is just for you," he says.

My heart swells.

Today, Paul and I are not a couple. I'm pretty sure that's what you are wondering. I wasn't interested in continuing in the direction we were going in. I wasn't attracted to him. Or maybe I was, but not enough. I try to ask myself why but I can't answer. Attraction, or the absence of it, isn't explainable. And I am free now. Autonomous. Untethered. I don't need to offer explanations to anyone for anything, ever again. This is the truest thing I've ever written, yet I still need to remind myself of it, every single day.

Still, the cup remains on my kitchen counter. It has no purpose, no function. Maybe I keep it here to remind me that, in the end, we all eventually get what we want, or what we think we want, or what we once thought we wanted. Or maybe I keep it here to remind me that my story is not over. That no story is ever over, that the camera keeps rolling, even if we've stopped paying attention. Maybe I want a reminder to pay attention.

Or maybe, I just like looking at my prize.

Amanda Klarsfeld *graduated from Tulane University with a concentration in creative writing. She has since worked as copywriter for multinational brands and a community news writer, food section writer and blogger for Sun-Sentinel, a Pulitzer Prize-winning newspaper. One year ago, Amanda returned to New York City, where she was born and raised, after almost thirty years in other, less exciting places.*

DANIEL INOUYE: PERSONAL JUSTICE ATTAINED

by Iris Lu

Daniel Inouye was 17 years old when he witnessed Japanese planes bomb Pearl Harbor. That day would "go down in infamy" for the US– and be life-altering for Inouye. In the wake of the attack, Inouye wanted to join the US military to fight back– but found he was ineligible to serve: the US War Department had reclassified all Japanese Americans as "Enemy Aliens" (PBS, The War – Daniel Inouye). This wave of suspicion and xenophobia would culminate with FDR's signing of Executive Order 9066, which sent over 120,000 Japanese Americans to internment camps (HISTORY -- How Japanese Americans Fought for—and Won—Redress for WWII Incarceration).

Inouye petitioned the government to lift the ban and allow him to fight. In need of reinforcements, the War Department conceded, allowing Inouye to enlist in the 442nd Infantry Regiment Combat Team of Nisei fighters. Over two years of deployment in Europe, Inouye would be shot in the stomach and lose an arm in the service of the country that he had fought to fight for. But despite fighting honorably, Inouye and his peers in the 442nd regiment returned home to the same discrimination as when they left. Inouye would later recall walking into a barbershop in San Francisco decorated with medals and being told "We don't serve Japs." (DKII, Senator Daniel Inouye & Family: Watergate Changed his Life).

In 2013, a year after his passing, Daniel Inouye became the first and only senator to receive both the Medal of Freedom and the Medal of Honor. Ostensibly, these medals were for the courage he showed on the battlefield. But Inouye's greatest act of courage would come when he returned home, fighting to ensure the violation of constitutional rights suffered by Japanese Americans during the war never happened again.

In 53 years of representing his home state of Hawaii Inouye was a consistent champion for democratic values, from his keynote at the 1968 Democratic National Convention where he warned against the dangers of suspicion and fear, to his seat on the Senate Select Committee investigating Watergate, where he cautioned the importance of safeguarding the election process and voter rights. These fights were not without a price. As the highest ranking Asian American member of congress, he was often met with the same vitriol he endured in the 1940s. "My son... used to enjoy answering the phone. But [now] I grab the phone, because...there are [phone calls] that are rather hateful. I don't want Danny... barraged by obscenities." (DKII, Watergate Hearings Opening Statement).

In 1978, Inouye began the most important chapter in his battle for civil rights: working with the Japanese American Citizens League (JACL) as a leader of the Redress Movement. The movement faced many challenges, beginning with divisions within the JACL itself. Haunted by their own moral shortcomings during WWII, many of the elder Nisei members were content to move on, popularizing words like shikataganai ("it can't be undone") (Japanese American Redress). The 3rd generation Sansei, on the other hand, recognized internment within the context of the broader civil rights movement

(NPR, The Unlikely Story Behind Japanese Americans fight for reparations), and believed reconciliation was essential– but were split between demanding a federal apology and demanding both an apology and monetary compensation. (Maki, How Japanese Americans Fought for—and Won—Redress for WWII Incarceration).

Redress also faced challenges from conservative revisionists like Lillian Baker, whose group Americans for Historical Accuracy claimed internment camps never existed, claimed pictures of the camps had been doctored, and argued its internees had been there voluntarily.

With a quiet courage that reflected his years of experience, Inouye realized the only way to move forward was to manifest a common, objective truth, suggesting "a federal commission to research and investigate the incarceration experience" (Maki, How Japanese Americans Fought for—and Won—Redress for WWII Incarceration). On August 2, 1979, Inouye co-sponsored Senate bill 1647 to form the Commission on Wartime Relocation and Internment of Civilians (CWRIC).

After two years the CWRIC released its report, "Personal Justice Denied," which chronicled the injustices suffered by Japanese-Americans during the war. The report elicited testimony from 750 witnesses across 10 US cities, with many sharing their stories for the first time. The report concluded internment was not done out of "military necessity" that had been claimed to defend Executive Order 9066, but from "race prejudice, war hysteria, and a failure of political leadership" (Personal Justice Denied). The report offered three recommendations: a presidential apology, a foundation to educate the American public, and a payment of $20,000 to every detainee.

Inouye's seniority in the senate helped rally support for the commission's recommendations– as did his role as Chairman of the Senate Select Committee on Secret Military Assistance to Iran and the Nicaraguan Opposition in the Summer of 1987. In his closing statement in the Iran Contra hearings, Inouye was discussing the abuse of power within the Reagan administration, but could just as well have been describing the dangerous logic that had led to Japanese internment: "'This is a dangerous world,' [the generals] said. That, my fellow citizens, is an excuse for autocracy, not for policy. Vigilance abroad does not require us to abandon our ideals or the rule of law at home. On the contrary, without our principles and without our ideals, we have little that is special or worthy to defend" (DKII, Iran-Contra Hearings Closing Statement). Just one month after Inouye cautioned of the dangers of autocracy in the Iran Contra hearings, a bill to enact the CWRIC's recommendations--named HR 442 in honor of the Nisei regiment in which Inouye served--came to the floor of Congress.

On August 10, 1988, President Reagan signed the Civil Liberties Act into law, granting a presidential apology and redress payments of $20,000 to every living Japanese American who had been affected by Executive Order 9066. (HISTORY, How Japanese Americans Fought for—and Won—Redress for WWII Incarceration). For Inouye, the bill was the culmination of almost 50 years fighting for democratic values both on and off the battlefield, righting not only the wrongs perpetrated against Japanese Americans, but serving as a reminder to protect the constitutional rights of all Americans. Today, against a rising tide of antidemocratic forces, the courage of leaders like Daniel Inouye must inspire us to fight abuses of power in the face of hysteria and fear, and make sure that democracy, universal suffrage, and equity remain a reality for all Americans.

FOUR MICRO NONFICTION PIECES

by Gail Hosking

Neruda at the Other End of the World

A young friend reads me Neruda from the western side of the mountains of Chile at 3:45 PM across the world from this hospital, this place where blue scrubs and wheel chairs, crutches and signs for the OR abound, where the afternoon temperature outside is 100, and I close my eyes and lean back in a lobby chair waiting for my partner's biopsy, a "procedure" they refer to it here, and I'm looking on my phone as everyone else does and I find my friend at the other end of the planet, smiling, reading love poems: drink sky behind pines, her voice as clear as the cold sky behind her, her cheeks rosy, her eyes bright, not a cloud to be seen, kisses like roses, hardened by passions, and I am gladdened, even as I wait for the news then drive my partner home through the thick Boston traffic in a rainstorm thinking about Neruda in a young woman's backpack, my life divided into dreams with parallel bodies, poetry and youth.

Almost

It's a school night on McKinley Street on your way to Raymond Street where your grandparents live. Your mothers and sisters are there already for dinner. You've just finished your homework, maybe a phone call to your horn-blowing boyfriend, so you set out walking with your hands in your jeans pocket. The spring air is warm, and you know you're headed towards summer as you stroll down a familiar street. The sky is dark gray, or maybe dark blue, but the streetlights have come on. In the near distance you see another teenager coming your way, and just as he nears, you say hi, and he immediately punches you in the gut, hard and fast. You keep walking with confusion—did this really happen? And if so, why? But you keep walking as if it didn't happen, only to hear his heavy footsteps running back towards you. Something in that moment altered reality, coated with terror and a new knowledge of trust. You run as fast as you have ever run before. Your heart feels like it's crashing in your chest, your legs suddenly strong and determined. You turn right onto Raymond and continue until you find the house, pound on the door, your head turning to see if the stranger is still there. Police are called. But nothing is ever said, nothing found out, only your innocence is taken away. Your nerves forever on edge in the dark. Dreams of strangers. Fearful surprises.

The Light Returns Me to Childhood

Like a mystery stored in my body, the light of today remembers the fullness of the sun over the base in North Carolina as young soldiers march by, and my father salutes the officers. Or the winter sun slowly peers over the Alps, one ray at a time so that the ice on my father's blue Opel station wagon melts, and the army brats come out in snowsuits to play "King of the Mountain" on top of a large snow pile swept to the end of the block. Sometimes the light hides behind clouds over Hitler's former SS base across the street as my mother takes down the diapers drying on the communal clothesline shared with the other army wives. The lights are timed in the hallways of each stairwell of our stucco apartment buildings because after the war electricity is in short supply. The pines along the barbed wire fence look black in the light of dawn. The sky changes by the hour. The trees stand so close together, I'm told, that their roots wrap around each other for support and comfort. Look, it's a metaphor like most things I study today. It's the forgotten search for implication. It's the raw ticking of time suspended between two countries. I keep translating everything I see these days into possibilities as I search the world for answers and study the puzzle of my own life. They say memory and regret can mingle. They say the body recalls what the mind tries to forget when the lights go out. They say the sun returns after storms.

Maybe a War, Maybe a Party, Maybe a Sandcastle

On the beach I listen to the French who came down to Mexico from Montreal, the men with their greased big bellies, the young all smooth and tattooed, the women with barely any bathing suits. I enter the emerald green or sometimes turquoise waters. The further out I go it gets darker, so I pause fearing sharks, a life-long fear. The tiny angel fish and needle-nose fish, the ones I recognize from fish tanks, move through the waters close to shore.

A man dressed all in white with a big-brimmed hat on the beach builds a heart, a peace sign, a mosque, buildings with entrances and windows in the sand, and then places international flags on every precipice. He adds small child-like figures like a pink pony, a nun, and a ninja warrior. People come to notice and talk with the artist. They take photographs and ask questions. By morning I suspect his art will be gone like a Zen mandala. Art for art's sake. The NOW, not the future. I should have asked.

Two nearby seniors juggle balls back and forth like teammates. When they finally stop, they bring fists together to say something about camaraderie or pure fun. People come by selling necklaces and chocolate bars and watermelon and stuffed animals and painted bowls. I want all of it and none, maybe desire it only to help their lives. Or to purchase souvenirs for my grandchildren. But I've brought no money with me purposely, so the choice is easier.

You would think all is well in the world, but amid this beach paradise with its French and German and English and Spanish spoken, two camouflaged soldiers walk by with their AK47s pointed to the ground. Their faces wrapped with a black scarf like terrorists. Wearing black boots, they walk up and down the beach as if looking for someone. When a beach mobile passes by later filled with three marines with rifles, no one seems to notice, but I feel like I've entered Chechnya, or Berlin, or Vienna, or Kiev or Zaire. I fear the calm before the storm. But who am I to point out the worst of mankind? Maybe they are here only to protect us. I lived once near Dachau and the Iron Curtain and learned to fear the worst. Fear still lingers all these years later. In the meanwhile, two women in bikinis carry bottles of wine as they walk by my beach chair. Maybe towards a party. Well beyond any war.

Gail Hosking *is the author of the memoir Snake's Daughter (U of Iowa Press) and two books of poems Retrieval and Adieu(Main Street Rag Press). MFA from Bennington Writing Seminars. Essays and poems have appeared in such places as Waxwing, Post Road, South Dakota Review, and The Healing Muse. Several pieces have been anthologized. Twice "most notable" in Best American Essays.*

THE MEANING OF LOVE

by Andrea Vutabwarova

Love appears to be this untamed force that I can't seem to pin down. The beauty of love is unparalleled, it is felt in every waking moment of our lives, stranger's smile on the street to the music that we listened to. Every waking moment of our lives are spent reveling in love- or the lack thereof. But somehow, this unparalleled beauty has horrors of its own. Somehow, love carries a dagger when it enters your life; it never leaves unscathed. Somehow, my greed for love grows larger.

My greed for love is insatiable; I tend to wonder if I will ever find the love that I so deeply desire. And my life overflows with love, from my family to my friends. The love in my life is bountiful. But the love in my life is also hypocritical, it comes with the tides. The love in my life has scarred me. To pine and yearn for a love that may never find me may be my greatest curse.

Love is just as human as the rest of us, maybe love is as deep as humanity itself. The key to understanding love from this perspective is to dive into the depths of what it means to be human. Humanity knows kindness, compassion, and empathy. But humanity also knows selfishness, greed and evil. Those things co-exist in our reality. So saying that love is capable of harm is not entirely untrue. Love may be so full of goodness that at times we ourselves cannot compute that it is in our reality. Love also has the capacity to be just as evil as the rest of humanity can be. Because much like the definition of humanity, to say that love is only good would be a lie. To fully acknowledge the human existence, we must first see that we are a selfish species, innately driven by self-interest.

If love is just as human as we are, that would imply that love is just as dynamic as the human race. No two love stories will ever be the same, each love story has its own set timeline, its own values and ideals that make it unique; each love story has its own unique face. That love evolves as the people evolve, and if the world gets its way, love becomes less hopeful as time goes on. Love is born through labor, through hard work, through the endless toil of creating life. Love is not an easy task one takes on, love is a lifestyle, despite the sorrows that the world may bring. Despite the trauma and flaws that a person inhibits. Despite the selfishness that exists within humanity.

Understanding love is understanding that it is not one dimensional. That because in life, we stumble and misstep, and rediscover who we are, love must be the same. Love is the constant rediscovery and discovery of each other. There can be no rules in love, only stumbles and missteps until you find someone to discover and rediscover. Understand that while love is good you can and will be harmed; grief will always be the price to pay for love.

In my quest to find or narrow down the definition of love, I have discovered the following: to love is to persevere. That is the very essence of what it means to love. And much like life, you must persevere in life in order to live it. Persevering through the trauma and agony of those that you love, persevering through the imperfections that add more depth and dimension to the people that you love, persevering because it is the only option when you love someone.

In order to love fully, maybe I need to stop looking at the ideal version of love. Maybe the ideal version of love, just like everything else in our current reality has been photoshopped and augmented into something it is not. Love is beautiful, but not without imperfection. Maybe all along I have admired love, but not actually loved it. Love is the essence that flows through the universe, "I love you" is both a declaration of devotion and stupidity.

Andrea Vutabwarova *is currently a student pursuing an undergraduate degree in accounting sciences. She has always had a deep fascination for written word and poetry, and often found herself deeply moved by it. Writing became a way for Andrea to make sense of the world from her perspective. She often writes prose or essays that help to highlight her current state of mind. When she's not writing, or studying, she enjoys crocheting, sewing or spending valuable time with her family and friends.*

GRANDPA'S FARM

by Jeff Hyndman

ROY W ROUSH greeted you as you pulled into the farm yard, his name emblazoned high up on the imposing red barn, just above the hay door. Nearby were five other outbuildings: a smaller, separate barn housed two tractors and various tractor implements, a chicken coop, a garage where a blue Buick Skylark was parked, a pumphouse and some distance away a pony shed within a fenced field. All of the farm buildings were wooden, painted red and covered by green asphalt shingles. A two-story, white clapboard house stood nearby with a screened-in porch and screen door, a petunia patch in the front yard and a sprawling white oak tree, which towered over the house.

This was my grandparents' farm. Growing up we visited the farm each summer for two weeks. The six of us piled into our Pontiac station wagon and made the ten hour journey to the farm, which sat outside the tiny town of Van Buren, Indiana, where some eight hundred people lived.

Grandpa was born to be a farmer, the only life he wanted or imagined. His 140 acres of corn, soybeans and wheat constituted the sole, everlasting Heaven he ever sought. Grandpa was a happy man.

Grandma, whose domain was the house and chicken coop, was a stout woman who always wore long flowery dresses, blocky black shoes, and glasses, which usually hung from a chain around her neck. She weighed twice as much as her rail-thin husband, with his bulbous nose and bemused countenance. She worked sunup to sundown cooking, cleaning, pegging laundry in the side yard, collecting eggs, butchering chickens for dinner and making the best pies I've ever tasted. Her mien conveyed gravitas; grandpa's, humor.

Upstairs in the farm house, a tall mahogany cupboard was filled with Ball Jars of tomatoes, corn, pickles, carrots, pumpkin and jams, all canned by grandma. It was also where we all slept, which we reached by walking up the unlit, slippery wooden stairs. There was but one bathroom in the house, which housed the smallest bathtub I'd ever seen, all of four feet long.

My brothers and sister and I loved going to the farm. There was so much to do and nowhere else was like it. The farm was rich in aromas, a potpourri of fragrances that hit us as soon as we opened the car door and set foot on the gravel driveway. The sweet smell of freshly cut hay, the earthy smell of cornfields, the gassy odor of cow manure, and the whiff of wild blueberry, all combined to convey to our sense of smell that we were on a working farm, far from the Eastern Seaboard from whence we came.

Like an observer with a window to the past, I can still see myself catapulting stones with my slingshot at crows who cawed at me disdainfully, or at rabbits I spooked from hedgerows. My brothers and I spent hours in the hayloft playing king of the mountain or swinging from the heavy rope that was used to hoist hay bales up and into it.

Grandpa kept a pony for us to ride with a saddle or in a pony cart. Dusty was the pony I remember best, a large pony and sometimes difficult to manage. Once, my sister and a cousin were riding in the pony cart when a car drove by on the gravel road in front of the farm—a rare occurrence— and startled Dusty, who tore off at a gallop and ended up in a ditch with the pony cart overturned. Thankfully, no one was injured, but grandpa turned bright red as he read the riot act to Dusty, as if Dusty would benefit from the tirade.

An equal, if not greater treat, was when Grandpa invited each of us to ride on his white International tractor while he cut hay or disced a field. It was a prodigious and tall tractor, and from our high vantage point we saw—in any direction we turned—endless flat, farm fields, the heart and soul of Indiana. The change from the highways and population centers of New Jersey to the gravel roads, towns and fields of Central Indiana seemed almost magical.

We always had a family reunion one evening during our stay. Roushs and Schweigerts, whose families were connected in a distant past that was fuzzy or forgotten. Aunts, uncles, cousins, children, in-laws, parents and grandparents came together to celebrate the good fortune of the clan and to swap stories and news. Picnic tables laden with delicious foods, including Grandma's pies—red raspberry, blueberry and strawberry. Homemade ice cream, Orange Crush and Grape Nehi in bottles, capped these feasts.

It was a grand occasion filled with laughter and conversations. We chased after fireflies under a canopy of stars; we ran around with sparklers left over from July 4th and we took turns cranking the handle for the homemade ice cream. We threw baseballs up ever so high on the barn roof, and with our mitts we raced to catch them on their way down. We had fun as only children can.

Indelible memories of those years are more vivid the older I get. It's as if life compensates us for our slowly failing bodies with lucid experiences from our past. Grandpa's farm is long gone, the fences and hedgerows and buildings vanished, washed away by time's relentless march, with only the house left, a rental in disrepair, on its way to history's dustbin.

When we're young, we live in the moment of such experiences and when we're old, we savor the memories. Inside of us is sort of a projector slide show with thousands of slides we can effortlessly pick and choose to see in our mind's eye. Grandpa sitting at the Formica kitchen table, balancing a saucer with hot coffee on it and watching him sip from it. His fingers crooked and arthritic, his hair white, his black rim glasses, and the same gray work shirt and pants, the only thing I ever saw him wear.

The last image I have of grandpa is when he was quite old. He appeared to be the ever- shrinking man, and it was likely the cancer that would take him in less than a year was already running rampant throughout his wiry body. It would be my last trip to the farm. I have a crystal clear picture of grandpa sitting on his smaller, slate gray Ford tractor in the forty acre field behind the main barn. It was sunset, with reddish fingers undulating in the sky above us. The farm was quiet. The tractor was stationery and grandpa was surrounded by twenty or so Black Angus cattle. He wore his customary gray cap and leather gloves, darkened by countless oil stains. I perched on the barnyard fence and watched him. I thought I could just barely hear him talking to the cattle.

I have little doubt that grandpa would not have liked to live in our world today. He was a man born in a different century. The complexity and rancor of today's world would not have appealed to him. He definitely would eschew the industrialization of farming.

Grandpa has always played an outsized role in my life and in my memory of him and the farm. I don't know if I've ever known anyone who absolutely fit in his time and place like grandpa did. I was lucky to have known him.

My wife and I have visited Van Buren over the years, where little has changed; the same post office, the same railroad through town and the single stoplight still watched over the only intersection. We stop by the cemetery to visit my grandparents' graves as well as the numerous Roushs and Sweigerts, scattered throughout the cemetery, going back three hundred years.

I wish they were all still with us. I think of them often. Uncle Dow—who always kept change in his pockets, which you could hear him jingling whenever he was standing. Sweet Aunt Doris, who smiled most of the time and smelled of perfume. My cousin Greg, who always wanted to arm wrestle me because he always won. And my endearing mother, who could sashay across the room with the best of them. My proud and quiet father; a pillar of strength. They were the best of us.

Jeff Hyndman *is a semi-retired IT person and a part time dog walker. He lives in an Atlanta suburb with his wife, Ellen, their dog, Carmella, and their cat, Chelsea, who pretty much runs the show. His essays have been published in a variety of literary magazines.*

POETRY

EU VI FERNANDO PESSOA NA RUA

by Arthur Powers

Eu vi Fernando Pessoa em Lisboa,
em Chiado, numa rua subindo
à Igreja do Carmo, sentado

numa mesinha de fora:
xícara de café, chapéu de palha,
cigarro na boca, bigode aparado

naquele rosto inconsequente –
mas olhos vivos, vendo outro mundo,
um leve sorriso nas esquinas da boca....

Em pleno 2022 –
eu vi Fernando Pessoa na rua,
em Lisboa, em Chiado....

Não fales comigo que ele é morto,
eu vi Fernando Pessoa em Lisboa,
em Chiado, na rua....

'Ta bom, 'ta bom...
Tu tens em mão
o atestado de óbito...

Mas tens tal atestado
para Alberto, para Álvaro,
para Ricardo? Não?

Não tens? Então
eles vivam ainda –
Fernando é somente

um quarto morto –
que significa? A maioria
de nós somos um quarto

morto! Ele três quartos
vivo é! E eu sei. Pois
vi Fernando Pessoa na rua.

CLIMATE CHANGE SENDS A POSTCARD TO LOST AMBITION

by H. A. Sappho

Climate Change Sends a Postcard to Lost Ambition

The emperor is a bad burrito.
All night long I sleep
on the stains of my pillow.
Predator and prey
row the red evening.
In the morning
when the ancients come
I am there
and so are you
my China shop bull.
The future is ours
and all for the low cost
of makeup and musclemen on the beach
watching the horizon float away
from yesterday's bright sky
with an entire city
dropping its handles.
Smokestacks and gas pipes
line the new day.
You think to yourself
that time is a cactus and the cactus
is the reincarnation of a scale
weighing the soul of a vegetable
against the onslaught of history
until memory makes up its mind

as well as yours
to park the future in the wrong garage
and walk across the desert
for a mechanic who knows
which way the wind blows.
It blows north
to the cliff at the top of the world
where not even regrets can survive.

Climate Change Kisses an Amputated Forest

Mind opens its garbage can.
Body pours in its refuse.
Centuries fume
across the burning landscape.
Tornadoes of smoke with flaming knees
invade the deeper forest.
Disappearance will have its way
with words choking the planet
using blades as definitions
for oblivion's foster family
growing its brood
with this paper in your hands.
Fire is the consequence of gluttony.
Know that to know anything
is to honor the humility
of uncertainty
willing to slow its stride
until a poised *now* appears
willing to reconsider everything
that came before a human thought.
But now is not that day.
Today the visible and the invisible
forms of disease encircle the globe
building thoughts into cities and cities
with the forest's amputees
burning rage and revenge
up to the cigarette sky
which will soon lower its suffocation
onto the bones of butterflies between
strafing deserts and surging seas.
The lungs of the planet are ready
to seek a new way.
The monk extends the loss of branches.
The saint preaches the law of drying seeds.
The penitent switches the crown of imagination.

The criminal replaces the trunks of ignorance with indifference
and fits new blades onto the Hydra limbs of avarice.
The last tree stands as a loosed second hand
from a clock swinging the future
between the charcoal ruins and birds
unable to live in the fevered air.
Accomplish maybe the wind says
and all this may yet change.

Climate Change Chases Our Ghosts into a Cave

We first shot the day
in its antelope legs.
After that
the heart of a cloud
was lassoed into dagger rain.
Next we branded the ocean
with refuse and ruin
until it reached the shore.
Then came the invisible herd
heading elsewhere
than the lowering sun.
Still running, its force
carried the lost parchments
to the Cave of Removals
where *this* and *now* hide
in the afterlife
of time's simulacra
concealed or named
by God, the one
who is several
nowheres at once.
Depending upon the mood
of the second or the season
we can no longer determine
where the Great Evening ends
or if it ever rests its shoulders
on a dream
of the first wings of spring
still racing around the globe
searching for what can be saved.

Climate Change Swims Blank Through the Malevolent Sea

Blank has had enough
of the repercussions.
A few decades later
evading the jellyfish armies
he reaches the butterfly shallows
of undersea wings,
intricate, hard-edged
mechanical blunders
of evolution's former ambition
to confirm the rumor
that somewhere even higher
above the new waterline
was a civilization of two-legged beings
as vast as the eight-armed one he once knew
below the waterline.
Now he is only a proof
of the correlation between
ghosts and memories
and what the equation equals
in the long aftermath
of dissolving numbers.
And he wonders how long
after the last memory is gone
does it take
an eight-armed ghost to finally be
the last one to disappear
from the brown vinegar sea.

H. A. Sappho *is a native of Los Angeles with expat time spent in Prague, Berlin, and Hanoi. His baseline interest is archetypal psychology. These poems are from a completed book, In the Pandemic's Caboose. Currently he is at work on FAUST, Part 3.*

THE STAR

by Youssef Oubihi

A Peck

By all means
Let my journey begins
With a peck,
On the right cheek
On the left cheek
On the upper lip
On the bottom lip
On both—
When both lips meet
Soft and sweet
Ah that peachy pink—
Stop! Don't think,
Taste the flavour
Then continue
The endeavour
With a new

Peck to pick,
On the side
Of the neck
With a kiss
Say less
Side to side
One to the left
One to the right
The path is clear
Forming a line
Like a pier
I cannot miss
Nor can I hide
What starts to melt
Inside
Once I felt
The beats
Of your heart
The warmth
Of your skin
Splitting me apart
Calling me in

The Star

In a quiet cloudless night
I saw a star with a gleaming light,
I shouted to the star: " what shall I do?
Shall I hold it or shall I let it go? "

After a brief moment of silence it said:
(While its wonderful glow was well spread)
"Listen, you are not asking the right question,
A wrong answer for a wrong question;

Listen, she made you talk to me from that far,
She made you look for an answer from a star.
You are ultimately taken by her,
You will never be able to let her go, sir! "

Youssef Oubihi *is a poet and a master student of Studies in Literary and Cultural Encounters at Sultan Moulay Slimane University in Beni-Mellal, Morocco. He grew up in the Souss region, where he breathed, imbibed and absorbed poetry from its magic air, sea, and land. His philosophy of poetry can be put thus: poetry for those who can taste its flavours is more than a way of life; it is life itself."*

GRATITUDE

by Alexander Etheridge

In the Late Hour

Look, everything is moving so
quickly, it seems still—
In a short time, this
will be a long time ago.
Vast cities and whole
deserts are vanishing
without an echo.
Lifetimes pass
in the split-second before we wake.
Too late was
yesterday—right now
is gone into
dim memory, swifter
than a welder's spark.
Look,
it's already happened,

you and I
are lost
to another age.

John Coltrane

I think of him again,
head bowed in the studio,
or on a smokey stage—
Hushed mourner, tightrope
walker, grand
wailer.
Ecstatic on the sax, he summons

echoes of Eden,
bringing them close enough
for us to touch.

Rover, seeker,
astral traveler—his scriptures

burning wild in the air,

cutting sapphires from silence,
pushing the far gates
open
to a strange glow,

a molten river—our primitive hearts
joining his prophecy, his

light, his *sound*
of light, a strobing glimpse
of a higher world

beyond the roads of time.

Gratitude

After you've set the book down,
It's all right if we only
remember the paper cuts.

It's all right if Eliot stands under
a bare bulb for days
writing two lines.

We should thank our suffering—
Chopin coughed up blood
composing his last mazurka.

We come from an ancient family
of weepers—A certain grief
gave birth to us all.

A flash of agony stokes the coals
in the heart's furnace. We burn
like the scrolls of Alexandria.

It's OK to break down before
the poem is over. Everything we've lost
carries us on the wind.

The Stranger

A window opens
and the curtains
rustle at 3AM

We can be taken
from out of our dreams
or from our

plane of oblivion
One dark may lead
to a deeper dark

What happens
when death ends
our every sense

Do we wake
into a new
unimagined sight

Does our mind
blend tracelessly
into infinity

What becomes of
our last moment
in the oceans

past time
Will our memories
attend us

Or will we only
know worlds
of cold rubble

in the ancient
mind of
obliteration

Given World

At last you meet her, and now
your story begins—
She is September's first breeze
coming through a window,
and doors opening
to light
from the far side of dawn.

She is a fireglow
like newborn suns.

There's a voice you can
almost hear, saying
You're not yet gone

Open your other eyes
and watch stars vanishing in
a star's light—
It's morning again.
Wake now
in her forever

She is a willow
from salvation's forest, and there's newly fallen rain
in her hair.
She's walking with you
in the risen light,
and everything lost
to the years, each slow grief,
at once feels worth it.
This

is the first day,
and now the world belongs

to you and her alone.

***Alexander Etheridge** has been developing his poems and translations since 1998. His poems have been featured in The Potomac Review, Museum of Americana, Ink Sac, Welter Journal, The Cafe Review, The Madrigal, Abridged Magazine, Susurrus Magazine, The Journal, Roi Faineant Press, and many others. He was the winner of the Struck Match Poetry Prize in 1999, and a finalist for the Kingdoms in the Wild Poetry Prize in 2022. He is the author of, God Said Fire, and, Snowfire and Home.*

LOVE IS A NEON LIGHT

by Ann Huang

Love is a neon light

(after Rene Magritte's *Ceci n'est pas une pipe)*

the scent
of your
garden

the ex-
qui-
site

side of
our life
the love

of my life
the life
of yours

so damn
puffed out
from soil

so damn
washed off
to Pacific

ocean~
without
trace~~

who cares
what
now?

Last Debacle (June 1st, 2023)

(After A.E. Stallings "Frist Miracle")

His soul is like a garnet stone
Shining, indelibly bound to who has made it reborn—

The discovery of a foreign hardness so marvelous
Wandering lust beyond the pig-feet calluses

Melting into the Popocatepetl or juxtaposing his fate
With the procession, many decades are preceding his mate.

His liver shrunk his heart and painted his bed sheets
Whereas he received her love in million beats;

He meant to renew his cosmic ordinance; however
He forfeited his candor with fleeting anger.

Circle of Life: We had a Great Run

My ocean
Green
My baby
Gone
Your body
Died

A body
Next to
None
Our dog
Wanting
You

The
Bloody
Shot
We're
Played
Out

Love wasted
Love
Love
Love
Love for
Your eyes

You're a
Ghost
I am your
Shadow
Inevitable
Time

Go to
Shanghai
After death
After life
Circle of
Life

Resurrecting
Love
Please
Resurrected
For me
I needed to look into your eyes one last time!

Now it's you who's exiting

You always talk about
standing near the exit sign
when I was doing a reading

Now it's you who's
Exiting
So swiftly and decisively

You knew it was an act
To tell me otherwise
That you had to leave me

Alone in this world of
Cruelty and carelessness
You can't be there

For me where I needed
You like the salty water
For a fish

And now it's fish
Without salt
You see me off

Perhaps in a bit
Of anger because of
My child-like naïveté

Thinking that I could
Save you from an
Illness that even doctors

Can't cure
Please stand with me
To the end where

We get swept away
by Our
Ocean of Love!

Why are you so beautiful and so far?

God- you're a cruelty
Such a cruelty
I'm shaking so bad
Why are so confident and then weak
Why are you so selfless and then selfish

What are you made of
Iron or paper
Things are turning and turning
On me
I can't keep my shakiness away

I spent nights after nights in couch
Wishing you could climb up my balcony and touch me

You never did it but always joked around
I'm so tired of waiting or writing
I want to feel you
Not remember how I felt

I want to be with you
Not wishing to be with you
I want to shout at your convenience
Of status quo

I hate and love you
Because you are my friend
Not only my lover
You are so warm and tender
That I could melt you in my mouth

Stop acting like you care
You need to act like you dare

***Ann Huang** is a multilingual Chinese American poet, filmmaker and visual artist based in Newport Beach, CA. Her poetry has been featured in Denver Quarterly, Ruth Stone, CONFRONTATION, Poets Choice, and Contemporary Verse 2. She's Ephemera's June 2023 Poet. Her latest manuscript Garden by The Glass Door is the Wisconsin Poetry Series' 2024 Semi-Finalist. Her collection of poems, Saffron Splash, is forthcoming in 2024 from The Raw Art Review.*

THE FIRST DAY OF SPRING

by Elizabeth Derrick Smith

Dinnertime

At the table, my baby girl squeezes her fists,
    letting the warm potatoes ooze through her small fingers.
Chewing, grinning, she points to the cheese,
    she slaps the cabbage,
she squishes the peas until she has written upon her tray,
    in her own elegant language,
an exclamation of the pleasures of the body.

The First Day of Spring

The lily in my kitchen
Sags and crowds along the edge
Of the pot, as if burdened

By its caretaker, who reads a magazine
By the window instead of pruning, fertilizing,
Watering, or fretting over the snow currently falling.

Flimsy, brown-tipped leaves
Simply surviving
Until the sun comes again.

The Autumn Leaves

Too many sing *the falling leaves*
drift by the window,
and too many guitars and pianos—
orchestras, even—roll along, as if
the notes were tumbling on the lawn.

Autumn leaves really are red and gold
and dying as the air gets cold.
The nights are longer, and
the pears are in their last days before
the snap into winter.

Yet fall also brings us
inside, where we are sheltered,
together and smiling, against the frozen darkness
by golden decorations, turkey, onions
with sage, imported oranges, and cinnamon sticks—

Moments we sometimes long for while flirting
in a garden of purple flowers
amid the ferocious heat of a summer lust.

A Longing

Sometimes I speak to our mustard
Seedlings on the doorstep as I water them,
Recalling the night
At the ball game when we
Laughed so hard that the sauce
Slipped from your hot dog
And onto my sleeve.

Returning to Vancouver Island

Today, at Willow's Beach, the breeze combines
The scent of trees with that of ocean tide
As I now search for shells—the purple kind
That look like spoons. My daughters dig beside
The waves with little trucks we've borrowed, while
My husband snaps a picture. A woman walks
A dog. A family picnics. Couples smile
And wet their feet. A boy collects some rocks.
But I don't hear our siblings laugh or chat
Or pray with us like when we all lived here,
And I don't see my nieces playing that
They're ponies. Once, we were together here.
I guess when housing jumped and income slacked,
The only question left was when to pack.

***Elizabeth Derrick Smith** is a freelance editor and writer with a bachelor's degree in English from Brigham Young University. Her work has been published in BYU Studies Quarterly, The Pinnacle, and Pensive Journal. In 2020, she co-founded a free online literary journal, where she promotes works by emerging writers and well as her own: thepensieve.site. She currently lives in Utah with her husband and daughters.*

HOW THE FUTURE EMERGES

by Mark Vogel

How the future emerges

no need to document the exact second the day
leaps alive like a switch turned on —
all the world in synch. No need to connect
the dots as the alive sky races over Appalachian ridges,
somehow illuminates a cabin porch
where a six-year-old in yellow/gold light
babbles, her playful speech responding to directions
only she can hear, teaching (slow)
her future students what they need to know.
Simultaneously, light is the connection
three thousand miles further west
weaving weightless through Pacific shore
evolving clouds—
a teen dances on yellow rocks, sure a calm
master has arrived—who, in one gesture
will free an ancient logjam
in a timeless reach through chaos—
creating California art out of polished driftwood,
even as further east, two thousand miles inland
in the Great Middle, winds and weather come
from afar, an unencumbered front pushing
away big river stagnation, the day once
again open to possibility where
none before existed. Kids on bikes on
KC boulevards sensing possibility flying
with abandon, sure time is endless on
the knife-edge of speed.
For already light and clouds move quick

on a living map drifting north and east,
where a fourth-grader's nervous story leaks on
a Chicago school stage. Tentative at first
in the spotlight acting out her ambitious drama,
her voice grows strong, a confident smile proves
her generation already is taking charge.
All contained in the quilt even further south
where a Florida sun slow-boils the park's wet air.
A ball held high in a grandfather's hand/
a boy standing poised and ready, holding
his kid's glove like a pro. Sure the ball will
be thrown over and over, he crouches like a dog
ready to play. Slow motion, the release,
the seams revolving in golden light.

Taunt the Rattler

Once begun, the long maturing first inklings
are quickly forgotten in the mischievous rush
to preserve the sensuousness of days to come. Long
before anyone hands out names, every generation invents sex.
Before we know how to be sacred and still live in sin,
how could breathlessness be defined? Only in retrospect
are the first inklings remembered. Like the day Millie Ragsdale
came for us third grade boys in the lab school locker room
shared with the university PE class. Maybe because
teachers knew everything—Millie sensed we would be
standing agog, taking in college guys stripped to pubic hair,
asses, sweaty jock straps all a-kink on the floor.
Seeing with wide eyes what we would someday become.
Millie there to shield us from ugly exposure—
to guide us back to classroom seats, knowing how
boys grow wild, peering through the obscure
kinky door left wide open to the elements. No matter,
for at the time no merit badges were awarded for
graduating into newly mature landscapes. But somehow
sex was involved then, and two years later also
when the wind brought the river grit close,
and we taunted newcomer Chris, who had no right
to be so boy-cute, and the center of attention,
but not home-grown enough to fit in our jostling herd.
We tied him to a playground tree—taking turns
spitting on him. So fucking clever, we yelled,
"If you can't handle this, go back to the circus."
Until we were caught and forced to be reflective,
though the month-long afterschool punishment taught
us nothing. A year later Chris drifted down the river
flowing to the Gulf where all of eros began. By then
we were lost in new lands—so many dangerous
first looks/slow reveals/accepting the evolving
game-changing truth this hometown was not the center
of the world. Seventh grade innocence still real,
though hands sought out what they wanted, and everyone
everyday was naked/caught in the white Sunday School

light with no place to go but ahead. Comical how we still turned red at the hint of exposure/but pushed on anyway. Movie moments when the world washed over, we were delirious in the wild evening winds.

While we danced

we tell the story we've memorized by heart,
we know when to insert facts and what emotions
are better left in our bodies.
Tsering Wangmo Dhompa in **Poetry**,
Vol. 289, Number 1, Spring 2020, (p.13).

The black cat's wide oval eyes memorized for long enough
the moving skin of our lives, not at all predictable
except in our monthly tragedies.
Years ago on a tramp round the vile haunts,
I discovered a kitten sleeping,
half-stupefied in a den of infamy. When
I reached to pet behind her ears she crawled close,
then readily came home, and for some time
pretended to be domesticated, much like my lover
who at the time latched on, insisted on sex
that hurt (me). Because pounding takes its toll,
soon enough time jumps, and rolls, with speedups
and voids until a narrative page turns over,
and both the cat and lover are gone.

Right now, I regret her absence, how she brushed against
my legs, as I recreate moments of peace,
relishing how so little happened in the lull before this
recent upheaval when the universe turned over,
insisting on concrete and concertina wire
to ward off explosions and bodies in the park.

In some different future we might well go back
and live by our animal names—mouse pig rat dog,
instead of hiding in camouflaged clothes,
creating little movies, then lurching from oblivion
cleaned up, ready to perform. In some
different future, eyes will focus enough to see
the dream's stuffed carny animals again come alive.

But today, the awful quiet can't stop the next
language assault, power games revealing some bully's
great win. We have to learn again how to love,
knowing like Robert Creeley, it's only a matter of miles.
That soon enough a mysterious smile will again
appear, ignorant about everything yesterday
we felt was real. But ready for more.

I want to be very light where I'm going

And deny the mad world that stuffs the bag of chaos—
    diminishes with a hard sentence, teases with
lies believed, when daily the madness thrives like a virus.
    Why must we be tested? How many wounds

in this season moving on, before healing growth is complete,
    and the cold drops down from above like
a painful habit? Already stink bugs that never used to be
    a problem crawl under sills, insisting

our home is theirs. Now one flies awkward, crashes on
    the wall, then so brazen advances on furniture—
on me writing, trying to find the meditation.
    How surreal when insects blunder close,

smelling up the poetic abstraction. In the movie
    others wait at the window, eager to prove
I know so little—only that decades ago (in one storied scene)
    I was top dog for a small crowd when the day's

etched label felt permanent, like the cross sewn on
    the grey donkey's back. But today, no great symbols
speak, only three bugs floating in the toilet, still alive,
    about to be sent into the depths. Their lingering

perfume on my palm paints this weightless winter light
    with bald humor. I know ill-tempered Canada geese
are not so beautiful, their long green shits soiling the ground.
    Like some humans—not so pretty close-up,

where often enough, memories are an assault—pointing to
    Ukrainian streets littered with civilians shot
in the head. Here a lost child sees geese high above in
    great V's—honks drifting from clouds mixing

into afternoon music. From a distance the postcard remains
    a poignant sepia scene—a sacred (temporary)
mystery real enough, so I am aware I want only to be light
    where I am going, comical stick legs moving

to a plan, on the great shore. Out on the water rough fish
    bigger than life rise to the surface, and a grin
(as art) builds slow in gentle air—
    as if it is destined to take off and fly.

Mark Vogel *lives at the back of a Blue Ridge holler with his wife, Susan Weinberg, an accomplished fiction, and creative non-fiction, writer, and two foster sons. He currently is an Emeritus Professor of English at Appalachian State University in Boone, North Carolina. Poems and short stories have appeared in several dozen literary journals.*

ON THE GREEN LINE, A VIOLINIST STRIKES

by EmmaRose Zilla

on the green line, a violinist strikes

a gee-sharp. i lower my book, Oliviera's *Dayspring*, dog
ear the wilted page. here, the spruce-plucker pauses, looks
at me as though i am something predictable, that somehow,
through
that rib, neck and scroll, he knows my secret: i am not all that
complex – *i can see right through you, girl,* his chord seems
to whittle. and i can't help but think that he is right. lately,
my scenarios are ugly existentials: brane universes and whom
they may concern, entanglements and thousand-kilometre
distances and taut, gingham ribbons. *small.* i say. *think small.*
at
zaftig's deli, i eat the best reuben of my life. except
for the sauerkraut, which always manages to catch like death
midbite. yesterday, i am kissing a boy who said he loves
me. it feels like cheating a hole-in-one, tipping the pocked
ball
using my breath down the waterfall through the flimsy castle
i shuffle on the trolley, clutching the chrysanthemums for my
mother
and laughing at the absurdity of the word *cry-sahn-thee-mum,*
which really should not exist. in my head i recite fragile

equilibriums of dihydrogen and carbon monoxide and
pota*see*um
dichromate. if this violinist were to ask me how i'm feeling,
though, i would not give him the long version.

self-portrait of a brutally soft girl

do you realise Godhood is just like Girlhood? an ugly, divine
rage / not marred by bloody, pray-torn knees, but tokens of her age
/ God lies in the midst of her lacquered heart. She will not fracture
against / gentle Hell. / She will not beg to be diluted, no bastard
plea will breathe into existence: what is a girl but a prelude to
shattering? / true: that we're a sad, secret kind of dying, / that there
is something female about being dead / writhing, wondering,
weakening of / good daughters blamed for their skin & their touch
/ solace only in the night woven in their mothers' hands /
watch & burn as your silence / seeds into this
new
light.

***EmmaRose Zilla** is a high school junior from Boston, Massachusetts – though she originally hails from the cosmopolitan city of Hong Kong. She loves free-verse poetry, and her work has been recognised by the Kenyon Young Writers Program and the Scholastic Arts & Writing Awards. In her free time when she's not writing, she's probably swimming, playing the piano, or haunting her local bookstore.*

WHERE ARE YOU, CHILDHOOD

by Tishkin Grigory Vladimirovich

Where Are You, Childhood

Said the mother to her son,
"Come and eat your porridge, dear."
But I'm in no rush for such fun,
The situation's pretty clear.
I'd rather go outside to play,
And have a football match instead.
Than eat my porridge right away,
I'll see if my friend's been fed.
Perhaps he's finished with his meal,
And we can skillfully kick the ball.
Together, we share this zeal,
Our games are the best of all.
Tomorrow we will go again,
Down to the river, just us two.
To catch a pike in the glen,

Much better than candy to chew.

The mosquitoes swarm around,

Trying to bite us, it's their scheme.

But we won't fear a single sound,

We'll fish together, like a dream!

Look, it bites! Pull it fast,

I shout to my friend, don't delay.

"I've got it, don't help, I'll cast,

Or you'll scare all the fish away."

So we roam, my friend and I,

From football to fishing's call.

Soon to school, with heads held high,

To show our cleverness to all.

And at home, mom waits for us,

The dumplings ready, hot and right.

I breathe the smell with joy and trust,

No mom's better, she's my delight!

The Suit of Love

When I was just eighteen years old,
Life was a garden in full bloom,
I wanted a girl's hand to hold,
And joy dispelled all trace of gloom.
My energy was like a stream,
A fountain soaring to the sky,
Life moved at a pace like a dream,
I wished for my dreams to come by.
I dreamed of love, immensely grand,
And felt a woman's warm embrace,
I'd touch and kiss with tender hands,
My blood would rush in fervent race.
My youthful days were full of zest,
I soared on dreams with boundless height,
But now that joy has gone to rest,
I kiss my loves in dreams at night.
Unfading tenderness and fire,
Unyielding passion, bound by fate,
The burning love will not retire,
For love will come and set me straight.

The Scent of Love

The delight of love and hope's embrace,
In tender youth's sweet prime,
A storm in May’s blossoming place,
And nightingale's song through time.
To my gentle woman, a song I sing,
Intoxicated by love's sweet scent,
With this beautiful news I bring,
A longing for love, in harmony, sent.
One thing alone torments my heart,
To bow to her with utmost grace,
Modesty’s lessons do impart,
And love's chime I embrace.
Angels united us above,
With her, I'm struck by love.

Tishkin Grigory Vladimirovich, writer Poet and singer:

I was born in 1974 19th of August in Ukraine. Russian by nationality. I write a romantic poetry since my childhood of 7 years old age. I have been writing poetry about love and poetry on the other topics such as fairy tales for children humoristic poems, poems about war also I was writing philosophical poetry. Also I was writing erotic poetry. I was writing poetry for my friends I was dedicating my poetry to my beloved women and to my parents. I am famous Poet in Russia. I have been awarded with three medals by the Union of writers of Russia. I have been awarded with the medal of Dostoevsky medal of Nekrasov and medal of Pushkin. I have published poetry works in Russia. And I have my published poetry works in Ukraine. My poetry will be translated into the French language and published in France. I write Poetry in the English Russian and Ukrainian languages. I have won many Poetry competitions and contests. I have my YouTube Channel which is called Poetry Channel of Tishkin Grigory. I am posting my songs and my poems on my YouTube Channel. I wrote a book with the set of my poetry which I named "Poetry of my Love". My motto sounds like this: "I was born a Poet and I will be a Poet till the end, I will be writing poetry to make all people happy keeping my honor!"

Made in the USA
Columbia, SC
06 November 2024

45858304R00236